EBURY PRESS

SITA: A TALE OF ANCIENT LOVE

Bhanumathi Narasimhan is the younger sister of Gurudev Sri Sri Ravi Shankar. She shares his vision of a stress-free, violence-free planet. She is a meditation teacher. Bhanumathi leads the women welfare and childcare initiatives at Art of Living, which now supports 723 schools with over 72,000 underprivileged children. An author of bestselling books, which have been translated into twenty-two world languages, she holds a master's degree in Sanskrit literature from Bangalore University. She is a singer and has also created soulful albums of sacred chants and melodious bhajans. She lives in Bangalore and connects with her readers on Instagram, @bhanu_narasimhan.

ADVANCE PRAISE FOR THE BOOK

'The story of Bhanu-ji's *Sita* flows with the effortless grace of a perfectly harmonious melody and touches the heart while creating reverence in the mind. Goddess Sita is the epitome of sacrifice and renunciation. She took the test of fire to prove her kindness and forgiveness. This book depicts love, longing and a purity of godliness like the perfect notes of a song!'—Asha Bhosle, singer

'In Bhanu-ji's *Sita*, we see a refreshing phenomenon of Sita's mind that wakes you up with the sharpness of lighting and the gentleness of a flower petal all at once. A closeness that speaks to you as one'—Ashwiny Iyer Tiwari, film-maker and writer

'I feel honoured to review this wonderful piece of art. Since I was a child, I have heard and read the holy Ramayana several times but the way Bhanu-ji has narrated the epic is a real eye-opener. She brings to life the infinite paradigms of love'—Chandni Joshi, gender, rights and policy specialist, Nepal

'*Sita* by Bhanumathi Narasimhan is a gripping narrative of one of the most inspirational characters. We often view the Ramayana era from a twenty-first-century perspective. But here is a brilliant depiction of Sita, the quintessential Indian feminine spirit, that gives you a real-time feel of a different era. It is written in a language that is easy to read and comprehend. A wonderful and educative read'—Dr Devi Shetty, chairman and executive director, Narayana Health

'The writing is soul-touching, gentle and healing. It is almost magical how all the characters came alive in front of me. It brought back memories of when I played Sita. A book to be read and kept. A splendid piece of art written by Bhanu-ji'—Dipika Chiklia Topiwala, former member of Lok Sabha, and actor who played the role of Sita in Ramanand Sagar's *Ramayan*

'This is a spirited and enduring Sita who is calmly recollecting her transformation at various stages of her life. She is the queen who teaches us how to live life no matter how difficult the situation gets'—Farheen Ahmad, journalist, Bahrain

'*Sita* by Bhanu Didi took me to the early days of my dance choreography where I portrayed the young Sita in Pushpvatika. Emotions of love and attachment were sparked by this performance. Bhanu Didi has captured these emotions very well. Bhanu Didi's exposure in Gurudev's ashram, a haven of spirituality, and her lifelong association with Gurudev make her eminently suitable to describe such tender emotions in her brilliant book. It need be hardly emphasized that such tender anecdotes seldom occupy a prime place in the Ramayana and Bhanu Didi has filled this gap admirably'—Hema Malini, member of Lok Sabha, actor, director, dancer

'Romance, drama, the human mind, spiritual values and nature's beauty—the interplay of these five elements is seamless in the narration, which remains true to the historic representation'—Dr D.K. Hari and Dr D.K. Hema Hari, founders, Bharat Gyan

'Sita's deep connection with nature, with people around her is so personal yet makes one feel a sense of expansion, of being part of something universal. Her commitment to her love and to staying positive is truly remarkable and empowering. Bhanu-ji has brought out the subtle strength that every woman possesses through her narration of Sita'—Katrina Kaif, actor

'Bhanu-ji's *Sita* shows you that strength doesn't lie in just armies and weapons, nor sheer physical prowess. Strength lies in a mind that is unfazed by adversity, unblemished by negativity, ever pure and reflecting the perfection inherent in creation'—Kiran Bedi, former lieutenant governor of Puducherry

'Bhanu Didi's *Sita: A Tale of Ancient Love*, is a divine account of less-touched-upon aspects of Sita's life. Through this tale, Didi takes you on an ethereal ride that will make you feel a part of the surreal, exquisite world of ancient times, where Rama and Sita fell in love. It is a tale of love, longing and sacrifice that will instil a sense of calmness'—Meenakshi Lekhi, minister of external affairs, Government of India

'In the Ramayana, Sita's love and respect for Shri Rama, and her sacrifice and suffering because of her abduction by Ravana, show the entire gamut of human emotion in a relationship between husband and wife. But when the husband is the king and bound by duty to the people, the relationship becomes very complex. In this book, the author explains the relationship from Sita's side. A very sensitive and insightful interpretation'—T.V. Mohandas Pai, chairman, Manipal Global Education

'Sita's divine radiance lit up the darkest of forests and even Ravana's Ashoka Vatika while she was kept captive there. Her infinite love for Rama was her compass to live life with grace even in the most testing times. Bhanu Didi's narrative of Sita will empower every woman to realize that as nurturers women are intrinsically blessed with a wellspring of courage that emerges whenever life puts forth a test. Therefore, one must never let any trial or tribulation shake the belief that we have about our courage or conviction'—Preetha Reddy, executive vice chairperson, Apollo Hospitals

'A refreshing new perspective of the Ramayana from the point of view of Sita. Sensitively written, the narration makes the ancient epic accessible to modern audiences with a distinctly feminine point of view while underscoring the essence of Indic gender values'—Shashi Shekhar V., CEO, Prasar Bharati (Doordarshan)

'*Sita* by Bhanumathi-ji has shown us the way to understand and experience Lord Rama who embodies the supreme consciousness through Mother Sita's love in a simple and potent way. Great truths are explained in a language we understand. Jai Sita Ram!'—Sri Shanmuga Shivachariar

'*Annalum nokkinaan, avalum nokkinaal*. This legendary verse from Kamba Ramayanam comes to life in this book that so beautifully describes the landmark moment when the two pairs of eyes—of the lord and Sita—meet to etch a story of love and compassion forever! Bhanumathi-ji takes us through the journey of Sita, her outlook and acceptance with grace in each of the situations she is put into. The kaleidoscopic outlay is so absorbing that one feels transported to the very place, and the heart follows every step of Sita in anticipation of her next move! The freshness of this narrative once again communicates that our epics will continue to engage and inspire over centuries to come!'—Sudha Raghunathan, Carnatic singer

'*Sita* by Bhanumathi-ji is deeply stirring and weaves an intricate tapestry of sensitivity with strength and wisdom as the story unfolds'—Sushmita Sen, actor

'*Sita* by Bhanumathi-ji has achieved what very few books can. It has taken a centuries-old tale and told it again so well that it seems new . . . Fresh, lyrical, poetic, philosophical and deeply beautiful, this is a book that will stay like a fragrance long after it is returned to the shelf. Evocative, deeply emotional and moving, you will feel each turmoil and triumph that the characters go through'—Yatindra Mishra, poet, royal family of Ayodhya

'This book on Sita is a recognition of the honourable role of women. In the Balinese tradition and culture, women are very highly respected. May this inspiring book enhance the realization of gender equality'—Anak Agung Ngurah Oka Ratmadi, 'Cok Rat', former head of the Bali House of Representatives, Indonesia

SITA

A tale of
ANCIENT LOVE

BHANUMATHI
NARASIMHAN

EBURY
PRESS

An imprint of Penguin Random House

EBURY PRESS

USA | Canada | UK | Ireland | Australia
New Zealand | India | South Africa | China

Ebury Press is part of the Penguin Random House group of companies
whose addresses can be found at global.penguinrandomhouse.com

Published by Penguin Random House India Pvt. Ltd
4th Floor, Capital Tower 1, MG Road,
Gurugram 122 002, Haryana, India

First published in Ebury Press by Penguin Random House India 2021

Copyright © Bhanumathi Narasimhan 2021

All rights reserved

10 9 8 7 6 5 4 3 2 1

This is a work of fiction. Names, characters, places and incidents are either the
product of the author's imagination or are used fictitiously and any resemblance
to any actual person, living or dead, events or locales is entirely coincidental.

ISBN 9780143455288

Typeset in Bembo Std by Manipal Technologies Limited, Manipal

This book is sold subject to the condition that it shall not, by way of trade
or otherwise, be lent, resold, hired out, or otherwise circulated without the
publisher's prior consent in any form of binding or cover other than that in
which it is published and without a similar condition including this condition
being imposed on the subsequent purchaser.

www.penguin.co.in

This book is a retelling of mythological stories, some of which have origins in religious texts. The views and opinions expressed in the book are those of the author only and do not reflect or represent the views and opinions held by any other person. This book is based on a variety of sources including published materials, stories from religious texts as well as stories that have been passed on from generation to generation orally. This book reflects the author's own understanding and conception of such stories, and the stories are presented in a simplified form, in a manner accessible to readers. The objective of this book is not to hurt any sentiments or be biased in favour of or against any particular person, region, caste, society, gender, creed, nation or religion.

'Love is not an emotion. It is your very existence.'
—*Gurudev Sri Sri Ravi Shankar*

Prologue

Time stood still,
The soul danced,
As they locked eyes with each other;
One glance spoke volumes
Carrying the thread of past, present and future

An electric moment
An exchange of energy
But whom to unite with

When all is part of Infinity?

Spring was in full bloom
All around and within
Birds burst into song
Petals showered her, and him

A fountain of joy
A cool feeling
Just a glance created havoc
A conflict between being and merging

How strange it is
Two strangers meet
And become one in a glance

They part to meet, and meet to part

They never really were apart

There was no two
Yet they rejoiced in every meeting

Each glance was ever new

Perhaps this is divine love . . .

1

A Garden in the Mind

Sita stood watching as two butterflies danced in the air. Flapping their delicate wings, they made circles, one above the other, near the base of a tall gooseberry tree. The butterflies eventually soared into the sky. Her eyes followed them for a few feet and danced over to a little squirrel precariously balanced on a branch, chasing a buzzing bee away. His bushy tail arched over his honey-brown body, almost covering his adorable face. His tail moved forward and backward in an involuntary rhythm while his eyes were focussed on his winged friend. Sita smiled to herself, amused by the intricate play of the squirrel and the bee. A gentle, cool breeze whistled through the trees, and the leaves rustled as if to make the sound of the waves in the ocean. A shower of a hundred soft lilac-coloured petals floated down from the jacaranda trees, instantly covering the ground. A few special ones floated tenderly towards Sita and rested on her outstretched, soft palms. Sita's eyes closed and she dived deep within as the gentle touch of the petals enveloped her being in waves of beauty. And in that inner silence, the soundless vibration of the sacred word 'Ram' rose in soft ripples of bliss. A single tear flowed from Sita's eyes, sweetened by her devotion and longing for her beloved.

Ashoka Vatika is an enchanting garden tucked away in a secret corner of Ravana's extravagant palace in Lanka. Spring had arrived in its full glory. *Champaka*, *nagalingapushpa*, *uddalaka*, varieties of jasmine and many other flowers were in full bloom. Tree branches were bent low with the weight of delicious mangoes in abundant bunches. Pomegranate trees with their luscious pink treasures and slim guava trees laden with fruit had hundreds of parrots hovering contentedly over them. They flew in groups from one side of the garden to another, chattering all along. Small herds of deer fed on the lush green grass and sweet fruits as the young fawns sprang about playfully. They gently approached Sita, beckoning her to pet them. They nudged her with their soft brown snouts and closed their eyes in pleasure when she stroked their necks. Peacocks emerged from the thickets, seeking her attention by opening up their resplendent feathers into graceful arcs. And in that perfect moment, as they danced with gentle excitement, their colourful feathers would quiver and settle back into position. All the colours seemed ready to jump out and capture the eyes of anyone moving about in the vicinity. The intoxicated cuckoos sang relentlessly as if competing with the melodious notes of hundreds of sunbirds, bulbuls and other singing birds. The buzzing honeybees droned like a tanpura, offering the note for the songs of the birds. 'Hummmmmm,' went Sita in an attempt to match her pitch with the bees. She avoided stepping on the gleaming white, cold pathways etched with gold and precious gems. She preferred the comforting feel of the soft earth under her feet. Nature was her respite and constant companion in her time away from her beloved.

She strolled towards the lotus pond that was home to a variety of water birds, including graceful swans and *chakravaka* ducks. They cackled away, spreading their wings to shake off a thousand tiny droplets of water. A few of these droplets landed on the wide lotus leaves, where they curved themselves into perfect spheres, each glistening with the rays of the sun like pearls strewn here and there. Sita's eyes captured every detail but nothing left an impression on her mind, just as the lotus leaves, though they were in the water, remained untouched by it. There was only one impression in her consciousness, her beloved Rama, and he filled her completely.

'Siiitaaaaaaa . . .' The hoarse voice of the rakshasa woman who guarded Sita thundered through the trees. Jolted out of her reverie, Sita composed herself and started walking towards the direction of the sound. The encirclement of golden *ashoka* trees, with their thick foliage, came into view. She went in with her head bowed and walked towards the *simsupa* (rosewood) tree that stood in the centre.

The earth had formed a smooth mound below the tree for Sita to be comfortably seated upon. She took her place there and leaned back against the solid tree trunk for support. The tree responded with its kind but firm touch, radiating the love and warmth of a protective mother for her newborn.

And here, surrounded by ugly, coarse, insensitive rakshasis, Sita was held captive. They were not ugly because they had deformed faces or protruding teeth and unclean hair or twisted nails. They were ugly because they refused to acknowledge the beauty that surrounded them; they were blind to the divinity in the person whom they held captive. They felt no kindness or love—their hearts were filled with fear, and they took pride in the terror that their demon king struck in the hearts of all beings. They had no knowledge of truth or untruth, of eternal or temporal, of dharma or adharma. Sita glanced at their lacklustre eyes and felt only compassion. Her mother, Sunayana, must have known this was how they were. She wouldn't judge people. In a remarkably uncomplicated way she would just accept that things and people were what they were, and move on. Sita's thoughts floated back to precious childhood moments spent in the company of her loving parents.

Sita would have been a six-years-old. She was wearing her favourite mustard-coloured lehenga with a thick dark green border, and a soft maroon blouse in a velvet-like material with puffed sleeves and intricate motifs embroidered with golden zari. It was her favourite blouse! Her mother had braided her long, flowy black hair and decorated it with fresh jasmine flowers. She could still feel the soft but firm touch of her mother's fingers on her hair. Her mother had the most refined fingernails, so well-groomed. Actually, everything about her mother was perfect. She was always so presentable and dignified. Her long hair would be tied up in a neat bun and fully adorned with flowers and jewelled hair accessories. Her taste in jewellery was impeccable. She never wore ostentatious pieces. Sita had her mother's taste in jewellery. She preferred it delicate and light.

Urmila, her younger sister, was playing with their mother's jewellery while their mother was busy with Sita's hair. Of course, the jewellery was too big for her tiny frame, but she had worn all the long necklaces with big ornate pendants on top of one another. The bangles were oversized for her and went all the way up her arms. She wore everything that she could get her hands on as she pretended to be an asura queen. 'All this gold is now mine! I am not giving anything back to you!' she said, trying to put on a gruff voice, but giggling instead. Sita and Sunayana laughed as Urmila clumsily pranced around the room with her nose up in the air, trying to stay in character. She was actually quite amusing! Even children were aware that the asuras were enamoured more by material wealth than by dharma.

'Why did God make asuras like this, Ma?' Sita asked innocently. 'That is how it is, Sita,' replied Sunayana. 'We have to be careful and keep a healthy distance from them.' King Janaka had just walked in, drawn by the sound of laughter, and overheard this conversation. Sunayana saw him entering and shared Sita's enquiries with him. 'Maybe you can explain this to your darling daughter!' Sita's braid was finished and she was admiring the way her mother had placed the jasmine flowers without crushing a single petal. She now looked up at her father and moved towards where he was standing, awaiting his response. Holding her chin, he first took a moment to absorb and admire every detail of his daughter's angelic face, and then bade her sit comfortably. He felt proud of her. He sat beside her and said, 'My child! The world is full of opposites. But it is not birth that makes one an asura. One's thoughts, words and deeds are important.' He pointed to a small lamp that was lit near the idol of Devi Parvati in Sunayana's chamber. 'See, you can light a lamp and add more light to a place, but darkness is just the absence of light, isn't it? In the same way, it is the absence of virtues and dharma that turns the mind towards negative tendencies. Prahlada was born to the most powerful asura king, Hiranyakashipu, and yet, he was the most ardent devotee of Lord Vishnu! He is certainly not an asura. It is the lack of kindness, dispassion, truth, generosity, gratitude and devotion, and the inability to uphold one's dharma that turns the mind towards negativity.'

'Would these asura ladies ever turn towards the light?' wondered Sita as she returned to the present and watched them gossiping among themselves, while occasionally giving her mean and fearsome sidelong glances in Ashoka Vatika.

As a child, Sita and her sisters would regale each other with stories about gods and goddesses, brave kings and beautiful queens, magical beings, great rishis and with stories of distant lands. They would enact different characters, write their own dialogues, and dress each other in costumes that they would fashion themselves. They even made up their own songs and dances as part of their stories.

Sita was particularly good at embodying a role. Whichever character she was given, she would bring it to life. Sometimes the others would wonder whether Sita really was the person she was pretending to be. Especially while enacting stories of the Devi, Sita's face would assume an ethereal glow. Her eyes would change and become luminous. She would move as if her feet were gliding over the earth. Her whole stance would change and radiate unparalleled conviction. The others felt a natural urge to bow down to her. Even the ladies-in-waiting and the palace guards would offer obeisance to her. Sunayana and Janaka would watch from a distance and know in their hearts that their daughter was no ordinary child.

2

Daughter of the Earth

It was customary in Mithila for the king to till the land with his golden plough at the start of the sowing season. All the farmers would come together and pray to the earth, the water, the sun, the wind and the skies above. The offering of prayer was made to the golden plough.

After the prayers, Janaka lifted the plough and started tilling the land to the chanting of Vedic mantras and the sound of conches, bells, trumpets and drums. The farmers followed him reverently. After the first few steps, however, the plough got stuck. An unexpected yet pleasant feeling arose in Janaka's heart. He did not try to force the plough forward. Instead, he knelt down and began digging with his bare hands. The farmers jumped in to help him, and soon, they uncovered a mysterious, solid wooden box. The box itself looked as if an ancient tree had fashioned it from its own trunk. The grains and rings in the wood seemed to tell tales of hundreds of years of existence as the tree had stood witness to life as it unfolded. There were no hinges or handles, nor was the box of any particular shape, though one could say it was nearing an oval.

Janaka ran his fingers over the surface of the box and felt its texture. With mounting curiosity and a sense of deep reverence, he bent to lift the box out of the earth. He was prepared to use his full strength but was surprised when the box found its way into his arms effortlessly. It was light as a feather. He placed it gently on the ground to open it. The cover came away easily. Janaka's eyes grew wide with amazement at what he saw. The box was lined with soft red silk, and within it, wrapped in fine white muslin cloth, was a tiny baby girl with pink cheeks and curly black hair.

Janaka gently extended his hand to her, and her tiny fingers wrapped around his index finger as she gurgled sweetly. Janaka's heart overflowed with love. He felt a wave of joy bubble up under his skin and exhilarate his entire being. He had never felt anything like it before. He instinctively closed his eyes to savour the moment. And in that same instant, he saw much more than he had ever seen with his eyes open. He saw millions of seeds sprouting, flowers blooming, little birds hatching out of eggs. He felt part of all the innumerable droplets of water that rose from the oceans into the sky to become puffy rain clouds. He felt the solidity and stability of every tree trunk on the planet, he felt the dynamic surge of energy in every flowing river, he felt the unshakeable majesty of every mountain, he felt the fears and joys of every animal roaming the forests, he saw the uncountable number of thoughts floating around like clouds and passing through human minds. He felt one with the earth he stood upon; one with the water that flowed upon the earth; one with the fire and light in creation; one with all the air in the atmosphere, gentle here, vigorous there, cool at some places, harsh and dry elsewhere; for one instant, he felt connected to all of creation.

Janaka opened his eyes barely a moment later, but felt as if aeons had passed. He could clearly feel the delicate touch of the baby's finger that still held him, yet he could not feel himself. The name Vaidehi echoed in the cave of his heart. Videha meant one who has transcended the body, one who has an expanded awareness. Mithila was also called Videha—the kingdom whose people were of a heightened consciousness. This child had effortlessly moved him into that beautiful space by her very presence. With great effort, he brought his awareness back to the conscious plane and tried to stay grounded. With utmost reverence, mentally seeking permission from the Divine Mother to hold the child in his arms, he lifted her up and looked into her eyes with a smile. As he gazed at her moon-like face, a tiny droplet of water from the heavens landed on the forehead of the child. She squeezed her half-open eyes shut in response to the droplet. The king looked up and saw the rapid gathering of dark cumulus clouds in the sky. A few drops landed on his face too. The farmers cheered in chorus. Rain was the harbinger of prosperity. The harvest would be plentiful. For the people of Mithila, it was an invitation to celebrate. The child was clearly the bearer of good fortune. She was their Lakshmi.

King Janaka and his wife Sunayana had not had any children of their own thus far. He brought the child home and placed her in Sunayana's arms. 'She is ours, Sunayana. Mother Earth has bestowed her upon us.' Sunayana looked at Janaka, utterly bewildered. He shared the whole story with her. 'Who would ever expect to find a child in a box?' exclaimed Sunayana. 'Are you sure that her parents are not nearby? Is it appropriate for us to adopt her without knowing her origin or lineage?' She turned to look into the baby's beautiful face as she said this and slowly, a voice in her heart grew stronger and louder. She found herself saying, 'Could we keep her? She is the daughter I have always longed for!' She took the child in her arms and held her close. There was a stirring in her heart and she felt a sense of completeness. 'She has made me a mother,' said Sunayana, her voice choked and tears of gratitude flowing from her eyes as she looked into the innocent eyes of the child. 'I don't think she was ever born, Sunayana,' said Janaka. 'This child is a special being who has chosen us as parents to fulfil a divine purpose. Time will reveal the path that she will tread. Let us fulfil our responsibility as parents. I will request Guru Shatananda for his guidance and blessings on this matter.'

Acharya Shatananda was the son of Maharishi Gautama and Devi Ahalya. He was a wise and soft-spoken rishi who guided Janaka on all matters of importance. Sunayana had arranged for a small wooden cradle for the child. The cradle was lined with soft cotton mattresses and contained tiny bolsters on either side. The baby was cosily wrapped up in a fresh piece of yellow cloth and was fast asleep. The acharya arrived and approached the cradle. He stood gazing at the child. Both Janaka and Sunayana patiently watched him for a sign, an indication of what they should do. But they were not prepared for what came next. The acharya joined his palms and bowed down to the child. Janaka and Sunayana looked at each other in bewilderment and stood speechless. 'Name her Sita, Janaka,' said the acharya, turning to the new parents. 'As the crown jewel of Videha, you may address her as Vaidehi. As your daughter, she will be known as Janaki.' He raised his hands and blessed the joyous couple before he left.

In the following days, several rishis, munis and great *tapasvis* visited the palace to get a glimpse of the child of the earth. 'Teach her all you know, Janaka. She is the source of all wisdom,' said one saint. 'She will bring prosperity wherever she is! Her touch will bring abundance,' said another. 'She will inspire valour and uphold dharma in the coming times,' added another rishi. 'Success will be the natural fruit of all that she undertakes. Good fortune follows her like a calf following its mother,' prophesied another.

'The earth she walks on is equal to gold, Janaka. Cherish every moment you have in her presence, O blessed king!' said a yogi who came to see her. Janaka and Sunayana were overwhelmed with gratitude.

The cooing, crying and gurgling of the infant filled the corridors of the palace and playing with, dressing up and admiring the little princess became the prime occupation of the royal household's women. During festivals, the common people would queue up to catch a glimpse of the child.

Sunayana was an ardent devotee of Devi Parvati. She had a beautiful idol of the goddess in her chamber. Each morning began with a prayer to her. Sita would sit with Sunayana to pray. She would pick up one flower after another and hand it to Sunayana to offer. She would ring the little bell when it was time for *aarti*. She loved to try to catch the little clouds of fragrant smoke that would rise from the incense cones. Fresh sweets, fruits and rice with ghee in a golden cup would be kept ready as an offering. Sita would sit next to her mother with her palms joined together in prayer. Whatever Sunayana chanted, Sita would pretend to follow her and a series of adorable sounds would tumble out of her tiny mouth. Once in a while, she would sneak a sweet or two into her mouth in the middle of the puja. She would shut her eyes when she was eating, as if no one else would notice her if her eyes were closed!

One day, the laddoos were exceptionally fragrant and Sita was also a little hungry. So she quietly popped the first one in her mouth and got ready for the second when she saw her mother looking at her out of the corner of her eyes. She quietly returned the laddoo to the plate. After the puja, Sunayana patiently explained to Sita that one ought to wait for the food to be offered to the divine before eating it. Her personal handmaid was listening to everything. She did not want to interrupt Sunayana, but the moment the queen finished, she said, 'Maharani! The child is the devi herself! She has made all the prasad sweeter by eating it. I have not seen God before. But when I see her, my heart tells me that she is the one! Please don't scold her.' Sunayana's eyes became moist on hearing the words of the simple woman. The handmaid continued, 'Have you noticed, Maharani, the flowers on the idol are fresh even the next morning whenever Sita has touched them? Every day, when I take the container of water to clean it after the puja, I find that the water is sweet and fragrant. I have stopped throwing that water away. Instead, all of us share it among ourselves as prasad!' Sunayana's heart overflowed with joy and gratitude. She bowed down to Devi Parvati and offered her delicate emotions at her lotus feet.

Though Sita was being held captive in Ravana's garden now, they would bring her food in a golden plate every day. And every day, the plate would remain untouched. Sita never took even a sip of water from the palace kitchens. The Rakshasis who guarded her did not care. They would enjoy the food themselves and return the plates as if Sita had eaten everything. But the small animals and birds noticed Sita's refusal. When the Rakshasis were asleep, little squirrels would run down the trunk of the simsupa tree and drop nuts into her lap. They would wait to see if Sita accepted their offering or not. The sparrows and sunbirds would carry tiny berries in their beaks and place them on the ground near Sita, just as if they were bringing food for their young ones. Sita could not refuse their offerings. She would wash those berries and nuts in the water from the nearby stream and eat them. This was all the food that she consumed throughout her confinement in Ashoka Vatika.

3

Fragrant Memories

Even as a child, Sita took a keen interest in cooking. When she was just four, a good part of her play schedule included spending time in Mithila's palace kitchens. She had a special stool made for her to stand on and supervise the cooking! She would innocently give her suggestions for the menu and suggest experimenting with different herbs and spices in the various dishes that were being prepared. She would drop the herbs into the large vessels with her little hands and feel satisfied with the fragrance that arose. All the cooks would wait for her every morning. The kitchen became cleaner, the cooks were better dressed, nobody missed work and there were no latecomers. The food tasted better and those who ate it derived satisfaction and delight from their meals. Sunayana observed all these changes with a keen eye.

One day, young Sita prepared kheer for her parents. She had mixed all the ingredients herself. As usual, Sunayana served lunch to Janaka and the kheer came at the end.

Janaka was already full, but Sunayana encouraged him to have at least one spoonful. Sita was expectantly watching him to see his response. Janaka had one mouthful, then another and another; he soon finished the whole cup and then wanted more. 'Sunayana, you have outdone yourself today!' said Janaka. 'This kheer is delicious! Could you serve me some more, please?' Sunayana gestured to Sita and asked her to serve her father. Delighted, she served him a tiny spoonful. 'Do you know who has made the kheer today?' asked Sunayana with a big smile, with her eyes indicating towards their beautiful daughter. Janaka beamed with pride. 'You have taught her well, Sunayana!' exclaimed Janaka. He never hesitated to praise others and, as was his inclusive attitude, created a pleasant and loving atmosphere for Sita to grow up in.

Her beloved, like her father, was very inclusive. She had once prepared kheer for him as well. On having a spoonful, he immediately called his brothers and their wives, and proudly made them all taste it. He personally took some to his mother's chamber and asked her to taste it as well. King Dasharatha too enjoyed kheer that day. He then asked Sita to prepare it for all the palace staff in the royal kitchen. Sita's kheer was the topic of the day.

She had managed to make kheer once even in the forest. It was just her, her beloved and Lakshmana—or so she thought. The great king of the vultures, Jatayu, happened to pay them a visit and he too was offered kheer. Whatever her beloved relished, he wanted to share with everyone. It so happened that many passing saints stopped by for kheer that day. 'Did you give some to your favourite woodpecker?' 'Yes,' replied Sita with a smile, 'the sparrows and bulbuls got some too. And the newborn fawn liked it too!' Lakshmana smiled, shaking his head. 'You will ask Bhabhi to cook for the whole forest, Bhaiya!'

Lakshmana loved Sita's cooking but he never ate much. His diet was meagre. He felt that a full stomach did not allow him to be alert, and he was committed to standing guard at all times. The only break he took was to meditate. He barely slept. Sita's mind drifted fondly towards Urmila, her darling sister. She was such a bundle of joy and enthusiasm. Whatever Sita did, she would follow suit. Their garden in Mithila had countless varieties of butterflies. There was one secret little enclosure which was a haven for butterflies. Hundreds of butterflies in all colours and sizes rested on the leaves of the tall, leafy plants, and when the girls entered, they would all rise up in circles, flapping their multi-hued wings. The girls' hearts would soar along with the wings of the butterflies and they would stretch out their arms with their eyes wide open in wonder, waiting for a few to settle down on their hands.

A butterfly had once settled on Urmila's hand as she stood in the balcony of her room in the palace of Ayodhya. That excited her greatly because she missed her butterflies in Mithila. Ayodhya was a big city, but there weren't many secret gardens and butterfly havens around. Lakshmana entered her room and saw her standing still with her hand outstretched. He noticed the butterfly and smiled to himself. 'Swami, come quickly! Look at the blue spots on her wings!

She is so stunning!' Lakshmana moved closer, silently so as not to startle the butterfly. A few seconds later, it flew away and Urmila turned to her husband with a broad, contented smile.

'Urmila, I have something to tell you. I am going to the forest with Bhaiya,' said Lakshmana. 'Will you be back for dinner, my lord?' she asked in her sweet and chirpy voice. Lakshmana could not but smile. He held her by her shoulders and looked into her eyes with tender love. 'Your innocence is my greatest joy, Urmila!' Lakshmana had a direct manner. 'I need your help—will you do what I ask of you?' Urmila sensed that something was amiss, but she was prepared to stand by her husband come what may. She loved him dearly. 'Yes, tell me . . .'

'Mother Kaikeyi has banished Bhaiya to the forest for fourteen years. Bhabhi is going with him. So am I. The forest is not a safe place and I have to stand guard over them and stay alert night and day. I cannot afford to sleep. I need you to pay my debt to Nidra Devi. Will you do this for me?'

Urmila had no time to think. She stood rooted to the ground in shock. The world around her was crumbling. Even her tears did not find the strength to flow.

'Don't let your tears flow, Urmila. I won't be able to bear it. Be my strength,' said Lakshmana with deep concern.

Urmila suddenly felt more grown-up and mature. 'Swami . . . It is my honour to be useful to you, to Bhaiya and Bhabhi in this hour of trial. I will wait for you.'

Sita felt so proud of her sister. Her penance was incomparable. As for Lakshmana, Sita loved him like a son.

She wondered at his devotion to his elder brother, and deeply respected his dispassion and valour. At least he was still with her beloved now. He would take care of him and be his strongest support. However, she wasn't very sure of his culinary skills. What were they eating? How were they managing without her? They were always ready to take care of others, but what about themselves? Her reverie was broken by the tap-tapping of a friendly woodpecker on his daily visit to the simsupa tree. The bird was content to just have Sita's attention for a few minutes before flying away. Was this little bird from the same family of woodpeckers who visited her in the forest? The bird tapped the trunk with its beak as if in response and tilted its head to look at her. One of its kind lived outside her window even in Mithila. For now, the company of this innocent bird was her biggest solace.

4

Sunny Days and Starry Nights

It was the crack of dawn in the peaceful city of Mithila when Sita awoke to the tapping of her woodpecker friend on a nearby tree. She turned over on her bed and gazed out of the window. The bird looked bright and beautiful, with the characteristic blue tuft of hair on its head. She smiled, stretched and breathed out deeply. Easing herself out of her cosy bed, she walked over to the window.

She liked watching the sun rise. She imagined the sun sending out a million rays towards the earth to gently wake up all the flowers and the leaves, the butterflies and the birds. She thought of the little buds, tickled by the warmth of the golden rays, pushing out their petals one by one. She turned her attention to an enormous beehive hanging from the branch of a nearby tree. As she watched, the entire hive started swaying back and forth in the gentle breeze, but not a bee was disturbed or thrown about. The colony of thousands of bees moved as a single unit. What must the queen bee be telling her little worker bees? And what a life they led, Sita wondered: flying from one flower to another in search of tiny drops of nectar. Her father always told her to look for the honey hidden in each event in their lives. It may be a flower with thorns or stuck in mud or full of pollen dust or with a delightful fragrance: regardless, the bee was focused on the little drops of nectar alone. 'We should learn from the bees,' he would say.

Her room was on the first floor. It was a spacious room and tastefully decorated. The floor-length curtains were a golden colour, with delicate floral patterns woven all over them. The floor was covered with soft silk rugs into which her feet sank comfortably. Her bed was big enough for herself, Urmila and her two cousin sisters, Mandavi and Shrutakirti. It was a tall four-poster wooden bed with an ornate headboard and sheer curtains on all sides. Her feet wouldn't reach the ground when she was seated on it. She had to jump down.

Sita was a light sleeper. She had a large window by her bed through which the night sky was visible. On many occasions, she would gaze endlessly at the moon and the stars. She made friends with them and felt an uncanny closeness with them. With her gaze fixed on the starry skies, sometimes she would feel as if she was floating amidst them. She would reach out and touch her headboard or anything solid, just to make sure she was still on the ground.

These were the same stars and remained with her still in Ashoka Vatika, as she lay on the platform under the canopy of trees, staring into the night sky. The rakshasas usually slept late and arose even later. But the rakshasis who guarded her would leave her alone and go home to make merry. Only one or two still stayed at the entrance to the garden. Just their absence made the garden so much more pleasant and intimate. She wondered if Rama was looking at the night sky too. The very thought that they might both be gazing together at the same stars sent a rush of joy into her heart. There were many barriers that separated them physically, but these little twinkling relatives of hers connected her instantly to her beloved. She closed her eyes with a smile on her face. She mentally dwelt upon every detail of her beloved and found deep solace in the image. He was tall. But when she looked up at him, Sita could not see anything beyond him. He was the tallest of all. His hair was like silk, ebony black, and fell to his shoulders in rich curls. Sita, always walking one step behind him, would admire the way they danced jauntily with every step that Rama took. His face glowed with a cool radiance that even the moon could not match. Sita had seen lotuses bloom at night when the light from Rama fell upon them, and lilies blooming in the day from his cooling presence! She would laugh at the way he confused the flowers. He would look at her innocently when he heard her tinkling laughter and she would once again lose herself in his eyes. There was nothing more beautiful in this creation than those eyes. They were like oceans into which Sita felt pulled, like a wave receding to its depth. What would break her reverie was his voice—soft, deep and full. Though gentle, the authority in it was unmistakable. His command was her wish. The human mind is like a forest, with many complex thoughts, feelings, concepts and ideas tangled and interwoven within it. Finding a clear path is not always easy. But for Sita, it didn't matter because her beloved led the way. She simply followed in his footsteps.

Her mind drifted to one night in the forest of Panchavati. The sky was absolutely clear and it seemed as if the entire Milky Way was visible. Rama and Lakshmana were gazing up at the stars while lying on simple beds of *kusha* grass that Lakshmana had prepared outside their hut. Sita was seated on a rock that had been placed near a tree, which served as a backrest. Sita was telling them about how she and Urmila would patiently wait for the sight of a shooting star to make a wish upon. The brothers were enjoying the innocent recollections when they suddenly spotted a shooting star and excitedly pointed it out to Sita.

> Counting more than the stars in the universe
> Again and again they arise
> Filling every inch of immeasurable space
> When in the self you do not reside,

said Rama and looked at Lakshmana and Sita with raised eyebrows, as if asking them to solve the puzzle.

'This one is easy, Bhaiya! Desires,' announced Lakshmana. 'Here is one for you.'

> An instantaneous bubble
> Stretching across lifetimes
> Never in the moment
> Forever colours your sight.

'Nice one, Lakshmana. The answer is impressions. But this is not the case for those whose mind is like a pure crystal, whose intellect is not stuck. They are untouched by events, like droplets of water on a lotus leaf,' said Rama. 'Such minds are rare, Bhaiya. It is a blessing to meet even one person who is that refined,' replied Lakshmana. 'I am surrounded by two such people, Lakshmana,' said Rama and looked at Lakshmana and Sita fondly. 'But that is because our minds are filled with only you! There is no place for any other impressions. So it is you who have really saved us!' said Sita. Sita's words echoed Lakshmana's thoughts. 'That is the absolute truth, Bhaiya!' Lakshmana uttered fervently. Rama's smile broadened and his eyes sparkled with love.

'Your turn now, Sita,' said Rama, and both brothers looked at her in anticipation. 'Hmm . . .' thought Sita for a moment, and then recited,

As you hear it, it flows
When you share it, it grows
Live it and life glows.

Lakshmana instantly said, 'This is for me, Bhaiya. This puzzle is not applicable to you.' Rama raised one eyebrow and looked at Lakshmana for an explanation. 'For a devotee, knowledge flows in their life when they listen to their master. It grows when they share with others what they have learnt. And their life glows when that knowledge is integrated into their life as wisdom. But the master is the source of wisdom itself! He is the light in the life of the devotee. There is nothing to grow or deplete for the master!'

Rama turned to Sita and said, 'You have to pose a question that I can also answer, Sita! Ask again!'

Sita smiled and said, 'This one is just for you!'

Smaller than the smallest
Larger than the largest
Finer than the finest
The self-luminous sun of all.

Lakshmana could not help laughing aloud. 'What is so funny, Lakshmana?' asked Rama. 'Bhabhi has just described you and called it a puzzle! Of course your ways are most puzzling, but the thought of you trying to solve a puzzle to which you yourself are the answer is quite hilarious! It reminded me of our mothers who would wonder aloud, "Who is the sweetest of all, who is the cutest of all?" and so on, when the answer was always the baby itself! Bhabhi has sung your praises in a more sophisticated way, that's all!'

'Will you let me answer at least one, Lakshmana? You are being impossible!' said Rama. Lakshmana continued laughing and looked at Sita, waiting for her to come up with the next puzzle. She too was enjoying Lakshmana's arguments. His love had such an endearing and wise flavour.

'What now?' thought Sita, and in that question was the answer to what she could ask next. She said,

A place you have never been before
Nor can you go hereafter
Slow down to get there
You cannot go faster.

'You are so good at this, Bhabhi!' said Lakshmana and waited for Rama to answer. Rama smiled and said,

The field of all possibilities
So infinite and deep
Is contained in the present moment

If your mind is elsewhere
You might as well be asleep.

'Isn't it time you rested a bit anyway, my lord?' said Sita. 'Just one more, Sita!' replied Rama. 'Let Lakshmana ask,' said Sita, looking at him the way a mother involves her child in every activity.

'OK! Here goes . . .' said Lakshmana.

Unseen yet tangible
Rest if you have to catch it
Deeper rest if you can hold it
Let it go and come as you watch it
Aha! The witness! Perhaps you found it!

Rama and Sita both took a deep breath at the same time and all three burst out laughing. 'That was a befitting ode to the breath, Lakshmana,' said Rama. 'The first act of life, the last act of life and the witness to life as well!'

Years had gone by since that beautiful night but the memory lingered in her mind so clearly. Sita, casting one more look at the night sky in Ashoka Vatika, closed her eyes and became aware of her breath, which was growing slower and deeper as she moved into a kind of stillness that bespoke complete rest. Sita was turning inward when she felt the earth tremble slightly beneath her. The tremor had a certain rhythm to it. Her reverie broke with a start as she realized they were footsteps. Was it who she thought it was? Her heart trembled and her body tightened. She had nowhere to hide. She sat as close to the tree as she could possibly be and prayed to Devi Parvati to give her strength, to be by her side. The footsteps became louder and sounded almost like drumbeats. There was one loud beat followed by a tumble of sounds that were rather chaotic. But the heavy first step never missed a beat. A certain step followed by uncertain ones, orderliness followed by chaos, clarity followed by confusion: Ravana was not coming alone. His purpose was defined. Those who followed him knew only that they had to follow him. They had no greater purpose.

Sita's resistance radiated from her being like an unseen wall of fire around her. Ravana walked along the white paved footpaths and entered the grove. He was tall. Very tall. He had the appearance of a black mountain. His skin was dark and smooth. His eyes were piercing beams of harsh light. They refused to see the world as it was. They were veiled by the umpteen impressions that clouded his mind. Ravana called himself the master of the whole world, but he had no say over his own mind. He thought that even the gods were there to do his bidding, but he was a slave of his unfulfilled desires. Yet, he was powerful. Deeper than the veil that covered his heart was a fountain of tremendous energy. Like the sun that shines equally on all life without judgement, this energy, which sprung from his self, powered his existence irrespective of the quality of his life. This energy coursed through every cell of his being and he glowed with unparalleled arrogance, which made him appear taller still. Yet, his being was limited. He felt no connection to the earth he walked on or the skies that were a roof over his head. He thought of them as objects that belonged to him. He could not perceive the infinity beyond the materiality of his life.

He was well-dressed, adorned as a king should be. The choice of jewellery was careful and expensive. He did not carry any weapons. His feet stopped at a distance of ten feet from Sita. Though all he wanted was to take her and make her his own, he could move no further. He looked at her with unblinking eyes. Clad in a simple sari, her beautiful long black hair fell below her waist, eyebrows arched like Cupid's bow, and her delicate lips quivered like his own heart at her sight. He felt a sudden softness in his heart. She was so petite and helpless, but her beauty was more powerful than anything else he had ever experienced. There was nothing in the world that he wanted more than her.

There were over a hundred women from the palace who had followed him with uncertain footsteps. They were dressed in loosely clad silks and wore abundant gold. But they looked like they had dressed hastily. They seemed drunk and wore contented smirks that struggled to hide their curiosity about Sita. These were not ordinary palace maids. These were the women he sported with. They were also merely objects for him. They stood on all sides but a few steps behind him. They were utterly confused by the sight of Sita. A burning rage of jealousy rose from the pits of their stomachs. They looked at Sita as if she were nothing. But they craved the attention that she received from their lord. Ravana stood immobile between these two fires.

'Look at me, Sita. I have come,' Ravana spoke in a clear and controlled voice. 'Do not grieve or worry. Everything that is mine is already yours. Command me. I will place the world at your feet. I will give you pleasures beyond your imagination. I am strong but do not be afraid of my strength. To you, my touch will be softer than silk.' Sita cringed at his words and retreated even further within herself.

The heat of the fire that she now radiated became stronger and almost perceptible to the senses. Ravana felt it push him back while his arrogance egged him on. The flame of his desire, like a coiled serpent, raised its hood and its heat burnt him from within. His whole body felt weakened. She said nothing. She refused to even look at him. She was so distant. Probably the only place in the world that he had not conquered and could not ever reach. 'How pure she is . . .' he thought, and at that moment, a wave of coolness swept over him and he just wanted to leave her alone. His arrogance resisted this feeling but his heart said, 'Give her time. She is worth waiting for.'

'I will come again. You look tired today. Rest well.' Saying this, he turned to leave. The confused mass of women spread out on both sides to clear a path between them for their king and hastily followed after him like a mindless herd.

Sita's eyes were still shut, but she loosened her fist, her shoulders relaxed, and her body unclenched itself. Tears streamed down her face and she held on to the memory of her beloved for comfort.

After several long minutes, when the silence of the night once again engulfed the garden, she gradually opened her eyes to look up at the sky. Many dark clouds had covered and cast a veil over the sparkling light, but they were slowly receding now. With each little star that came out twinkling, she felt the sparkle of hope shine in her heart again.

5

An Ethereal Bond

It was over two decades back when Sita had first felt the presence of Ravana. Janaka had announced the *swayamvara* for his dearest daughter. Whoever would be able to lift and string the Shiva-Dhanush (the bow of Shiva) would be her suitor. Kings and princes from distant lands arrived in Mithila to attempt the formidable challenge.

Sita felt a special connection with the Shiva-Dhanush. The bow was over 16 feet long and had an aura of absolute tranquillity and unshakeable strength. It was kept on an ornately decorated platform in a hall built specially for it. Her father did regular Rudra pujas (prayers to Lord Shiva) in that hall. The bow was sacred beyond expression. Even as a child, whenever they would go to the hall for the puja, Sita would keep gazing at the bow. She would not be able to take her eyes away from it. Even when she could barely walk, she was overcome with the urge to touch it. While all the elders were busy in the puja, she climbed down from her mother's lap and slowly moved towards the bow. With her tiny, soft fingers, she reached out and touched it. The bow responded to her touch and shook lightly. It felt like a feather in her hands, but the vibrations from the movement of the bow instantly sent out ripples of energy across the entire room. Janaka rose in shock. In a fraction of a second, he reached his daughter's side. It had taken days of prayer and over a hundred of his men to shift the bow from one end of the room to another. And here, it had shaken at the touch of a baby!

He took the child in his arms and looked at her face. Sita wore an ethereal smile and had a distant look in her eyes. Though he was carrying her, he felt like he was holding empty space in his hands. In fact, it was not empty space but pure energy. Sita was in a trance. Guru Shatananda came over to where Janaka was standing with the child. His palms were filled with flower petals which he showered on her. An assistant pandit gave him an aarti plate with which he circumambulated her. She had an otherworldly smile throughout. A few seconds later, she returned to her wakeful state, gurgling and pulling playfully at her father's beard.

The Shiva-Dhanush had been in the care of the kings of Mithila for several generations. Janaka's ancestor, King Devaratha, had received the bow from the devas with detailed instructions on how to preserve it carefully. The divine bow had an earthly purpose and it seemed like the time for the realization of its mission had arrived. Janaka was unsure as to how it would reveal its purpose, but he was patient and prepared.

As a young girl, Sita would wander into the bow's room by herself. The palace guards saw when she came and kept Janaka informed. But Janaka realized that there was a special connection between Sita and the bow, so he never stopped or questioned her. Sita would approach the bow with great reverence. She would sit next to it and share all her secrets. She would talk about all her adventures in nature and share details of the divine moments that she felt only the bow could understand.

One fine morning, she went for a walk by herself on a pathway lined with jacaranda trees. Innumerable petals that had fallen from the flower-laden branches carpeted the ground. Though they fell in no particular order, the pathway did not appear to be at all in disarray. Instead, it looked perfectly arranged, as if by design. Beyond this pathway was a huge banyan tree. While the roots of a tree remain and grow, the leaves and the flowers come and go with the seasons. The constant roots are hidden like the self and the changing foliage is like the mind with all its varying thoughts and feelings. But this tree had aerial roots. She felt as if the tree was telling her that the self need not always be hidden. Occasionally, in some chosen beings, it shines forth more obviously than in others. The tree kindled a connection to infinity within her. Following the branches of the tree, her eyes travelled to the vast blue sky. Anything that kindled the experience of vastness in her transported Sita to a timeless, transcendental state of consciousness. The Shiva-Dhanush resonated with that very state of her being. In its presence, she felt closer to her self.

But Janaka and Sunayana would make sure she wasn't in the bow room for too long. They would send someone to call her to play or try out some new dresses or help with some decoration or admire an exotic flower—anything that brought her back to an everyday plane of existence.

One day, Sita and her sisters were playing with a ball in the garden. It was soft and colourful and her sisters laughed as much as they ran while throwing the ball around. Urmila was good at this game and threw the ball the farthest. One of her throws sent it straight into the bow room, bouncing past the palace guards and all the way inside. It found a cosy resting place beneath the Shiva-Dhanush. The giggling group of girls came running close behind, entering the hallowed hall. Noticing where the ball was nestled, Sita went ahead, casually lifted the bow with one hand, removed the ball with the other and handed it to her sisters. She placed the bow back carefully and the girls ran out to play.

Janaka and the powerful sage Parashurama happened to be on the first floor of the bow room when the girls entered. They heard the commotion and peeped over the balcony to see what was happening. Janaka keenly observed the sage's reactions to the playful activity that was unfolding below. When the sage saw Sita lifting the bow with one hand, his eyebrows furrowed for a moment, and then relaxed in the next as his face brightened with a big smile. 'Janaka,' said the sage, 'I see that you are not surprised by what you just saw. But I am sure that you realize that this was no mean feat for a child to perform. The bow has permitted her gentle hands to lift it. The bow feels a deep connection with her. It will choose her suitor, for the course of life on this planet itself will be defined in that very moment. When the time comes, announce that the one who wields the bow of Shiva and manages to string it will be the one who qualifies for Sita's hand in marriage. Rest assured, this is not just a test of physical strength or power, for the bow is far more powerful than any being on this planet. Instead, it is a test of one's strength of character and purity of being. The bow is here for a divine purpose and will fulfil it by revealing to the world the one who has come to uphold dharma!' Janaka, his palms joined together, bowed to the great sage and accepted his guidance and foresight. It gave him great solace to know that his most significant responsibility as a father was now entirely shouldered by the divine. Janaka had no trace of arrogance and was a witness to his enormous duties. He felt that he was an instrument in the hands of the divine. Still, moments like these were an opportunity to experience gratitude.

Years later, when it was time for Sita to be betrothed, the grand bow was moved to the main durbar of the palace. It was placed in the middle of the hall on a raised platform for all to see and admire. Kings and princes from various kingdoms occupied the thrones that had been placed for them on either side of the bow along the length of the hall. The sages were seated to the right of Janaka and his ministers to his left. The women, including Sita, could witness the proceedings through a curtained balcony on the first floor. A small number of Mithila's citizens were also allowed in the main durbar so that they may later narrate the happenings to the rest of the public, which eagerly awaited every last detail of this grand event. Poets, painters and sculptors had also been invited to capture special moments from the day and immortalize them in verse and art.

Janaka stood up and welcomed all those who had gathered to witness the momentous day, and with the blowing of the conch, declared the commencement of the swayamvara. The word 'swayamvara' denotes the right of a girl to select her groom, her complete freedom to choose her life partner based on her own judgement. Sita chose to trust the bow completely. She had faith that the bow knew her better than she perhaps remembered herself. After all, the bow had a memory that spanned lifetimes.

It was into this hall that the demon king had barged in uninvited. The light in the hall seemed to dim upon his arrival. His footsteps resounded like thunderclaps. The guards at the door shrunk at his sight. All the guests rose from their seats in alarm. The serpent-head of fear raised its hood and some of the kings in the hall felt weak in the knees. Janaka was, however, the perfect host. He composed himself and offered a respectable seat to the demon king, who looked like darkness sculpted, ego consolidated. He was the centre of all attention. 'I have not come to take a seat, Janaka. Let me be done with your childish test and be gone with my bride,' said Ravana with a smirk, his eyes feverishly searching for a glimpse of Sita. Upon his arrival, Sita had felt the heaviness in the energy of the hall and had retreated behind the thick drapes, no longer visible from the floor below. She was repulsed by his very presence.

Fear gripped Sunayana's heart and she clasped Sita tightly. 'I cannot give my daughter to this demon, come what may! O Devi Parvati! Please do something. Save us from this plight. Surely Sita deserves better than this!' Tears of supplication flowed profusely from Sunayana's eyes. The sisters huddled closer to their mother, all with the same prayer in their hearts. Sita remained resolute in her faith in the wisdom of the bow.

Ravana, an ardent devotee of Lord Shiva, took quick steps towards the Shiva-Dhanush and with one hand, in a casual manner, moved to lift it. The bow did not budge an inch. Ravana's eyes narrowed. He faced the bow and applied some strength. Nothing. His anger mounted and he used both his hands and all his strength. The bow simply stayed still. His anger rose to its peak, his eyes flashed red, his nostrils flared up, and in a fierce, deep-throated voice, a gut-wrenching cry escaped from his being as he bent forward in a final attempt to lift the divine bow: 'Har Har Mahadev!' The bow responded. It shook ever so slightly, and the ground beneath it shook along with it. The tremors were felt by all those present in the hall, and those standing held on to nearby pillars to keep their balance.

Ravana turned to Janaka and roared, 'You have planned this swayamvara only to insult the entire race of warriors alive on this planet. A bow that remains unmoved by me: what hope do mere mortals or even gods have to be able to wield it, let alone string it? This is the bow of Rudra, my *ishta devata*. And for this one reason, I forgive you for your insolence.'

Defeated but not deterred, Ravana stormed out of the hall. The air in the hall became lighter. The lights seemed to brighten again. The women, who had been holding their breaths above, finally let go. Janaka sat back on his throne with a sigh of relief. Sunayana was filled with gratitude. Sita, whose eyes were shut, slowly opened them.

She had avoided seeing Ravana that day. But his presence was unmistakable and unchanged to this day. If at all, it was darker now, but adding darkness to a black night had no meaning.

6

Infinity in a Seed

Sita eagerly awaited the winter months of Mithila. The skies were clearer and countless twinkling lights bejewelled the night. Sita and Urmila would huddle together in bed under the skylight in Sita's room. They tucked their feet into the soft silk coverlet and their hair lay loosely scattered on the plush cotton pillows as they waited for a fleeting glimpse of shooting stars. Those celestial streaks would appear out of nowhere and arch across the sky, leaving a momentary trail of light, disappearing into nothingness, all in a matter of seconds. If the sisters managed to get over the excitement of seeing the shooting stars, they would remember to make a wish. 'Didi, what did you wish for?' asked Urmila. Sita's fingers wrapped themselves around Urmila's as she disclosed, 'I wished that we could be together even after our marriages, Urmila. When you are with me, I never feel alone.' Urmila rolled over and hugged her elder sister fondly, saying, 'I wonder which star can make that happen! We should ask Guru Shatananda tomorrow in our astrology class.'

'Look, Urmila! One more!' Another shooting star whizzed past in the sky. Enjoying this grand spectacle of nature, the two sisters eventually drifted off into a peaceful sleep.

They had to rise early for their classes. They learnt music, dance, painting, cooking, literature, poetry; they learnt to play the veena; they had classes in martial arts, archery, swordsmanship and horse-riding; they were educated on Raja Dharma, the Puranas, Vastu Shastra, *jyotish* (astrology), environmental sciences, the basics of Ayurveda (sufficient to make home remedies); along with all these, they practised yoga, pranayama, meditation and were introduced to Vedanta. They learnt about creation and the various beings of light that governed different aspects of life, and how the balance between the energies of these beings had to be maintained for prosperity, peace and happiness. Sita was intelligent and perceptive. Her intuitive abilities were well beyond her years. Her teachers recognized this and taught her accordingly. She was sensitive and grasped what was being communicated even before the words were uttered. She would often help her sisters and the other children in her study group whenever they struggled with a particular concept.

Janaka was very particular about the education of his daughters. He had organized a grand debate and discussion among *brahmavadins*, the wise ones, in his durbar. The winner of the debate would be awarded 1,000 cows. But in his mind, he had planned this to be the best way to choose the right teacher for the children. Many great scholars from distant lands arrived in Mithila. The reward was a ceremonial requirement, but scholars came because they knew that a debate organized by Janaka would be enriching and add to their knowledge. The great Rishi Yagnavalkya graced the occasion. Brahmavadini Gargi had also come to take up the challenge.

Sita was drawn to Gargi. Clad in a simple sari, with long, flowing black hair, a bright spot of *chandan* on her forehead and kumkum below it, and adorned with a tulsi mala, she was exceptionally radiant.

In the early stages of the debate, Gargi engaged Rishi Yagnavalkya in a series of questions whose answers led deeper and deeper into the very basis of creation.

Sita was curious to hear Gargi's conversation with the great rishi. She rushed into the durbar and quietly took a seat. The conversation had already begun. Gargi had stepped down from her seat and into the central area of the hall, directly below Yagnavalkya's seat. Though it was a debate, she was asking questions and receiving answers. So, she stood reverentially in front of the rishi.

She was his contemporary and addressed him by his name.

'Yagnavalkya,' she continued, 'if all this is pervaded by water, then what is water pervaded by?' Her voice was clear, sonorous and full of strength. When she spoke of water pervading everything, Sita felt one with the water element in the universe. She felt its fluidity, its coolness, and she flowed with it. Her mind was subtler than the water that she experienced.

'By air, Gargi,' came the reply.

The water became air and Sita moved with the gentle breeze. She was one with the air that moved in and out of every living being in the world, and felt the expansion in her consciousness. Her mind was subtler than the air.

'And by what is air pervaded?' asked Gargi. 'By the sky,' came the reply.

Sita's awareness instantly filled the space of the entire durbar and then expanded to all of Mithila, then to the whole planet and into the vast expanse of outer space that contained countless such planets and stars. She was in a state of expanded awareness. Her mind was subtler than space.

'And by what is the sky pervaded?' 'By the world of the Gandharvas.'

The Gandharvas were the keepers of harmonious sound, the melody and the rhythm that form the heart of all creation, the source of life. The sense of sound is an inherent quality of space. There is a sound that is produced due to friction, when molecules collide, and there is a sound that is inherent in nature. This sound is heard only when the individual identity dissolves and a harmonious oneness is experienced. Sita rejoiced in this melody of the self.

'And by what, Yagnavalkya, is the world of Gandharvas pervaded?'

'By the world of the sun, Gargi.'

The radiance of the sun shone in the core of Sita's being. And it was not the radiance of just one, but of a thousand suns from every world shining together.

'And by what is the world of the sun pervaded?' 'By the world of the moon.'

The coolness of a million moons filled Sita's being at that very moment.

'And by what is the world of the moon pervaded?' 'By the world of the stars.'

The memory of the shooting stars in the vast expanse of space filled Sita's consciousness, and every cell of her being beamed.

'And by what is the world of the stars pervaded?' 'By the world of the gods, Gargi.'

Sita was transported to a world beyond the physical, where the celestials existed as pure beings of light and energy.

'And by what is the world of gods pervaded, Yagnavalkya?' 'By the world of Indra, Gargi.'

Guided by the words of Yagnavalkya, Sita experienced the state of Indra as the collective consciousness, which is filled with awareness and dynamism. And there was not just one but many Indras, one for every world. A world of Indras.

'And by what is the world of Indra pervaded?' 'By the world of Prajapati.'

Sita would often wonder who it was that made the sun rise each day. 'Those who lived millions of years before me saw this very sun, and those who will come in the future will also see the same sun rise every day,' she pondered. It was the same sun, yet ever new. No two sunrises were ever the same! And in his kingdom, there was not just one such sun but thousands of them. Who made the moon revolve around the earth and cast the reflection of the sun, transforming the heat into such pleasing coolness? Who made the rivers flow, the birds chirp and the flowers blossom? Who was it who put an entire tree into a seed, and so many seeds in each tree? Each tree was like a universe in itself, and with every seed, another universe could emerge. The tree was contained, unmanifest, in the seed. The roots of the tree were like Brahma; the trunk, branches and leaves like Vishnu; and the fruits like Shiva. From within the fruit, the seed emerged again. The beginning was in the end. The cycle was eternal.

These conversations had a tremendous impact on Sita's brilliant intellect. She began to understand and experience the spherical nature of creation—that everything was interconnected and interdependent. Sita turned her attention back to Gargi. 'And by what is Prajapati pervaded?' 'By the Hiranyagarbha, O Gargi!'

Sita felt a tingling sensation in her feet. The ground beneath her was coming alive. There was a phenomenal amount of movement in the millions of tiny particles of earth that made up the little portion of the ground which her feet rested on. It was as if they had all started dancing together in utter joy. She looked down and her gaze was fixed. As she continued looking at the ground, it began to part, and she felt as if she were going deeper and deeper into it. She held her gaze and began seeing a golden light. The light filled her consciousness—there was no durbar, no dialogue, no earth, no sky—just her and the golden light. The light was full of love and was calling out to her. She was drawn to it, like a bee to nectar. She felt the urge to simply dissolve into the light. She closed her eyes and was about to let go when she heard an inner voice that said, 'Not now.' It was the same voice, time and again. And it was the same light, time and again. But yes. Not now.

The Hiranyagarbha is the golden cosmic womb. Sita felt her own presence inside the cosmic womb, as if she were inside the womb of her mother. This was a space of solidified faith. The mother knows the child within the womb, but the child does not know the mother. Sita felt infinitely secure in the womb of the divine. She did not try to know the divinity. She simply experienced Her presence in every cell of her being.

Sita realized her divinity. Only divinity can recognize divinity. That is why even though every individual is of the same divine spark, one has to go inward to realize this. Then the realization that everything is pervaded by the divine, everything is in the divine, dawns. All that knowledge becomes an experience only when you go to your source. It is like going into the womb again. That is the Hiranyagarbha. That is the beginning and that is the end.

Gargi had a smile on her face that glowed even brighter with the light of wisdom from the rishi. There was excitement in her voice as she asked further questions, because she knew she was getting closer and closer to the deepest secret of this creation.

'And by what is the Hiranyagarbha pervaded, Yagnavalkya?'

'Do not question further, Gargi! Stop, before your head falls off! You are entering a space where words will fall short. These are subjects that are not meant to be spoken about.'

Gargi accepted his words, bowed down to him and held her peace. There were few in the court who really thought that Gargi stopped her questioning because she didn't want her head to roll off. There were only a chosen few who realized that Yagnavalkya meant that these were subjects beyond the realm of the intellect and best comprehended through experience. Any attempt at verbal explanation would only result in a distortion of the truth.

Other sages like Aslava and Uddalaka questioned Yagnavalkya on other topics and received befitting answers to all. With no one left to challenge him further, Gargi stood up again. 'With the permission of all the scholars assembled here, I would like to pose just two more questions to Yagnavalkya, equivalent to the arrows of the scions. If he is able to answer them, then he certainly cannot be defeated by anyone in the subject of the Brahman, the supreme consciousness.'

With the authority vested in her by all those gathered, she posed the first question to Yagnavalkya. The entire gathering waited with bated breath for Gargi's question. What could she ask that might render the great sage answerless? While most of the scholars deemed that failure, for Sita, that was often the state of her own mind! She would look at the bright dewdrops that settled on the fresh green leaves every morning, beholding a little rainbow within them, and become answerless. She would gaze into the eyes of a newborn calf and be rendered answerless. Her breath would catch in wonder at having discovered a new flower and she would be answerless. She would look at the full moon, drinking in its coolness, allow herself to be showered from head to toe by refreshing lunar beams, and be made answerless. Most of creation left her answerless. And she enjoyed being in that state of wonder. She was also wondering what Gargi would ask the great sage.

'Yagnavalkya, what pervades the sutra (reference to Prajapati) which is above the heavens and below the earth, which is heaven and earth, and is that which is between them, and is that which was, is and will be?'

'The unmanifest akasha (space), Gargi.'

Sita had gone for her morning stroll in the garden that day and found hundreds of gooseberries on the gooseberry tree. Squirrels running on the branches shook the tiny fruits so that they dropped to the ground. Sita admired the delicate leaves on the branches. A slight gap, like a thin line, was visible between the leaves that were arranged together. As she gazed steadily at the patterns of the leaves, her attention shifted from the individual leaves themselves to the space between them. At that very instant, she realized that this space was connected and undivided: it was all just one. A paradigm shift took place in her consciousness. Her individual identity dissolved in the undivided space. When she heard the words of the rishi, she realized that while her attention was on the leaves, the experience of space was limited. You can 'see' space only when it is limited. When you connect with the undivided space, 'you' dissolve, and there is the experience of the unseen oneness. There is no beginning and no end.

'And what pervades the unmanifest space?' asked Gargi.

Yagnavalkya remained silent for a moment. He was in a predicament. Those who know the Brahman will not speak of it. Those who speak of it, definitely do not know it. Yet, if he did not answer Gargi, he would be deemed defeated, bereft of the knowledge of the Brahman, and that was not the case. And yet, if he were to speak, how would he explain the indescribable? How does one describe the unfathomable? How do you limit to words the purview of infinity?

Sita recollected seeing the passion-flower creepers during her visit to the garden. They had been planted only recently and had already grown so tall! She had counted seven buds on just one of the creepers. She was seeing them grow so fast, yet she had not seen them growing. Who was behind all this mysterious beauty? It was truly unfathomable.

The rain is visible, the rivers are visible, where the river joins the ocean can be seen. But the water evaporating from the ocean cannot be perceived. There is an aspect that is seen and another that is unseen. They coexist in creation. It cannot be explained. And it is all moving in a cycle, one after the other, without a beginning or an end. Imperishable.

Everything is run by the Brahman, but it cannot be explained. It is like cooking without knowing the recipe. She was living it, but it was not expressible. Be it a weed or a plant, they both had a place in creation and they both grew. Sita felt that she was a part of that divinity. She felt a sense of belonging with everything. For in that space, you begin to understand a little of this deep mystery.

Yagnavalkya said, 'That, O Gargi, is what the knowers of the Brahman call the imperishable.' The way Gargi questioned him on the basis of the authority given by the scholars, Yagnavalkya gave his answer as that which has been said by those who know. He continued, 'It is neither gross nor subtle, neither short nor long, neither shadow nor darkness, neither air nor space, it is unattached and unimpressionable; it is without taste or smell, without eyes or ears, without tongue or mind; it is non-effulgent, without vital breath or a mouth, without measure, and without interior or exterior. It does not eat anything, nor is it eaten by anyone.'

Yagnavalkya continued, 'Under the lordship of the imperishable Brahman, the sun and the moon are held in their positions, heaven and earth are held in their positions, moments, minutes, days and nights, weeks, fortnights, months, seasons and years are held in their positions . . .'

The idea of holding time in its position was interesting for Sita. For those who were on the ground floor of the hall, the events occurring there were in the present moment. Standing by the window of her room on the first floor, she would have seen much more. She imagined herself standing on top of the nearby hill, a place she had visited on a picnic with her parents and sister. They could see the entire city of Mithila from there. It was nearing evening and a thousand little lamps were being lit in every house. It looked like the stars had come down to the earth. Sita had thought of events as past, present and future; one that is behind us, the now, and that which is yet to come. But the idea of the past and the future also being held in their positions meant that everything was there right now: like the view from the hilltop, the rishis must also have access to time in its full scale!

Yajnavalkya continued to describe the imperishable in many ways. He concluded by saying that it is never seen, but is the seer; it is never heard, but is the hearer; it is never thought of, but is the thinker; it is never known, but is the knower. There is no other seer, hearer, thinker or knower. And by this imperishable Brahman, the unmanifested space is pervaded.

Sita's thoughts drifted back to the seed. Though the tree is in the seed, if you break the seed, you won't find anything inside it. She felt that maybe he meant in a nutshell that the Brahman is the seed form of the entire creation. Sita understood it like that.

Gargi stood with a radiant smile and bowed to Yagnavalkya. She addressed the entire gathering of venerable scholars and requested Janaka to declare the sage the unparalleled victor.

When the debate concluded, Sita ran out of the hall and went straight to the kitchen to check on what had been prepared for lunch for the revered scholars and rishis.

Along with her mother, she would also serve them food
that day.

Sita knew that she would be learning from the great
Yagnavalkya, but she also wanted to learn from Gargi. She
went up to her father and shared her wish with him. Janaka
took Sita with him and approached the Brahmavadini.

'Why do you wish to learn from me, child? I was not
the winner of the debate,' asked Gargi. She had a radiant
bearing and curious smile.

Sita said, 'O revered one, from what I understood of
the conversation, I feel that there can be no loser in a debate
on the Brahman. Either you have shared knowledge, or you
have gained supreme knowledge. It is a win–win situation.'

Both Janaka and Gargi were pleased with her reply.

'Further, life is full of duality. Both success and failure
will be part of it. And you accepted defeat in a manner that
was graceful and dignified. You celebrated the victory of
Rishi Yagnavalkya as if it were your own. I want to learn
this from you.'

Gargi was astounded by the maturity and wisdom of
the child. She addressed Janaka and said, 'Janaka, you are
blessed to have her as your daughter. I wonder if there is
anything she doesn't already know that I can teach her, but
it will be my pleasure to have her company. I accept your
request. But do seek the permission of Rishi Yagnavalkya
too!' Janaka accepted her guidance and agreed to do so.

When they returned to the palace, the guards came
rushing to Janaka to tell him that the cows which were
to be gifted to Yagnavalkya had gone missing. They had

somehow been driven into the forest and the guards were unable to trace them. What would they tell the great sage?

Sita stepped forward and asked Janaka if she could go and bring them back. The idea of a visit to the forest was exciting and she knew that the cows would listen to her. Janaka took a moment to decide, because the forest was not a safe place for an eight-year-old. But Sita was not ordinary either. He did not want to dampen her enthusiasm. He agreed on the condition that she would stay close to the guards and not wander off alone. Sita asked if Urmila could also go with her. Janaka smiled. The sisters were inseparable.

When Sunayana found out, she was quite upset. 'You forget that your children are daughters, not sons!' she reprimanded Janaka, choking with emotion, and went off to her room to pray to the Devi for their safety. Every few minutes, she asked if they had returned or not.

The girls, however, were thoroughly enjoying themselves. They mounted their horses, which had shiny hooves, and rode away. The forest was welcoming to them. There was a certain inexpressible beauty in untamed nature. There was an orderliness that was not linear. Those with intuitive intelligence felt at home. Those who depended on just their outer senses were alert and experienced a tinge of fear. The girls did not follow the typical rules. They raced into the forest as if it were their grandparents' backyard. The head of the guards tried warning Sita, but she just laughed at him sweetly and rode on. Their hair flying behind them, the girls looked like forest deities in their own kingdom. They rode towards what seemed like a thicket of tall, thorny bushes, but as they went nearer, new, unseen pathways emerged. The guards were sure these had never existed before. They turned back to see if the pathways were magically closing or disappearing behind them. Flocks of colourful birds flew along with them. Squirrels, mongoose, beavers, all came out to catch a glimpse of the riders. Urmila was a dreamer. In her mind, a handsome prince was already in the forest trying to follow her trail. Riding a tall chestnut stallion and armed with a bow and arrows, she felt he might catch up with them any moment. She even turned back to see if he might really be there, and giggled to herself upon realizing what she was doing. Sita was watching her out of the corner of her eye and knew that she was in her distant dreamland again.

When they reached a certain point, Sita slowed down for the horses to walk. The silence was tangible. The sound of the hooves crushing the autumn leaves beneath their feet was loud. The trees were tall, and the sunrays split into a shower of a thousand beams as they filtered through the canopy above. They entered a clearing where all the different directions seemed the same. Sita dismounted and started walking on foot. Everyone else followed suit. She walked on confidently. She turned left here and right elsewhere with great assurance, as if she had the map of the forest in her palms. While the guards were unsure about where they were heading, they felt reassured in Sita's presence. They trusted her.

In time, they heard the sound of a gurgling stream in the distance. There was a good chance that the cows would be found there. But water attracted all kinds of other animals too. They would have to be careful. Sita walked on. When they were about 500 metres away from the stream, she told the guards to stop and wait there, but to keep an eye on her throughout. She told Urmila also to stay back. They agreed and Sita walked ahead, alone. She moved on the ground like a cloud in the sky. She looked supremely graceful and ethereal. Her footsteps did not make a single sound. She walked lightly. She knew she was being watched. Not just by the guards and Urmila, but also by a pair of shining eyes that were hidden behind the tall grass. It was in a crouching position, ears up, eyes following her every move carefully. Sita stopped in her tracks when she was about 50 metres away from the majestic beast. He jumped out of his hiding place and landed about 2 metres in front of Sita. It was stunningly beautiful, with gleaming orange and black stripes on its body. It looked at Sita and growled gently. She did not move an inch. She looked back at the tiger with intense focus. Her mind connected with the cat's. The tiger sensed the peace and the calm, and its muscles relaxed. Its stance changed. It raised its head, claws withdrawn, and just continued to look at Sita. A few seconds later, it turned and walked back into the tall grass and was once again hidden. All this happened so fast that there was no time for anyone else to react. Sita had sensed the tiger and had the guards stop only so they wouldn't harm it. The cows were busy quenching their thirst in the stream. And when they saw Sita, the entire herd started running towards her. She turned and started walking back with 4,000 hooves following her.

It was a sight to see. Not only had she saved the tiger, she had also saved the cows from being hunted. The guards surrounded the herd from all sides and Sita led the way out of the forest. Janaka's pride and Sunayana's relief were both immeasurable when they saw Sita returning with the cows.

That night, all of Mithila would be telling and retelling the story of their fearless princess and celebrating her safe return. Children would ask their grandmothers to repeat it. They would pretend to be the herd of cows, the tiger and then Sita, and enact the whole story. Men would speak of her valour, women would fold their palms and praise her as a goddess, poets would write songs about her graceful confidence, and little girls would pretend that cats were tigers and walk bravely around them.

Sita was lying on her bed gazing at the stars as usual. They resembled the eyes of the tiger tonight. Her lips curved into a half-smile at the thought of the cat's majesty, power and grace, and how dignified the tigress felt when she walked away. Still hearing the sound of the gurgling stream in her mind, she went to sleep.

7

A Silent Answer

Sita sat by the stream in Ashoka Vatika with her hands in its cool, gushing waters. The gentle flow of the water caressed her tender fingers. The stream itself was hundreds of years old, yet its flowing water was ever-new. The water from this stream and a few others converged at one end of the garden, beyond which was a huge waterfall. From the edge of the garden, Sita could see the mist rising from below. The cool spray of the water on her face was refreshing. The sound of the water was music to her ears and soothing to the soul. She would often see elephants coming with their calves to stand below the waterfall and playfully splash each other. It was amusing to watch them. Their trumpeting could be heard amid the thrashing of the falling water. Beyond the waterfall the water would simply flow into the sea, but that was not visible from where Sita stood.

She wondered if the droplets that touched her hands would remember that they had met her. Perhaps these drops would rise from the ocean, form clouds, travel to where her beloved was and gently pour down on him as rain. When he would look up at the sky, these droplets would fall on his soft face, and in that instant he would feel her presence. Oh! How much she missed him! Tears of longing welled up in her eyes. She saw a baby elephant trying to avoid the splashing of its older siblings and she started smiling, even as the tears were rolling down her cheeks. Sita's longing was ever-new, just like the flowing water. Her longing for Rama was not born of a memory of the past; it was a continuously flowing river of love. It was present in this moment, just as her mind was in the present moment. Just as she witnessed the birds, flowers, flowing waters and playing elephants outside, she observed her thoughts, feelings and emotions welling inside. The garden within her was equally, if not more, colourful and vibrant. She explored and immersed herself in both worlds completely, and was a silent witness to both. The witness in her was fully aware and kept her grounded to the present. It made her sensitive to everything that was happening around her, and helped her stay centred even when faced with mounting challenges.

While she stood watching the falling water, she sensed someone approaching. She half-turned and saw a lady wearing a pretty turquoise-blue sari with a golden border, diamond earrings and necklaces, diamond-studded bangles and anklets. Turquoise and diamonds made a good combination, she felt. Even rubies of a lighter pink shade would have looked nice, but the diamonds were just right. She was older than Sita, refined and quite beautiful. She was definitely a mother. She exuded the maturity that comes naturally from having become a mother. She was certainly royalty, but she did not have the air of arrogance that the rest of Ravana's family and followers carried about themselves.

Sita looked at her in silence. She was scrutinizing Sita, absorbing every detail from head to toe. 'You are young,' she said directly. Sita was not sure how to respond. She maintained her silence, but was not withdrawn. This lady was majestic. She looked like she was carved out of ivory.

'I am Mandodari, Sita, wife of Ravana, the lord of Lanka,' she introduced herself. Sita was even more unsure of what to say or do now. She just waited silently.

'Everything has changed since you have come, Sita. The affairs of the three worlds and their dominion had occupied my husband's mind till a few weeks back. Now he thinks only of you.'

Sita was repulsed at her words. She looked down. She couldn't shut her ears out of respect for this lady, but she didn't want to hear anymore.

'I have heard that you continue to resist and refuse my lord. There are thousands of women who would do anything to get the kind of attention from him that you have received. But he doesn't care to even look at them. His ears have turned deaf to the words of love that any of his women may have for him. He searches among them for even one who has your eyelashes, or perhaps similar fingernails,' she said, as she looked down at her own. 'Intoxicants have failed to give him any pleasure. The sight of the moon burns him. He would have normally taken whatever he wanted by force, but he will not even touch you without your permission.'

She continued, 'He has no interest in the affairs of the kingdom. He does not even enjoy eating, and has lost his sleep. Even the sight of his dearest son does not improve his spirits.' There was an uneasy silence between them for a few seconds before Mandodari continued.

'I wanted to see you because you have my husband's heart. But I see that all he has is an image of your form in his mind.

'You are a virtuous lady. Your purity shines forth from your being. I know not your husband, but I can see that he is with you every moment. The virtue of a wife is her biggest armour. Her loyalty forces nature to fulfil her wishes. Your husband will come. I will try to warn mine but I doubt he will listen. You perhaps do not care for my words, but I wanted to tell you that he is a good king and a good husband. He has brought prosperity to the people of Lanka. They love him. Do not think entirely ill of him, Sita.'

Sita was amazed at the loyalty of this woman to her husband. Who was she trying to convince about the goodness of her husband? If she was jealous, she didn't show it. She wanted for her husband what he wanted for himself, even if it cost her dearly. Ravana was lucky to have her as his wife. It was unfortunate that he did not see it. Sita heard her in silence. Mandodari seemed as if she had mentally prepared herself for this encounter, including what she might say, but she hadn't come to interact with Sita. She just wanted to see her. For the moment, she had said all that she wanted to. 'I will take your leave now. This garden is magnificent. And I cannot but notice that it has become even more charming since you have occupied it. The flowers are in full bloom, the trees are yielding more fruit, the varieties of songbirds have increased and so have the multicoloured butterflies. The lotuses seem to bloom on seeing you instead of the sun. As the daughter of the renowned architect Mayan, I have a keen eye trained to notice such details.'

She sighed deeply, turned away from Sita and walked away towards the gate of the garden. Sita watched her as she left. It was clear that Ravana confided in Mandodari. She was intelligent and had the strength and capacity to advise him. She valued dharma and was not blind to the consequences that Ravana would have to face. But for the moment, there wasn't any more to do.

Sita moved on in search of the tall hibiscus plants with huge yellow flowers. One of them had been infected and she had applied some herbs to it to revive it. She wanted to go and check on her plant. Even in Mithila, the palace gardener would call her and ask her to tend to plants that were not doing well. This was an evening routine for her. She would go on rounds to check all the nagalingapushpa trees, the mango groves and chikoo trees, the banana and the jackfruit trees; she would wonder how such a big fruit hung so high up in the tree on such a thin stem. The gardener would be waiting for her and would show her all the new harvest from the vegetable plantations. He would also have her touch certain plants because he needed them to be healed. Seeds were sown after Sita touched them; their yield improved dramatically. He was convinced there was magic in her hands. She had a patch of brahmakamalas in her garden that would bloom with the rising moon, and had a mystical fragrance. This flower was a secret of the night. One had to be awake while the world was asleep to catch this flower in all its glory. The plant itself was not attractive. The leaves were long, thick and rubbery, and grew in any odd direction. And the flower would come out of anywhere in the leaf itself. But the flower's texture was utterly soft, the petals delicate and pure white: one could not imagine such a beautiful flower emerging from such a nondescript plant. The plant seemed to symbolize Sita's life. It had taken so many unexpected turns, just like the leaves of this plant. But in every situation, pleasant or unpleasant, Sita had blossomed.

8

Playing the Heartstrings

Every morning, at the break of dawn, Sita would go to the stream in Ashoka Vatika to perform her morning *sandhyavandan*. As she gazed upon the sun, chanting the Gayatri mantra, she would pray for the light of divinity to illuminate her intellect and keep it free from doubt or negativity. She would imagine herself as a pillar of light, and whatever she looked upon in those few moments glowed with the same golden hue of the sun. Everything in creation was nourished by the sun, and its radiance reflected back upon Sita wherever she looked. The thought of the sun was an immense reassurance to Sita, reminding her that her beloved was on his way to her. The family of Ayodhya were descendants of the sun, and Rama was the crowning glory of their lineage.

After offering her oblations, she sat by the stream watching a graceful swan swimming towards her. She started humming the Raga Bhairav gently. It was a morning melody and she felt the birds would enjoy it too. There was a parrot that perched on a nearby branch to listen to her. On the other side of her, a proud peacock strutted past and opened his feathers to dance. Whom should she sing to? All three were vying for her attention. She was somehow reminded of her three mothers-in-law at the palace of Ayodhya. Kaushalya was like the swan, always dignified, with the discretion to skilfully separate right from wrong. Sumitra was the knowledgeable princess from Kashi who could remember and quote verses from the scriptures, just like the parrot who could remember and reproduce whatever it heard. And Kaikeyi was like the proud peacock, stunningly beautiful and the most attractive. Kaikeyi had not had much friction with Kaushalya, but when she saw Sita she felt jealous for the first time. She wished with all her heart that Sita were *her* daughter-in-law. She wanted to have the first right to her company. But then, when she would see Rama all her jealousy would simply vanish, and she would be back to her contented state.

Sita sang very well. One day, she was invited to sing to all the three mothers. And just like the three birds, the mothers listened attentively and also took note of whom Sita was looking at while singing. Who was she singing to? A giggle escaped Sita as she remembered those moments. Rama had entered the room but stood quietly behind her. She had not heard him enter, but his presence filled her heart. She stopped looking at the mothers and closed her eyes, allowing the song to flow through her. The notes of the raga came forth like a fountain of love and showered the mothers with its sweet nectar. When she was done, the stillness in the room was deep and blissful. After a few minutes, Kaikeyi commented, 'Did you notice how the quality of her singing changed when Rama entered the room?' Sita turned instantly to see where he was and turned pink when she realized he was right behind her. 'No, Kaikeyi, she didn't know that Rama had come. It was not Rama in the room, but Rama in her heart that made all the difference,' said Kaushalya. 'But certainly, Didi, the cool of the night is felt even if you do not see the moon. Rama's very presence changes the state of your mind and elevates it even if you are not conscious that he is there. His connection with our soul is far more subtle than what can be perceived or expressed by the senses,' said Sumitra. 'Only divinity recognizes divinity everywhere,' added Rama. 'I am blessed to have mothers who see only the divine everywhere—even in their own sons and daughters!' Sita enjoyed this conversation of mutual praise and smiled contentedly.

In her heart, she sang her verses of love which only Rama heard.

Two hearts blended
the melody of the veena arose

Two feelings merged
tune and rhythm became one

Dreams became real
and reality felt like a dream

The boat drifted ahead
and reached the shore.

Kaushalya was a *gunagrahi*. She only saw the positive in every person or situation. This trait was essential to maintaining harmony in a family as large as theirs living in a huge palace like Ayodhya's. Dasharatha was an ambitious king. He was a good ruler but also sought the comfort of worldly pleasures. Sita's father Janaka was different. He did not seek to extend his borders and rule the entire land. He was a raja rishi. The only comfort he sought was that of the supreme self.

Her beloved was also like her father. Kaushalya had told her about the time when Rama was younger and went into a kind of depression. He was not interested in any material comforts or achievements. He wondered about the purpose of life, the secret of creation, the nature of the divine—he did not relate to his father's views on the world and its purpose. Dasharatha doted on Rama but did not recognize his deep spiritual thirst. He was worried about Rama's state of mind and took him to Guru Vasishta. Rama felt comfortable in the presence of the sage.

The conversation that followed between Rama and Vasishta was hailed as Yoga Vasishta. 'I don't really know what they discussed, my dear,' said Kaushalya, 'except that it was about the nature of the self. But what I do know is that I am grateful Rama is joyous and dynamic again. He has never asked for anything for himself, Sita. I have never seen him need anything or anybody. He is devoted to his father like a dutiful son should be. He loves and respects all the mothers and will care for our every need. His younger brother Lakshmana is an extension of his own self—like his own hand or leg. Wherever Rama goes, Lakshmana follows. But I see a change in him that I have never seen before. When I see how he looks at you, my heart melts, Sita. The love that he has for you is a thousand times more powerful than the love a mother feels for her newborn. He loves you more dearly than life itself. He may have bound himself to the world by duty, but he is bound to you by love. I have never seen him happier. I had actually thought that nothing in the world really mattered to my dispassionate son. In a way, that remains true. For you, Sita, are not of this world! I am grateful to the Devi for bringing you into our life.' Sita bowed to her mother-in-law and touched her feet for her blessings. She felt both gratitude and contentment.

The palace of Ayodhya was like a maze. One could easily lose one's way as one room led to another in a seemingly endless fashion. But one had to first seek permission to go to another's room. In Mithila, Sita was used to walking into her mother's room anytime. But here, things were more formal. There were three mothers. It wasn't really known where the king would be. She wasn't always sure about the right time to approach them either. So Sita usually visited them only if she was called or when Rama took her with him. In any case, she had created her own little world around her.

It was the same in Ashoka Vatika. Sita had made her own world within the garden. She placed her attention on nature and remained positive. In the initial days, the rakshasi guards would barely allow her to move freely. They were scary. They did not exude even an ounce of grace. If they had it their way, they would have eaten her for breakfast. They intimidated her in every possible way and took particular pleasure in her discomfort and disgust. They feared Ravana and, strangely, relished the terror he inflicted upon them. They ate anything that moved and were drunk for most of the day. Unclean, unkempt, foul-smelling and foul-mouthed—their company was depressing for Sita. But even among them, there were three who kept a quiet distance from her. They stood guard and avoided talking to her. They watched her throughout and stopped any of the others from coming too close.

After the first few days, one of them approached her and in a distant manner, said, 'O daughter of Mithila, you consume nothing of what is served to you. Do you not want to maintain your health till your lord arrives?' Sita was taken by surprise. She could not believe that a rakshasi was speaking with such confidence about Rama's arrival. 'Who are you?' asked Sita, looking carefully into her eyes. 'I am Trijata, daughter of Vibhishana, the youngest brother of the lord of Lanka,' she replied. 'Do you have any news of my lord?' asked Sita eagerly. 'Nothing that I have heard. But from the strength and patient endurance I have seen in you, I am sure he is coming. Nobody refuses Ravana. These women try to scare you but, in fact, they fear you. They are jealous of you. They have never experienced the strength of the subtle and the pure. Just as rocks are hard, they are like this,' said Trijata.

'But you seem different, Trijata,' said Sita. 'Even the hardest of rocks is weathered and softened by the flowing water over time. Your company has kindled a feeling of friendliness in me. It feels nice. I have decided that I like you,' replied Trijata. 'Besides, my father and my mother, Sarama, have spoken to me about Lord Rama. They say that he is the incarnation of Lord Vishnu. If that is indeed the truth, then the end of the rakshasas is near.' Sita smiled and said, 'Not the end of rakshasas, Trijata, the end of adharma.' Trijata pondered over Sita's words. This meant that the lord was not their enemy. There was still hope. 'Is there anything I can do for you that will ease your stay in this garden?' enquired Trijata. 'Yes, if you can allow me freedom to move around within the boundaries of this garden, I promise you I will make no attempts to escape.' Trijata nodded and instructed the guards who stood watch. 'Kala is my sister. She and I will take turns to be here. While one of us stands guard, the others will not dare to trouble you.'

Trijata and Kala brought immense relief to Sita. She had found rare companions even amongst the asuras. She learnt a lot about their ways of life, beliefs and value systems, their folk songs, and how they brought up their children. Sita would occasionally advise Trijata and share her views on how things should be. She shared some home remedies that were useful for children. Trijata shared those recipes with a few asura women who needed help and they found that their children were indeed healed. The people of Lanka gradually gathered news of the radiant lady whom their king had kidnapped. The idea that she had magical healing powers also soon spread amongst the people. Those who were guarding Ashoka Vatika became popular among the commoners because they would share news of what was happening there. For the moment, they knew nothing of Rama, and so had no trace of fear of him.

Ravana called for Trijata and the other rakshasa women and told them to coax Sita to wed him. 'Tell her about me. Find out what she likes and speak to her in those terms,' he said. 'She keeps singing, my lord! She has a very sweet voice,' said one rakshasa woman. Ravana's face broke into a smile and he yearned to hear her sing. He would easily be able to match her sweetness with the strings of his veena. 'Trijata, does she know that I play the veena? Tell her, talk to her about me. What else does she like?' 'She likes all the birds and flowers; she is knowledgeable about herbs and medicines, my lord.'

'That means that she will be happy in Ashoka Vatika. She is in the right place,' mused Ravana. 'Trijata, what kind of jewellery does she like? Choose a few beautiful pieces and take them to her. Let her adorn herself and feel beautiful. She is a princess, she should dress like one. Take her some silks too, choose the softest. Take her whatever you can and talk to her, Trijata. Tomorrow is a full moon night. The heart yearns for romance and love at that time. I will come in the late hours, when the light of the moon shines directly above the grove, to meet her. Keep her ready and adorned.' The rakshasa women bowed to Ravana and exited the room with jewellery, silks and other gifts to be presented to Sita. They had a task at hand.

'Trijata, wait!' said Ravana. Trijata was his niece. He could speak to her a little more freely than he could to anyone else at the moment. He knew that Sita had softened towards Trijata. 'Yes, my lord,' said Trijata and retraced her steps into her uncle's chamber. 'Trijata, does she still yearn for that mortal husband of hers? Does she believe that he is actually going to find her?' 'Yes, my lord. Though separated physically, her heart knows no other. Whoever Rama may be, he is fortunate to have such a wife. I cannot imagine an ordinary man inspiring this kind of resilience and love.'

'He is not ordinary, Trijata,' said Ravana with a distant look in his eyes. 'I went to Mithila when Sita's swayamvara was announced. Her father had declared that the one who wielded the bow of Rudra and strung it would be her suitor. The bow did not allow me to lift it even one inch. But this mere mortal broke the bow into two pieces. I was not there when it happened, but I heard the news. The bow allowed him to do this, Trijata. It was not a test of strength. You know that there is no one stronger than me. It was the will of Rudra. My lord chose that man over me. I have not seen him. Yet his formless presence fills my mind. Lanka is not easy to find. Yet I want him to come to me.' Ravana's voice was like a slow rumble that resembled the movement of the plates below the earth. The silence that followed was like the calm before the storm. He walked over to the window and looked at the moon. He was reminded of Sita and his voice softened again. 'I feel like I have known her for many lifetimes, Trijata. I feel like my purpose is to do her bidding. She is my queen. I can destroy the three worlds for her. Nobody has ever ruled over me like this. I cannot bear the love that she evokes. Yet I cannot touch her. There is no one to stop me, but my own mind fails me in her presence. She is delicate as a flower but has an impenetrable aura.' There were a few moments of silence as Ravana continued to look up at the moon. But the veins in his neck were tightening and turning green. 'The presence is not hers but that of the one she carries in her heart.' Ravana's fist was clenched and throbbing, 'I can feel him when I go near her.' Ravana sighed heavily and let go. 'He will come, Trijata,' said Ravana, again in a distant, low voice, 'but break her barrier before that. Do whatever you have to do. Break her barrier.' Trijata left quickly and silently.

She returned to the golden grove of Ashoka trees, which was in full bloom. The orange flowers seemed like a thousand flames in the sky. Sita saw her and gave her a warm and welcoming smile. 'You look troubled, Trijata. What is bothering you?' asked Sita. 'Never mind, Mythili, I am sure a few minutes in your company will make it all right!' replied Trijata. She sounded just like the palace staff in her father's house. The cooks, the gardeners, the palace maids, they would all just want to be around Sita for a few minutes, for all their troubles would fly away just by being with her. Her childhood days had been filled with much love and care and even here, amid great adversity, she had made friends. Trijata sent away all the other rakshasa women and told them to rest for the night. 'I will stand guard tonight,' she told them. She was their leader and they obeyed. They also knew that their king had given her a task to do.

Once they left, Trijata sat on the edge of the platform with her feet resting on the ground. Sita sat with her back resting against the simsupa tree. 'Sita, look at you: no jewellery, no fine silks, no adornment whatsoever, just these soiled clothes of bark. My heart pains to see you like this. Yet you look more radiant than the moon in the sky that is reaching its fullness.' Sita smiled at her, 'Whatever shines through me is the light of my lord, Trijata. I am also like the moon, reflecting the rays of the sun in my heart!'

'Devi,' said Trijata in a sincere voice,' if you permit me to ask, I would like to hear from you a little about your lord. If what my father says is true, may my life be blessed by hearing his glories! Tell me, how did he come to wed you?'

9

When Oceans Meet

'Didi, Didiii . . . where are you? Ma is calling us to her room. She wants us there right away!' Urmila was all dressed up and bursting with excitement. Sita's heart had been fluttering since her father had announced the swayamvara. She was excited and nervous at the same time. She rose from her seat by the window, through which she had been intently observing the flowering bush outside. It was littered with white five-petalled flowers with pink cores. Indulging her senses with their beauty and fragrance helped divert her mind. The sisters reached Sunayana's chamber. Sunayana turned from whatever she was doing when she heard the girls enter. The girls went to her and she embraced them with a kiss each on their foreheads. 'My beauties—how quickly you have grown!' she said as she admired her daughters. They felt secure in the arms of their mother. She would not let any sadness or discomfort ever befall them. 'Sita, your father has arranged for the puja of

Devi Parvati in our temple before the swayamvara begins. You must hurry now and pray to her with all your heart. The Divine Mother will show us the way.'

The girls took leave of their mother and went walking to the temple. It was on the outskirts of the palace garden. The temple, though guarded, was accessible to the people of Mithila too. The doors of the Devi were open to all. Still, the people of Mithila respected the private space of the royal family and came for darshan only after the king and his family had completed their designated rituals. Once in a while, the younger girls and children would come to catch a glimpse of Sita and exchange a word or two with her. Sita was very friendly and enjoyed a little chat with them. Some would bring her flowers and fruits from other parts of the country. Others would bring her small pieces of art that they had made themselves. They would fashion garlands out of flowers that they handpicked and give them to Sita to offer to Devi Parvati in her puja. They would bring savouries and sweets from home to give her if it was their birthday. They liked to celebrate with Sita. They would be eagerly waiting for her every day, and Sita also enjoyed meeting them. She always carried some small gifts from the palace with her to give to the girls and the children.

At times, their mothers would also come along and seek her blessings to heal their children. Sita would feel overwhelmed at their requests, but she would pray to the Devi and give her blessings, because she did not want to deny them their faith. And yet, the children were always healed after her touch. No one in Mithila seemed worried about illnesses because they felt assured that Sita's touch would heal them. Of course they took the prescribed medicines and herbs, but her presence brought strength to their hearts.

That day, Sita had worn a delicate yellow sari with intricate golden vines and flowers on the border and *parijata*-shaped small *butas* all over the body. The sari had a simple tissue pallu. She had worn a string of pearls around her neck and golden bangles adorned her slim wrists. Her mother had also given her two diamond bangles to wear that day. Her long hair was loosely braided, and a few stray strands had escaped the braids and curled up around her ears. Dark kajal highlighted the beautiful shape of her eyes. She wore a single large diamond as her nose ring. The kumkum on her forehead was perfectly circular and called attention to her clear forehead and perfectly arched eyebrows. Her cheeks glowed pink and her lips curved into a sweet smile. Actually, every atom of her beamed joy and youthfulness.

She reached the temple with her sister and they sat through the puja prayerfully. They adorned the Divine Mother with the garlands that were kept ready. The pandit gave them a lotus each, asked them to pray and make a wish, and then offer the lotus to the Devi. 'Didi, this is your chance! Please tell the Devi clearly what you want in a husband, how handsome, brave and righteous he should be. I prefer someone tall and without a moustache, but you see what you want; please be specific so it is easy for her to choose for you.' Urmila could not stop thinking about who would marry her dearest Didi. Sita closed her eyes, prayed sincerely and offered the lotus. 'What did you ask for, Didi? Did you tell her everything? Can you tell me too?' Urmila was bubbling with curiosity. 'The Devi knows who is best for me, Urmila. What do I know? I told her that I know she will take care of me and protect me always,' said Sita in a mature voice.

The sisters turned around and headed out of the temple. Sita walked a little slowly, her eyes to the ground. Urmila was bouncing away next to her like a ball of excitement. Sita patiently listened to her chatter and was happy she didn't have to participate. Urmila was giving her news of all the kings who had accepted the invitation and the far-off lands from where they were coming. They reached the steps of the temple and began to descend. Sita was enjoying listening to Urmila's descriptions and they gained speed as they went down the stairs. They were almost running down the last few steps of white marble when Sita caught her breath and stopped in her path. Standing before her was a young boy, perhaps in his late teens, with a bow in his hand. He was a few feet away from her, but she felt swept off her feet. Her eyes met his and in that moment she dissolved into him, like a river merging into the ocean. She could not feel herself, she had stopped breathing; the flow of her thoughts had come to a halt and her eyes had stilled. She had ceased to exist. There was only him and he was everywhere. There was no temple, no steps, no earth, no sky, no people, no voices, no other, no 'I'—Sita stood rooted to the ground and so did the young boy. 'Didi, Didi, let's go,' said Urmila, giggling at her sister. Her eyes met his younger brother's and they both smiled at each other shyly, acknowledging the moment their siblings were apparently sharing.

The boy smiled gently and broke Sita's trance. She looked down and caught sight of his feet. Her heart flowered, and she felt like bowing down. She felt like she was entering his feet and, once inside, she saw the vast, boundless ocean. In the ocean was a magnificent five-hooded serpent that had coiled itself into the shape of a bed. Resting on its coiled body was the Lord of the Universe himself, radiant beyond expression, and by his feet she caught a glimpse of herself. Just as she began to process this astounding experience, she felt a tug at her arm and, in a flash, returned to her wakeful state and turned to walk home. She did not look back nor lift her head on her way. She just wanted to run to the Shiva-Dhanush and share with it everything that had just happened. When they came close to the palace, Sita told Urmila to go to their room and wait. Urmila, though not wanting to leave her sister's side, reluctantly agreed. Sita ran to the hall where the bow was placed, went past all the guards and sat down next to it. The bow seemed to be glowing more than usual today. She offered her salutations to the bow and held it in her hands like a child holding her mother's finger. In that same instant a light as bright as a thousand rising suns filled the room and Sita's mind. Tears streamed down her face and every cell of her body pulsated with ecstasy. His image rose in her mind and the bow responded by emitting a surge of energy, like a bolt of lightning, that shot through Sita's body, rose above her head and sprinkled down like a fountain, drenching her in its cool, sparkling shower. The bow resonated with her heart. If infinity could be tangible, it was him. If love could be personified, it was him. If there was a pinnacle of beauty, it was him. If something meant more to her than life itself, it was him.

If there was something deeper than the oceans, it was in his eyes. The tears soon stopped and she felt a little settled. She gathered herself and stood up. She thought to return to her room where Urmila would be waiting for her. As she turned to leave, she saw her mother and Urmila standing quietly a few feet away. She ran into her mother's arms and Sunayana held her close. Mother and daughters walked back in silence to Sita's room and there, Sita recounted everything that had happened. Urmila told her how Sita had become entranced upon seeing him and added the details of his brother too. 'Ma, what has happened to me? Who is he? What shall we do now? My heart tells me that I belong to no other. But we didn't even ask his name,' said Sita. 'And Ma, they were dressed well, but we don't know if they were princes. Can they participate in the contest? Will Pitaji allow them? Will they even come to the swayamvara?' added Urmila. She was exploding with a thousand questions. 'Did you notice if they were carrying bows, Urmila?' asked Sita. 'Yes, Ma, I think they are Kshatriya boys. They looked valiant and bright,' said Urmila. Sunayana patiently listened to her daughters and thought it best to have a word with Janaka at the earliest. 'Wait here, my dears,' said Sunayana, 'and let me discuss this with your father. Let us see what the Divine Mother has in store for us!'

Sunayana left the girls and went in search of Janaka. She was considerably worried. Her precious daughter had clearly given her heart. She had already chosen her beloved. In fact, it didn't seem like she had to even choose. The boy had appeared a day before the swayamvara. Was this a coincidence or was it divine intervention? But the contest had been announced. Kings and princes had already arrived. They would certainly be ready to wage a war if Janaka went back on his word. Would they even permit that boy to try his hand with the bow, if he wasn't royalty? Who knew which king or prince was destined to wield it? The sage Parashurama had told them that the bow would choose the right person. In her heart, she prayed to the bow in all earnestness. If that boy was not a prince, would Sita lead an ordinary life too? She had overheard Janaka speaking of two young boys who had entered the city with Rishi Vishwamitra earlier that day. Were they the same?

Why were the boys with the rishi? Were they training to become ascetics? Though it was the life of a high-minded individual, it would be full of hardships . . . and Sita had lived the life of a princess! With endless questions racing through her mind, Sunayana entered Janaka's chamber. He was busy taking updates on the arrangements made for all the arriving guests. 'My lord, could I please have a moment with you in private?' requested Sunayana. Sensing her urgency, Janaka sent away his ministers and guards and turned towards Sunayana.

'Do you have news of two young boys who have come to Mithila?' enquired Sunayana. Though she had an inkling, she asked Janaka anyway. Since there were many arrivals into Mithila, they were all being tracked and reported. 'Yes, Sunayana,' replied Janaka. 'They have come accompanied by their guru, Rishi Vishwamitra. I went to receive the rishi as soon as I got news of his arrival. I offered my salutations to the great sage and invited him to grace the durbar tomorrow. He has kindly accepted. It is an auspicious omen, Sunayana, that the great rishi has arrived just in time to shower his blessings on our daughter.' 'Do you know who the boys are?' persisted Sunayana. 'No,' replied Janaka, 'they have come with the rishi, so they will be our guests too. But why do you ask?'

Sunayana narrated everything that had come to pass. Janaka smiled and said, 'Yes, the two boys looked like two suns walking on earth. The people of Mithila were gathering to gaze at them yesterday when they came out for a walk. The rishi had sent them out to explore the city. They carry bows and walk like lions. I was curious about them too. But I never expected them to steal my daughters' hearts like this!'

'But, my Lord, you have announced the contest. How will Sita wed another when she has given her heart to this boy?' asked Sunayana in great distress. 'Sunayana, remember the words of the great sage Parashurama. The bow will choose the right person for Sita. Let us wait and watch as the swayamvara unfolds. There is more to this than what you and I can perceive or control. Why would these boys arrive just when Sita and Urmila were descending the temple steps if there wasn't a higher plan at work?' said Janaka, placing his faith in the words of the wise ones and on destiny itself.

Sunayana felt strengthened by her husband's faith. She returned to Sita's room and advised the girls to pray with all their heart to Devi Parvati that the boy should come to the durbar tomorrow. Neither Sunayana nor Janaka doubted Sita's choice nor questioned her feelings. Their implicit trust created an open and harmonious atmosphere in the family. Sunayana quietly sent out her personal assistants to gather information on the boys. She knew that Janaka would do the same, but women observed details differently from men.

Sunayana wanted to find out everything she could about the two boys.

'Didi, that boy has a younger brother. Do you think he will marry me? We will be together wherever we go then! He smiled at me, you know . . .' Sita realized that, in her own way, Urmila too had found the prince of her heart. But all they could do for now was pray, and perhaps write some poetry!

Urmila was never patient enough to catch her finer thoughts and pen them down. But today, when her emotions were beyond anything she had experienced before, she sought the support of words to express the inexpressible.

Seated by the window, she stretched her head backwards, resting it on the sill facing the sky, and sang in a heart-warming voice,

> The winds of change
> whisper a new song in my ears

> They dance and swirl as they speak to me
> In jumbled words of love
>
> The fountain of youth springs up
> And my heart overflows
> I step into this new world
> A pathless path to love

Sita added to the rich moment with a verse of her own, spontaneously rendered in Raga Malhar. She saw herself in the mirror but somehow she felt that all of her was not reflected in it. She felt bigger than the form she saw in front of her. Sita closed her eyes, looked within and uttered,

> The mind rejoices in words
> Within the boundary of its meaning
> The river rejoices in flowing
> Within the boundary of its banks
> But the heart expands in love
> Boundless and infinite.

She picked up a few flower seeds that the gardener had given her and placed them in her palm. Urmila came near her, saw Sita contemplating the seeds, and said,

> The husk is broken
> The seed has sprouted
> The leaves seek the sky
> The heart is rooted.

Sita's voice became distant and contemplative as she added,

> The mind is set free
> The heart is bound
> The 'I' and 'mine' are lost
> Where true love is found
>
> The world dancing in abandon
> Is stunned and silent
> When deep love awakens
> It is the king! Pure and triumphant!

They had not eaten anything since morning, and it was almost lunchtime. So perhaps her hunger also expressed itself in her poetry. The girls normally ate with their mother, but today she was very busy with the preparations. Their food was brought to Sita's room. The sisters sat down to eat, but nothing was going in. Somehow they were finding it difficult to swallow anything. Maybe they could prepare and send some food for the sage and the boys? At least that way they could find out more about them. The girls decided this was a brilliant idea, cut their lunch short and went in search of their mother. She loved the idea.

She went up to Janaka and suggested that he pay a visit to the sage, welcome him by making an offering of a meal and fruits, as was customary. Janaka told her that it was already on his mind. The girls would have loved to go with him, but that would not be appropriate. Still, sending their father was better than being in utter suspense!

While Janaka was away, the sisters waited most impatiently. Sita had never felt such restlessness. She could not sit in one place. She was unable to admire her favourite flowers. The woodpecker sounded overly loud. The fragrance of the incense was too heady. She walked round and round in her room; she thought she would lie down but the angle of the pillow under her neck felt uncomfortable. Even the touch of the silk bedsheet was too much for her sensitive skin. She wanted to just get out and run. She asked Urmila if she wanted to go for a walk outside with her. Urmila agreed at first but then had second thoughts: 'What if Pitaji comes back while we are gone? Isn't it better to just wait here?' And the plans for their stroll were scrapped.

It was evening by the time Janaka returned. When the girls heard the sound of the chariot, they went running to meet him. Sunayana was already there. Janaka saw them and gave them a big, reassuring smile. Sunayana already felt relieved. She knew that the news would be good. They accompanied Janaka to his chamber and were eager to hear from him.

'You know,' began Janaka, 'the boys were shining like the sun and the moon descended upon the earth. They are gods in human garb. I am certain of this. Their very presence is calming and pleasant, and brings up a wave of joy in the heart. They carry their weapons like seasoned warriors, yet they exude such unparalleled peace. They are so young, yet so refined. Their behaviour was appropriate and the respect for their guru impeccable. I offered them all the sweets that you had sent.' He looked straight at Sita and said, 'You know, the elder boy took one piece of the coconut sweet that Sita had made. He didn't touch anything else.' Sita's heart grew wings. How did he know? It didn't matter. She was happy to believe that he knew and felt her love. Tears welled up in her eyes. She felt gratitude, as if the divine himself had accepted her offering.

'But did you find out who they are, my lord?' asked Sunayana. It seemed to her that Janaka was also enchanted by them. 'Yes, Sunayana, I was coming to that. Guru Shatananda and I approached the great Rishi Vishwamitra to welcome him and enquire about his comfort. Then I asked him about the boys. Sunayana, they are the sons of King Dasharatha. He will certainly bring them to the durbar tomorrow. He would like them to see the great bow of Shiva. The younger is named Lakshmana and the elder is Rama.'

His name echoed in the cave of Sita's heart. Her mind was utterly blank except for the name that was resounding in her being. What a beautiful name! Rama. Her mind repeated the name effortlessly as if it were a sacred mantra.

Having heard all the details of Janaka's visit, the women returned to their quarters contentedly. Urmila went off to her room to change for the night and Sita sat by herself in her chamber. Her solitude felt like a blessing, for now she could be alone with the thoughts of her beloved. It seemed as if time was simply not sufficient to rejoice in the memory of her love.

She reached out for some palm leaves and sat down to write. Her feelings were so fine and delicate that they found expression only in the form of poetic prose.

Rama, Rama, Rama. What a beautiful name!
How pure, how sacred,

Is that moment when you came
Into my life
As my very soul
You are my path, you are my goal
The wealth of radiance in me is Rama
The wealth of compassion, love, and gentleness
My heartstrings play the melody of bliss
A tune unheard, where words cease to exist
The pulse of my very existence
The core of my being is this
O gentle breeze,
Did you feel my breath freeze?
When I saw him
O infinite sky,
Did you see yourself in my eyes?
When I saw him
O twinkling stars
Did you see the light in his eyes?
When he saw me
A sparkling message of love untold
Unbearable, a tidal wave of emotions unfold
Too much to contain, impossible to hold
O brilliant sun,
Were you not but a shadow of the only one?
The one whom I saw
Like a river does my heart flow

Towards the ocean of bliss called Rama
To a cosmic rhythm does my heart beat,
And resonate with the sound of Rama
I lost myself
To be found in you, as you
Tell me my beloved

Is this really happening to me? Is this really true?

Brought back from her memories to Ashoka Vatika, Sita wondered if it was indeed true that she was now so far away, across the oceans, in an unknown land, imprisoned among demons, separated from her beloved. How she longed to be by his side once again!

It was nearing nightfall in Ashoka Vatika. Trijata had asked her a simple question that had opened up a flood of fond memories. The moon was nearly full and rising over the grove. She could clearly see the rabbit-like shape in it. She was reminded of Urmila, who would worry about how the rabbit got stuck in the moon. She would feel sad that the rabbit was alone there. Sita cheered her up by telling her that the big rabbit was Sita and a little rabbit, Urmila, was hiding behind the big rabbit. So the two rabbits were together, not alone. Urmila believed every word that Sita said and instantly, her worry dissolved into a smile. She liked the idea of being together with Sita on the moon and imagined the two of them jumping around, shaking their fluffy tails and nibbling on moon-carrots.

The rabbit was an illusion, the idea of it being alone was a bigger illusion, yet the emotion that it kindled in their hearts was real. The happiness that came from the thought of an illusory togetherness was real. The circumstances outside didn't matter. The only reality for Sita was her sense of togetherness with her beloved. And that sustained her.

Rama too had his own relationship with the moon. Kaushalya had told Sita the entire story. As a child of perhaps two, he had wanted the moon. The little baby kept pointing to the lustrous white, round ball in the sky and cried for it. They brought him wooden toy horses and elephants, little toy soldiers and dancing dolls, small noisy drums and many colourful balls, but nothing interested the child. His attention was only on the white ball in the sky. The mothers tried singing to him, distracting him with this and that—but he only looked at them as if wondering why they didn't understand what he was saying. It was so clear! He wanted the moon and that was all he needed. Dasharatha got news of the child's request and quickly came to his side. He carried him and sat him in his lap by the window. He told the palace maids to bring him a mirror. He held the round mirror in such a way that the moon's reflection fell on it. He showed it to the child, who was thrilled! Happy gurgles and laughter were heard instantly. The tears that were just moments ago still streaming down his cheeks had only just dried, and he was already smiling, touching the moon in the mirror. The moon was now in his hands. He moved the mirror here and there and pretended to catch the moon again and again. Dasharatha would ask, 'Oh, where did the moon go?' and pretend to search for it. The child would put the mirror in the right position and there it was again! The game went on for a while before the radiant child happily went to sleep in his father's lap.

Rama's presence was infinity itself. In his form, he was like the mirror within whom the reflection of infinity could be perceived. Infinity is intangible, but Rama was here. She could see him, touch him, hear his deep voice—it was Sita's personal relationship with infinity. Her relationship was one of unconditional love and absolute surrender. The memory of bowing down to his lotus feet filled her heart, and tears of devotion flowed profusely from her closed eyes. It was almost as if she were washing his feet with her tears.

Deep in the forest, Rama felt a sudden coolness at his feet, as if they were wet, and he felt the intensity of Sita's longing. The pain of the separation tore him apart, and he touched his heart. It was filled only with Sita. He looked up at the moon with tears in his eyes and said to himself, 'I am coming to you, Sita, I promise . . .'

10

Waves of Emotions

The next morning dawned and they all readied themselves to proceed to the durbar. The Shiva-Dhanush had been moved to the main durbar of Mithila. Sita was a combination of excitement, nervousness, prayer and poetry. All night she had only dreamt of the young prince, though she was not sure she had slept even a wink. She blamed the woodpecker for tap-tapping so early in the morning and waking her up. She blamed the stars for shining so brightly and not letting her sleep. She tossed and turned in all directions, put her head under the pillow to block all other distractions, but nothing helped. She remained wide awake.

Finally, it was time to go to the durbar. She wore a turquoise sari with sparkling dots embroidered all over. She liked the colour blue this morning because it was the colour of infinity, the colour that reminded her of how Rama had made her feel. She wore the diamond bangles that her mother had given her and matching diamond earrings and a necklace. She looked at herself in the mirror and realized how love-struck she was. She tore herself from her room and headed to the main hall along with her sister. She sat near her mother on the first floor.

Many kings and princes had gathered, but there was no sign of the young ascetics. Everyone else looked the same to Sita and even seemed hazy. With the blowing of the conch, the contest began. The first king was announced, his deeds of valour were described and he came forward with great confidence, but the bow did not move even a quarter of an inch, try as he might. The other kings laughed. He gave up and sat down. The next one stood up and was announced. The others now watched with a smirk on their faces. Would he fare any better? But no, it didn't seem that way. Kings came forward one after the other, though with flagging optimism, to try their luck. Sita felt the bow's disinterest in these kings.

Almost two hours had passed—still no sign of the sage and the young boys. Sunayana understood from Sita's eyes what her heart was longing for. She thought that maybe she should send someone to check on the sage. It was at this point that Ravana entered the hall. Sunayana quickly sent Sita inside. She did not want that monster to even so much as glance at her daughter. Sita sensed an alertness in the bow. It was aware and curious about him.

Sita's heart missed a beat. Why would the Shiva-Dhanush respond to this asura? Perhaps this asura was a devotee of Shiva. Most of them had received their boons from Brahma or Shiva and become powerful. Sita was worried now. She prayed to the Devi with all her heart. She did not want to see what was happening, nor how he looked. At one point, she heard a thunderous voice shouting 'Har Har Mahadev', and the bow shook. She felt the heavy energy in the bow rising like a tidal wave and the intensity of her prayer softening that force. The bow heard her, the grounds shook, but the bow settled back into its immovable position. Sita let go in utter relief and tears streamed down her face. A few minutes later, Ravana left the hall and Janaka announced a break for lunch. Sita rushed back to her room and flung herself on the bed, sobbing. The princes had not come. She felt inconsolable.

Sunayana was busy attending to the guests, but her heart was with her daughter. Urmila rushed in behind Sita and held her. Tears were streaming down her cheeks too. The sisters hugged each other and each took solace from the other. The afternoon passed quickly and it was time to gather in the durbar again. Sita settled her hair. At first she felt disinterested, but what if Rama came? She didn't want to look sullen, with puffy cheeks and messy hair. Her heart was still filled with hope. Urmila also felt the same. 'Their morning sadhana might have taken time, Didi,' said Urmila. 'They will come, I am sure of it! Don't forget how Rama was looking at you. I am telling you, it is not just you who have lost your heart. If you look carefully within, I am sure you will find his heart beating within you!' She made Sita smile. How she wished that everything Urmila said would come true.

They returned to the durbar and the contest resumed with the sound of the conch. Not a single king or prince had any luck with the bow. They were all defeated and felt a deep sense of resentment. One of them said, 'Janaka, you have invited all of us just to humiliate us.' Another said, 'Since no one was able to move the bow, we will fight and win the bride. If you try to stop us, you will have to fight all of us and lose whatever you have in the process!' Soon there was a clamour of loud voices and the agitated kings started protesting. The dissent in the hall was becoming uncontrollable. Janaka rose from his seat and spoke, 'I beseech you, O kings, take your seat. Do not dishonour the bow of Shiva. I would like to again call, in clear terms, any Kshatriya who would like to step forward to wield and string the bow. Is there no one in this august audience who is an able warrior? Is there not one among the men of strength here with the courage of a lion? Step forward now, for this is moment of truth.' The kings all stood in silence. No one moved. Janaka looked disappointed. 'Alas, the effort to find a suitor for my daughter among men has not borne fruit. It is a pity that the bow finds no man worthy of itself. Let it then be known that the lineage of Kshatriyas on the earth has none who can . . .'

'Stop! King Janaka, it is inappropriate for anyone to declare the race of Kshatriyas as incapable of the mere task of lifting this bow while my brother stands here.' It was the younger brother Lakshmana who spoke. He made his way forward from among the commoners. They had entered the hall while the kings had begun their protest and had quietly stood among the people of Mithila at the far end of the durbar. Sita's heart jumped at the voice of the charming lad. Where was his brother? When did they arrive? What had they been doing so far? Rishi Vishwamitra stepped forward. Janaka rose to welcome the great sage and offered him a seat among the other sages who were present. The older of the two brothers followed Vishwamitra out of the crowd, but stopped at the far end of the durbar, where his younger brother stood. They were the centre of attention. Janaka looked at the boy from head to toe and, in his heart completely approved of Sita's choice. Sunayana could not stop smiling and kept looking back and forth between the boy and Sita. He was tall, well-built, muscular, lithe, graceful, with a narrow waist, long arms, curly long hair that fell below his shoulders, eyes like lotuses, a broad forehead, a perfect nose, inexplicably radiant, with an aura of absolute peace, serenity solidified, and what a smile! 'Well, young man, if your brother's prowess is as you claim it to be, let him step forth to string the bow!' said Janaka. He was happy to see the boy and prayed to the Lord for his success.

'No, Janaka!' objected one of the kings. 'You insult us by allowing this lad, whose origin is unknown, to compete with us. Let him first identify himself, and then it can be determined whether he is worthy of this attempt.'

The boys looked at their guru but said nothing.

'See? I told you! They are unfit to stand among us. They don't have the courage to even speak of their fathers!' continued the brash king.

'Sit down, you fool!' thundered Vishwamitra. 'Have some patience! The boys are here under my care. They will not speak without my permission. They need not provide proof of their qualification for this contest. Yet, for the benefit of your doubting mind, they will tell you who they are!' He looked at Lakshmana and nodded gently.

Sita was looking straight at the young man, only half-hearing whatever was being said. It may have been important, for those gathered below, for him to announce his lineage, but she was in another world where only he existed. Whom to announce to if there was no other? While Vishwamitra was addressing the gathering, Rama took a moment to look up at where Sita was standing and their eyes met again. Their eyes were locked for one moment that was as long as eternity. Sita's hands and legs went weak, the floor beneath her disappeared and she felt like she was pulled towards him faster than the eye could see. There was a lump in her throat and her heart was pounding. In fact, it was thumping so loudly that she felt that all that was left of her was the heart.

'O respected King of Mithila,' said Lakshmana, 'I present to you the crowning glory of the lineage of the sun, the eldest son of the scion of the Raghus, the joy of the kingdom of Ayodhya, the upholder of dharma, the protector of the virtuous, the redeemer of Ahalya, the destroyer of the demoness Tadaka and many other asuras, a matchless warrior, of peerless countenance, and my elder brother, Sri Rama!'

Sunayana heard Lakshmana's proclamation and couldn't stop smiling. Everything would be perfect. She thanked the Devi and prayed with all her heart that this boy should lift the bow. Janaka also could not help smiling, but he restrained his joy, welcomed Rama graciously and invited him to the contest.

Lakshmana had observed Rama looking at Sita. He realized that his brother had made up his mind to lift the bow and wed Sita. He pressed his right toe firmly on the ground, focused his mind and invoked Adi Sesha, the divine serpent on whose head rests all of creation. He invoked Varaha, the incarnation of Vishnu who lifted and redeemed the earth from the netherworlds, where the asura Hiranyaksha had imprisoned her. He invoked Kurma, the turtle form of Lord Vishnu in which he provided stability to all creation when the great milky ocean was churned. He invoked the guardians of the ten directions to stand by, alert, in the form of white elephants. He commanded them all in his mind, saying, 'My lord, the lord of the universe, has decided to lift the bow of Shiva. Hold the earth and keep her stable. Be alert now and be prepared to contain the energy.'

Sita felt the pressure of Lakshmana's toe on the earth. She felt the excitement in the ground below her. She felt the sudden change in the space around her.

Rama bowed to the rishi, bowed to all who were gathered in the hall, and walked towards the bow. He joined his palms and bowed down to the bow. Sita sensed the lightness in the bow. The bow was behaving like a young damsel dancing in springtime, whirling with joy, her feet not even touching the ground. She thought the bow was going to jump into Rama's hands even before he reached out to lift it. The impatience was palpable. Sita almost laughed. Rama reached out to hold the bow and it was as if he was holding pure light. With absolute effortlessness, the bow was in his hands and he held it taut to string it. Every atom that made up the bow was dancing the dance of joy. It was as if Shiva himself was dancing the Ananda Tandava. When the lord dances, all of creation stands by in stunned silence. The entire audience stood up and watched in absolute wonderment. The energy in that space was rising by the second and expanding beyond the capacity of the five elements that gave physical form to the bow.

Holding the bow in his left hand, Rama pulled the string straight and reached out to tie it to the upper end. At the touch of his fingers the circle was complete, the bow emanated an aura of bliss and contentment, its purpose fulfilled, and sought to exist no further with a separate identity. The bow snapped with the sound of a thousand thunderbolts and its life force merged with Rama. It was a joyful union that shook the entire universe. Lakshmana was smiling, Sita was blushing, Janaka's heart rejoiced, tears of gratitude flowed from Sunayana's face, Urmila could not contain her excitement, Vishwamitra beamed with satisfaction, the kings were still frozen in astonishment and the people of Mithila were exuberant. Janaka stepped down from his throne and walked towards Rama. He was joined by Vishwamitra. Rama bowed to his guru and then to the king. Janaka held him with both his hands, gazed at his moon-like face with inexpressible joy and blessed him with all his heart. Sunayana called for the golden tray encrusted with precious gems on which rested the *jayamala*, the garland of victory. It was a garland of delicate jasmine flowers with an ethereal fragrance. She was waiting for Janaka to give her the sign. Janaka looked to Guru Shatananda for guidance. With a kindly nod of his head, the guru gave his permission and blessings. Sunayana and Urmila escorted Sita to the main hall below. When they were about 6 feet away from where Rama stood, Sunayana handed the garland to Sita. Sita's movements were like space moving within space. She held the garland in her hands, looked to Guru Shatananda and her parents for their permission, and took the auspicious steps towards her beloved. Rama's eyes were fixed on her and she could feel his gaze. She stopped about 2 feet in front of her lord, slowly looked up and raised the hands holding the garland. The eyes met again.

Conches blew, drums sounded, exotic fragrances wafted in the air, a cool breeze found its way into the hall, as Rama bowed his head to allow Sita to garland him. She lovingly placed the flowers around his neck. The moment was eternal and perfect.

But that moment too passed into a dream as a new drama began to unfold. The drumbeats were overpowered by bolts of thunder and ferocious rumbling. The crackle of lightning deafened the ears of the innocent inhabitants of Mithila. A whirlwind of dust swept across the land and blinded everybody. People ran into their homes and took shelter. The skies darkened and cumulous clouds in midnight blue covered the sun completely. Nature was reflecting the anger of a formidable being empowered by the merits of uninterrupted penance. His anger was akin to an active volcano spitting rivers of liquid fire and consuming everything in its path.

Sage Parashurama entered the hall burning with rage. He was broad-shouldered, well-built and muscular as a bull. The sacred thread, holy ash and deerskin adorned his body. He held a bow and arrows and a giant axe. He had matted locks, knitted brows and inflamed eyes. The kings assembled in the hall prostrated themselves on the ground as he walked by. Janaka rushed forward with Sita and touched his feet for his blessing. He softened on seeing Sita and blessed her with all his heart. The princes of Ayodhya came next. Parashurama was struck by the beauty of Rama and took an extra moment simply to gaze at his moon-like face. But he was not distracted for long. He saw the bow of Shiva broken into pieces and the fire of his anger rose again. 'Janaka! Who has dared to break the bow? Tell me now before I raze this entire city to the ground!' Sunayana was distraught. How was the sage going to be pacified now? She prayed with all her heart. Rama saw the distress on Janaka's face and the fear in Sunayana's eyes, and quickly stepped forward and said, 'It could only have been one who serves you. Only such a person would have the strength to break this bow. What is your command? Please tell me.'

'Rama! The one who has broken Shiva's bow is no less my enemy than Kartavirya, the thousand-armed arrogant king. I will vanquish him for having committed this foolish, thoughtless act,' roared Parashurama. Lakshmana intervened, 'Lord, I have broken many a bow even as a child. And this was such an old bow. Why do you waste your anger for such a trivial reason?' Parashurama's fury was fanned by Lakshmana's words. 'You fool! How dare you compare the bow of Shiva himself to some worthless toy that you broke? Have you no sense or control over your speech?'

'O revered one, to me, all bows are alike. This one was so old that it snapped at the very touch of my brother. He is not at fault. Please reserve your anger for where it has meaningful purpose,' continued Lakshmana.

Parashurama grew indignant at Lakshmana's words. 'You have no idea of my temper, nor of the strength of these arms which have destroyed relentlessly many an arrogant king and all their descendants. You are ill-mannered and brash, but I spare you, for you are a mere child. Vishwamitra, tell this student of yours to keep his mouth shut if he values his life!'

'O holy sage, you speak to me as if you would blow away a mountain with your breath. But they are all mere words. I started speaking to you with respect after seeing the weapons you carry, but I am putting up with whatever you say only because you bear the sacred thread and are a descendant of Bhrigu. The sons of Raghu would never display their valour in front of Brahmins, gods, devotees of Vishnu and cows. In any case, the arrows and axe are an unnecessary burden to you, whose words are sharper than lightning bolts.'

Parashurama could not believe what he was hearing. No mortal had ever dared to speak to him like this. And here was a mere boy, with absolutely no trace of fear. 'Vishwamitra, take him away this moment and tell him who I am. Do not blame me if he falls prey to my fury. Remove him from my sight at once!' shouted an enraged Parashurama. 'O son of Bhrigu, there is no need for my guru to trouble himself. You have already bragged about your exploits several times. You have grown stubborn with self-importance because you have not met your match. I would have tamed your fury effortlessly but as luck would have it, I cannot and will not fight you!' Lakshmana was incorrigible. Sita was amazed by the youngster's confidence. The sage did not seem fearsome anymore. She felt protective of Lakshmana. Sita felt emboldened by Lakshmana's valour.

Parashurama's fingers tightened around the handle of the axe. Rama sensed the surge of rising energy that would send the axe plummeting towards his brother and stepped in. 'My lord, have compassion towards this child who knows not what he speaks. You are the mature one, good-natured and forgiving . . .'

Lakshmana couldn't hide his laughter at Rama's words. The sage, who had seemed to begin cooling off at Rama's words, again fumed at Lakshmana. But Lakshmana had not had enough. He was speaking again. 'O illumined sage, of what use is your anger? If the broken bow bothers you so much, let us sit together and find a way to mend it!'

Janaka's face went ashen on hearing Lakshmana's words. Sita could not help smiling at his naughtiness. Those gathered in the hall could not believe what they were hearing. Though his words angered Parashurama yet again, he found his strength failing him. Lakshmana sensed him weakening. 'Rama, I spare him only because he is your younger brother . . .' Lakshmana's eyes gleamed with mischief when the sage started up his rant again, but Rama gave him a stern look, after which Lakshmana quietly went up to Vishwamitra and stood beside him silently. With one look, the lion had turned into a mouse. Sita noticed the exchange between the brothers and wanted to laugh out loud, but she contained herself. She wondered if her sister would ever listen to her like this! What had seemed like a dark, ominous cloud looming overhead had turned into an amusing spectacle. Sita was not afraid anymore. 'You young fool! My heart has never known tenderness before, but my hand fails me when I try to lift the axe against you,' Parashurama's words made the mouse-like Lakshmana smile again. He bowed to the rishi delightedly and said, 'O sage, you are so fiery even in your compassion, God save the one who has to witness your anger . . .'

'Don't open your mouth again!' shouted Parashurama. 'Out of my sight, you insolent brat!'' The sage turned to Rama and said, 'There is only one resolution to this, Rama. Fight me, for I will not relent without avenging the bow.' Rama patiently replied, 'I would have fought against a god, a king, a demon or even more powerful beings as I have no fear of death. But you are a venerable sage from the line of Bhrigu, and worthy of worship. I willingly offer my head to your axe if that is the service that I may do for you.'

Sita was not convinced about Rama's offering. Why did he have to say all this? Could he not just point out that the bow chose to break? As if Rama had heard her thoughts, he added, 'It was truly no fault of mine that the bow broke upon my mere touch!' With his attention focused on Rama, there was a shift in the sage's consciousness. He became sensitive to a presence that was beyond the ordinary. 'I will believe what you say if you are able to wield my bow, Rama. This is the bow of Vishnu himself, and equally powerful,' said the sage as he removed the bow from his side. But he was not prepared for what followed. As if the bow was waiting for this moment, it willingly passed into Rama's hands, who wielded it as if it were made of feather and light. Parashurama stood transfixed as his inner eye opened. The truth about Rama and his purpose was revealed to him. He joined his palms together and burst out, full of emotion, 'Glory to Sri Rama, in whose presence the heart blossoms like the lotus upon seeing the sun! Glory to the fire that will consume the forest of negativity! Glory to the light that will remove the darkness of ignorance and delusion! Glory to him who is an ocean of compassion and humility, friendliness and benevolence! Glory to him who bestows wisdom in his very presence! Glory to him whose name is sufficient to free the soul from the shackles of bondage! If all the mountains were to become my book and all the waters of the oceans the ink in my pen, it would still not be enough to write your praises! Pardon me for what I have spoken in my ignorance, dear brothers. Glory to the race of the Raghu!' Having sung such praises, the sage embraced and heartily blessed the brothers, exited the hall, and returned to the forest to continue his penance. However, he left his anger behind once and for all.

A wave of relief swept over the entire gathering as the sage left. Before anyone could wonder or ask about the miraculous transformation in the sage, Vishwamitra called to Janaka and asked him to immediately send word to Dasharatha about the events of the day. He also suggested to Shatananda and Janaka that Urmila's hand be given in marriage to Lakshmana. They were also a perfect match for each other. Janaka looked to Sunayana; both were overjoyed at the proposal. Urmila turned pink as a pomegranate and would have jumped and danced for joy. It took every bit of restraint in her to pretend to be demure and shy. Sita twined her fingers with Urmila's and clasped her hand tightly. The sisters could not have asked for more. Lakshmana's mischievousness was well-matched with Urmila's fun-loving, vibrant personality. Sita looked at him to gauge his reaction. He was trying to keep a straight face and was doing a bad job of it. He simply could not hide his smile. He saw the sisters looking at him and winked. The sisters burst out laughing and ran back to their room.

The air was full of love. Manmatha's arrow had found its mark. The girls had a soft blush on their cheeks. Their eyes spoke of a secret love that they carried in their hearts. Sunayana, gazing at them both, felt a joyous pang in her heart as she realized that her babies had grown up and were experiencing new and powerful emotions.

At first, Sita had thought of her new-found love as a beautiful feeling, a powerful emotion. But years later, as she sat watching the flowing waters of the stream in Ashoka Vatika, she was very clear that this love was her very existence. Trijata had walked with her, listening to her stories, and now stood behind her, giving her some space to just be by herself.

Sita's complete attention was on the sound of the flowing water. To her sensitive ears, it made the sound 'Rama'. She shifted her attention to the gentle wind, and its whistling also sounded like 'Rama' to her. As she walked, she was touched with the cool rays of the moon.

In that pleasant and calm space, a few melodious notes of the veena were carried by the breeze and mixed with the moonbeams like honey with milk. It was an evening raga and was rendered wonderfully. Sita listened to the music and, when it ended, asked Trijata about the musician. Trijata hesitated for a moment and sighed. She looked down at the ground and reluctantly said in a low voice, 'Devi, that was the lord of Lanka.' Sita's eyes widened a little in surprise. 'He plays the veena at the altar of his ishta, Lord Shiva,' explained Trijata. Sita sighed. 'Look, Trijata, such divine music flowing through someone whom we know to be a terror is enough to show you that the core of every being in creation is pure and innocent. Divinity resides in every heart. This divinity is truly the source of power. When one does not recognize this truth, arrogance takes over and pulls one into a downward spiral.'

Trijata was surprised. She had expected Sita to reject the sweetness of the music when told who the musician was. She told Sita so. 'Sita, I hesitated to tell you because I thought you would not want to listen to any music from Ravana.' Sita smiled. 'Yes, Trijata, for a moment I retracted my appreciation when I heard you, but the music was an offering to the divine. And it only brought me closer to my beloved. When the mind is pure, in that natural state, whatever flows through us is the voice of divinity. But when the small mind awakens, the dance of maya begins.'

Trijata witnessed Sita's unaffected, dispassionate state of mind and was astounded. She had thought of Sita as loving Rama and hating Ravana. But now she realized that her love for her lord was beyond that duality. Her lord was beyond just a person. For Sita, everything beautiful in creation was Rama. She felt the presence of her lord even in the music of the enemy. Ravana was not an opponent or adversary to Rama anymore. He had loomed large in Trijata's mind when she placed him opposite Rama. But now Ravana seemed very small because she saw him from Sita's point of view. Rama was bigger than any individual. There was nothing that could come between Sita and Rama because they were not two.

Trijata realized that Ravana would not amount to a blade of grass against Rama's strength. She was reminded of the incident with Rishi Agastya. She shared the same with Sita. 'You know, Sita, a few years back, when Ravana's atrocities were becoming unbearable, Rishi Agastya came up with a plan. He wanted to restrict Ravana's movements without waging a war. He knew Ravana considered himself an excellent musician. So the rishi invited him to compete. By the way, the rishi happens to be the uncle of the lord of Lanka. So, in an entirely natural manner, the rishi challenged him. If the rishi won, Ravana would have to pause his efforts to wage war and conquer more. If the rishi lost, he would be Ravana's slave and do his bidding. Ravana thought he had already conquered everything there was to be conquered and haughtily agreed. The thought of the short and stout rishi being his slave amused him. Arrogant as he was, he played from that space. The skill was unparalleled, the rendition perfect. But when the rishi started playing, he forgot about the competition and fixed his mind on the Divine Mother, his ishta. The music that flowed melted even Ravana's heart, and he accepted defeat. Since then, there has been some peace in the world. Though the asura hordes continue to loot and plunder, Ravana's activities have been curbed and restricted to Lanka. The rishi's devotion was far more powerful than the strength or skill of the lord of Lanka. I am beginning to see things in a different light, Sita. You have opened my eyes to the light, to the power of the subtle and the positive!' And she bowed to Sita.

The night was still young and Sita looked wide awake. So Trijata thought it might be okay to ask for more. 'Devi, can we continue the story? I would like to hear all the details of the wedding; such an auspicious moment! It would be such a blessing to see it through your eyes!' Sita did not mind sharing those memories with Trijata. It was more fun to share than to reminisce alone.

11

Touch of Life

Ahalya knew what loneliness meant better than anyone else. She had spent decades as a rock outside their own home. She had once been a very beautiful woman and she had known it. Married to the Rishi Gautama, she was leading a happy and contented life. However, the rishi was often away for long durations for further research in Vedic studies or when he went into penance. During those times, Ahalya felt lonely. Once, while the rishi was away, Indra appeared in their home in the guise of the rishi and took advantage of Ahalya. She felt that something was amiss but placed her trust in what she could see with her eyes instead of her intuitive intelligence. When the rishi returned, in his mind's eye, he saw what had passed. He was surprised that Ahalya's sensitivity had failed her to such an extent that she was unable to recognize the presence of an imposter in the garb of her husband. He realized that she was consumed by her loneliness and gave in to her senses. Ahalya too was overcome with guilt and remorse. She realized that she needed to go inward and repose in her being to be freed of the burden of this incident. The rishi was distraught for he knew what had to be done. He hardened his heart and cursed her to exist as a rock.

Her senses withdrew completely from the outer world, like a tortoise going into its shell. She was forced to push away everything that pulled her outwards. Instead, her mind was now focused inwards towards the centre of her consciousness. This new loneliness was just a step away from this beautiful place inside of her.

The rishi further said that her penance would be fulfilled, and she would return to her original form, when purified by the touch of the redeemer of all mankind, the lord of lords, when he descended upon the earth. Ahalya accepted the words of the rishi. The impressions of guilt would be wiped out in just a few years and not be carried over into other lifetimes. What was more, her mind would now just have one focus, to await the lord of lords, though she knew not his name or form. She never saw any faults in others and was also exceptionally patient. The rishi was aware of this. Her penance led her gradually into deep meditation. The rock came to be the most vibrant presence in the abandoned ashram of Rishi Gautama. It was here that Vishwamitra brought the two young princes.

'Whose ashram is this, O great rishi?' asked Rama as they approached the spot where the rock lay. 'Rishi Gautama once lived here, Rama,' replied Vishwamitra as he entered the ashram, followed by the princes. He walked up to the solitary rock and, standing around it, narrated the entire story of Ahalya. Rama looked at the rock and felt deeply pained about the sage's wife. At this moment, a gentle breeze stirred the dry leaves where he stood, and they rose and fell upon the rock along with the dust beneath Rama's feet. The stone instantly began to stir. It was sculpting itself into the form of a woman. 'Rama, it seems the very dust from your feet has purified Ahalya. Touch the rock with your feet and free her from her bondage,' said Vishwamitra. Rama felt embarrassed and uncomfortable. How could he touch the wife of a great rishi with his feet? It would be disrespectful. Vishwamitra gauged his sentiments. 'Rama, do it for her benefit. When the devotee surrenders to the Lord, lifetimes of karma are washed away. Since Ahalya cannot move towards you, it is upon you to set her free. Put aside your personal sense of righteousness for the sake of her liberation.' Rama felt better after hearing the words of his guru. In any case, he would have done his guru's bidding irrespective of his personal sense of right and wrong. That was the extent of his devotion to the guru. The tip of his right toe approached the rock, and its very aura completed the transformative process. The life force awakened in the rock that was Ahalya and she returned to her human form. She was shining with the light of the self. She bowed to Rama and tears of gratitude poured from her eyes. In a voice that emerged from the depths of silence, she said, 'Oh, Rama, you are the radiance in my heart! For years, I have felt your presence within me and that has nourished my soul. You have been my companion throughout and wiped away every unwanted impression from my mind. Now I rejoice in my purity and shine by your radiance! Blessed am I to be restored to life by your touch!'

Rishi Gautama appeared at this sacred moment. He rejoiced in seeing Ahalya and recognized the glow of the self within her. He was grateful to Rama for fulfilling the rishi's vow and redeeming Ahalya.

Guru Shatananda was the son of Rishi Gautama and Ahalya. He was overjoyed to hear of his mother's liberation. Janaka narrated the incident in detail to Sunayana, Sita and Urmila. They listened in stunned silence. 'Rama's touch turned a rock into a human being, and his touch broke the bow of Shiva into pieces. It is a touch that completes the evolution of beings, even inert, and hastens them towards liberation. He is no ordinary being, Sita,' observed Janaka. With a distant look in his eyes, he continued, 'He has come to this planet with a higher purpose.' He was now looking straight at Sita as he added, 'And you, my dearest child, have to stand by him throughout and help him uphold his dharma. A divine purpose may have enormous obstacles to overcome. The challenges may far exceed those within human capacity. The path may not be comfortable or predictable. There may be many hardships to face. But the only thing I feel strongly about is that nothing can be more fulfilling than his presence in your life.' He was looking into Sita's eyes as he spoke.

His little girl looked suddenly mature. His delicate child was glowing with inner strength. 'The only comfort I seek is him,' thought Sita, and said aloud, 'Yes, Pitaji, I understand.'

Urmila could not handle the idea of her sister even mentally preparing herself for difficulties. 'Don't worry, Didi! Nothing can actually ever trouble Rama. You should hear all the stories of how he fought with and destroyed the demons who were trying to disrupt Vishwamitra's yagna! They said that the asuras never even saw Rama's arrows because they were so fast!' Sunayana added, 'But I do wonder why the great rishi needed the help of two young boys to fight those asuras. He could have finished them off himself!' 'Yes, Ma! But I feel he did this so that the world would know Rama's glory. Such young princes, but what valour! The entire community of asuras has received a warning,' exclaimed Urmila. She cleared her throat, pretended to be the voice of the heavens and said, 'Here comes the one who will teach you a lesson and put you all in your place!'

Sita giggled. She had expected more gravitas in the voice from the heavens. Urmila sounded like the teacher's assistant at school who would try to get all the children to stop making mischief and sit quietly in one place. But then, dealing with asuras was probably child's play for Rama. So Urmila was in the right space after all! The thought made Sita smile even more fondly at Urmila. 'You look at me as if you think I'm being silly, Didi!' remarked Urmila, and felt compelled to justify herself. 'You should hear what the people are saying. It seems that while Rama was busy fighting the asuras, Rishi Vishwamitra was sitting and admiring the way his curly hair moved each time he released an arrow! He was not interested in the fight; he is as enchanted as the rest of us!' Janaka and Sunayana burst out laughing. Urmila's cheerful presence could lighten the atmosphere in any place, in any situation.

It had been over thirteen years since she had met her dear sister. Ahalya became a rock to purify herself, Urmila had slipped into *yoga nidra* willingly to pay her husband's debt to Nidra Devi. Her sister's sacrifice was as unparalleled as Lakshmana's devotion. Urmila was a gem, so precious, so rare. Trijata felt truly grateful that Sita recounted and shared these amazing incidents with her.

12

A Cosmic Connection

Sita retreated into her memories of her wedding. Sunayana had called Sita to her chamber. She had laid out many trays with jewellery displayed on them. She wanted to plan what Sita would wear for her wedding. Her maroon sari was already chosen. The embroidery on the blouse was being completed. Sunayana had chosen a few neckpieces but she wanted Sita to try them on. She had Sita sit on a small chair and began adorning her. She felt as if she was dressing up her ishta, Devi Parvati, in the form of a young girl. Whatever she put on her, Sunayana could look only at Sita's eyes and smile and wonder at how beautiful she looked. She forgot to make a note of which piece of jewellery looked better. In fact, whatever Sita wore looked like the most beautiful piece of jewellery ever. She was thoroughly confused. Janaka walked into the chamber and stood observing the mother and daughter quietly. Eventually, he could not help laughing at Sunayana. He told her, 'Sunayana, there are some whose worthiness is judged by the value of the objects they possess. But few are such that they add value to the objects that come into their purview. Sita adds beauty to whatever she wears. Here, let her wear this emerald necklace. Sita has always liked emeralds. I like it too. What do you think?' Sunayana was pleased with Janaka's choice and placed the emerald necklace around Sita's neck. Both parents stood behind Sita, adoring her reflection in the mirror. Sita saw their eyes in the reflection brimming with love and felt utterly happy. Now that the centrepiece had been chosen, Sunayana would easily choose the other matching pieces. Janaka told them that Dasharatha would arrive in two days. His messenger had come in advance to inform Janaka. He left to make preparations for their arrival. He also sent messengers to his brother Kushadwaja to arrive with his wife and two daughters for the occasion. Sita wandered off into the kitchen to see what was cooking. She felt like making laddoos.

All the cooks wanted to help her. In her hands, the ingredients would take a round shape effortlessly. When they were ready, she packed them in several containers. Her assistants, who were more like friends to her, all carried one container each and went on rounds of the palace with Sita, distributing the laddoos personally to all the palace guards. If anyone had offered a precious diamond to any of them at the same moment, they would not have even looked at the diamond. The guards accepted the laddoos reverentially and saved a few bites to take home to their families. The distribution of these sweets was a keenly awaited event in the palace. Every celebration or auspicious occasion meant that Sita would come around with prasad. When she was a child, Sunayana would accompany her and make her give one to everybody. She showed her how to smile at the person, give the offering with the right hand and also feel grateful when they accepted. It was all very graceful.

Sita took some laddoos for the gardener and his staff too. The gardener's wife would wait with her one-year-old baby girl to get a glimpse of Sita every day as she came out for her stroll. On some days, the child would be holding a flower and would hand it to Sita with a nearly toothless smile. Actually, she had two small teeth. Sita gave them some laddoos too and continued on her rounds.

The sisters had lunch with their mother. There was a lot of discussion about the gifts for the family members. They enumerated the colours that would suit each person best. The daughters chose a peacock-blue sari for Sunayana. Urmila would wear a red sari. Sita and Sunayana had chosen a diamond neckpiece for her. Janaka liked to wear pure white silk dhotis for all big occasions. They chose an auspicious mustard-yellow silk as the upper drape. Their entire day and the next was spent carefully choosing gifts for everybody.

The palace maid entered Sunayana's quarters to inform her that Janaka had requested her presence at the earliest. Sunayana left the choosing to her daughters and proceeded to Janaka's chamber. Guru Shatananda was there in discussion with Janaka. Sunayana bowed down to the rishi and took her seat beside her husband. 'Sunayana, Gurudev has studied the horoscope of Rama. He will share what he has seen with us.'

Guru Shatananda carefully unfolded the silk cloth on which the auspicious chart had been drawn. 'Rama has come to this planet under the *karka lagna* with the moon residing in the lagna and Jupiter exalted under the auspicious star Punarvasu.

'I will share with you the extraordinary characteristics of Rama as suggested by his horoscope. He is *purushottama*: the highest among all beings. Jupiter is the Lord of the ninth house representing dharma and is exalted in the lagna. The foremost aspect of his personality is his commitment to dharma. He is verily the embodiment of dharma and will follow it to the letter and in spirit. His knowledge of the sastras is thorough. His focus and commitment are unparalleled. Both Janaka and Sunayana listened attentively.

'An exalted sun shows that he will honour his word. He will create an extensive empire and re-establish dharma.' Both Sunayana and Janaka, observed the rishi's repeated emphasis on dharma as they quickly glanced at each other and turned back to the rishi.

'The presence of the moon in the lagna is an indication of his pleasing personality. He can win many battles without fighting. Even the enemy is likely to feel love towards him in his presence. He will also give a lot of importance to what is perceived by society.' Sunayana was pleased with the idea of not having to fight. Janaka sighed at the thought of acting on the unpredictable opinions of people.

'Now I will tell you about his relationship with Sita. The seventh house is associated with the spouse.

'Saturn is exalted in the fourth house and is the lord of the seventh house. Mars is exalted in the seventh house.

Both Saturn and Mars are associated with agriculture and give a clue for where to look for a wife for him. Janaka, you found Sita while tilling the land, isn't it?' Janaka nodded in assent.

'Mars is the lord of the fifth house, which represents the merits of the past life. The lord of the fifth house being exalted in the seventh indicates that theirs is a relationship across lifetimes. Further, Mars is the *adipathi* of *sama veda*. He is the embodiment of dedication and devotion. His exaltation is an indication of Sita's one-pointed devotion to Rama. Further, the lord of the seventh house is residing in the fourth house. This shows where you place your life partner. Rama has placed Sita in the throne of his heart. She will know what he wants even without him telling her: that is how aligned she will be with Rama. Perhaps this is divine love. Saturn is exalted in his fourth house and is also the lord of the seventh house, which is for marriage. Further, Saturn is aspecting the lagna too. Looking at this, one can clearly say that her life will revolve around Rama and she can even be called his greatest follower or devotee.' Sunayana did not know much about houses. But the fact that Sita was well-matched for Rama astrologically was sufficient.

'Shukra is exalted in the ninth house. This clearly shows that Rama will be extremely loving and caring towards Sita. He will involve her in everything. Jupiter and the moon together are aspecting the seventh house, which represents the life partner. Rama will always treat Sita with immense respect and love.' Sunayana thought this must be the case in Janaka's horoscope too for Janaka was very respectful and loving.

'The exalted Mars in the seventh house also indicates that Rama will fight great battles, if necessary, for his wife. He will stand by her in the face of any adversity. Since Jupiter, the lord of his ninth house, and the moon are aspected by Saturn and Mars with a malefic impact, there will be emotional turbulence and challenges that arise in their life through his father and mother. But what shines forth most predominantly is that his love for Sita will be the purest and the highest. The planet posited in the seventh house (Mars), the lord of the seventh house (Jupiter) and the significator (Venus), all are exalted. This indicates a love that is exalted, perhaps divine.' In Ayodhya, Sita would have three mothers, not just one. Sunayana hoped and prayed they would be loving to her dear daughter.

'Janaka, there is the presence of a strong enemy too. Rahu is debilitated in the sixth house, which is the house of the enemy. The lord of the sixth house is Jupiter. It is likely that a Brahmana of supreme intelligence, misusing that knowledge, will be his enemy. But do not fear, because there are all indications of a divine presence in Rama. He has come to the earth for a higher purpose, to redeem humanity from negative forces. The sun is aspecting Saturn in the seventh house and telling us that Sita too will be a fearless queen. Our young princess will be an idol for courage, Janaka.' Janaka's eyebrows were furrowed and he seemed to be in deep thought.

'And finally, Ketu in the twelfth house indicates that he will have no rebirth unless it is by his own choice. Janaka, even a commoner can feel the divinity in Rama's presence. In just a few days, he has won the hearts of the entire populace of Mithila. There is a continuous flow of people where Vishwamitra is housed with the boys; they just want to have his darshan. And Rama meets them patiently and with a smile. The people have taken offerings of sweets, fruits, flowers; weavers have woven special silks just for him; sculptors have carved idols to present to him; no one has gone empty-handed. The look in their eyes is as if they are going to the temple with an offering to the divine. There is talk among the people that they went wanting to ask him many questions, but that they went blank when they saw him. They see his smile and feel uplifted, as if all their worries are gone. Rama has been exceedingly patient in meeting all of them. This kind of affection is not ordinary, Janaka. His presence has kindled the spark of love and devotion in the entire city. Every man, woman and child has given their hearts to him, including me!' said Guru Shatananda, with an endearing smile. Janaka and Sunayana joined their palms and bowed down to their guru. He raised his right hand in a gesture of blessing.

13

Eternal Moments in the River of Time

The next day dawned to the sound of chariots entering the palace. Conches were blown and drums were beaten to announce the arrival of the king of Ayodhya. The great sages Vasishta, Vamadeva, Jabali, Markandeya and Katyayana accompanied Dasharatha to Mithila. Janaka had made careful arrangements for the royal entourage and for Dasharatha's army. He welcomed them appropriately along with his brother Kushadwaja and performed the pujas as prescribed by the scriptures before commencing the discussions.

As is customary, the great Rishi Vasishta described the lineage of the Raghus and Guru Shatananda described the lineage of the kings of Mithila. There was an air of great joy and happiness. Dasharatha, though a powerful king, recognized the greatness of Janaka's wisdom and the values that an alliance with him would bring to his empire.

Janaka subsequently addressed Rishi Vasishta, the spokesperson for the Raghus, and offered Sita's hand to

Rama and Urmila's hand to Lakshmana. The ceremonial offering was accepted joyously by the sage and the king. Soon after, sages Vishwamitra and Vasishta made another proposal to Janaka. Vishwamitra said, 'Janaka, your brother Kushadwaja has two daughters, Mandavi and Shrutakirti, who resemble goddesses walking on the earth. We would like them to be wedded to Dasharatha's sons Bharata and Shatrugna, respectively. They are also valiant princes of the line of Raghu. In this way, the alliance between the two families will strengthen further.' Hearing the advice of the great sages, Janaka and Kushadwaja felt exceedingly delighted. They looked to their guru, Shatananda, for his consent. He smiled and blessed them to go ahead. Janaka requested the permission of the sages to have the wedding ceremony for all the four couples on the same day.

The sages conceded and recommended that the wedding be held under the auspicious star Uttara Phalguni three days hence.

After all the important decisions had been taken, Dasharatha took leave to return to his camp, meet his sons and prepare for the ceremonies for his forefathers to be held the next morning to honour and thank the ancestors and seek their blessings.

Janaka shared all the details of the meeting with Sunayana. It was an occasion for great celebration. The sisters would be together and give each other company in the vast palace of Ayodhya. There was much to arrange within three days. Both Sunayana and Janaka set off to make preparations.

The entire city of Mithila was preparing for the wedding. Every house in each street in the city was decorated. People were busy shopping for new bangles, new sarees and dhotis, ordering flowers, deciding which jewellery to wear—there was just far too much to do.

The wedding hall was readied with four ceremonial fires for the four couples. Each area was adorned with fragrant flower decorations and yellow was the predominant colour.

On the auspicious day, Rama wore a yellow silk dhoti with a grand red-and-green border. The upper drape was a light blue silk brocade. Sita wore a maroon tissue sari with a thousand butas. It was of a soft, shining fabric with a flowing drape. She also wore an intricately embroidered *odhani* (additional silk cloth worn across the head). Her blouse was golden-yellow and also heavily embroidered with gold zari. It was in contrast to the sari but complemented it well. On her arms she wore golden armlets studded with diamonds and rubies. Her bangles were arranged carefully. Some were plain gold, some studded with diamonds, some with a combination of diamonds and emeralds and some with rubies. The ruby bangle reminded her of pomegranates and the amazing way in which each little seed, surrounded by the lovely pink pulp, is packed in the fruit. She wore delicate diamond finger rings and jingling anklets. Her ornate waistband was also studded with precious gems. She wore all the jewellery that Sunayana wanted her to wear. Her mother had a very refined taste and Sita was comfortable with her choice. All the three mothers in Ayodhya had also sent her long chains to wear. Kaushalya sent her an ornate pendant studded with emeralds and diamonds. Sumitra sent her a ruby choker and Kaikeyi sent her a neckpiece in a lovely blue sapphire. Her mother gave her a *navaratna* pendant with all the colours. The precious stones in her tiara had an extra shine in them on this day. Intricate mehndi designs had been drawn on her delicate hands. Her sisters had made Sita sit with her eyes closed and drawn the sun, the moon, the stars, various flowers and everything that they could think of that Sita was fond of in nature. Somewhere in between, they had written Rama's name and, when they were done, Sita had to search for it. She couldn't really see where 'Rama' was written between all the wiggly lines. While the sisters were making fun of her, Sunayana walked in and told her that because his name was etched in her heart, all she had to do was close her eyes! Once her mehndi was done, Sita took the bowl with the paste and started going around applying little round patches of mehndi on the palms of all the ladies of the palace staff. They all queued up with their palms outstretched and Sita smilingly applied the paste. The colour of the mehndi would fade in a few days, but the memory of Sita's touch would remain in their hearts and add colour to their lives time and again.

Sunayana's heart was brimming with joy. At the same time, she knew that her daughter would now be the daughter of another house and she struggled to contain the tears that threatened to come bursting out. Somehow, she managed to conceal them with a broad smile. And when she smiled, her eyes also smiled. Even then, a few tears that escaped her beautiful eyes were tears of joy, because she knew with certainty that the perfect suitor for Sita was Rama. She could wish for nothing more than that. But she did remember the first day she had seen the child in that wooden box, and when Janaka had handed the child to her. Sita had felt like a flower, a feather. She thought, 'Is this the same child? How time has flown! Today, she is the most beautiful girl.' Sunayana was proud of her, but at the same time, her motherly heart missed a beat at the thought of sending her off to Ayodhya. She consoled herself that instead of one mother here, she would have three mothers there. She saw a mental image of the three mothers and her heart felt comforted. Still, she wondered if any other mother could care for her Sita like she could. She told herself, 'How pretentious of me! To think no one else could be more loving . . .' And as her days passed mentally wrestling with such thoughts, the moment they had all waited for arrived. It was all so ethereal. No words could really capture the magic of the wedding of Rama and Sita. There were many flowers and fruits, sweets and vibrant decorations. Everywhere was abundance. All the guests were well-cared for and very well-fed. Mithila had never seen such a celebration. All the four sisters had garlands of lovely jasmine buds with small bunches of *kanakambara* flowers. The orange was in stunning contrast to the white flowers and was twined with golden thread. There was also a garland of fragrant champaka flowers with golden beads.

When Janaka called them, adorned from head to toe, they walked into the sacred altar one by one. Sita, who came first, was escorted by Sunayana. Her head was bowed in shyness but she wore a sweet smile. Janaka guided her to stand in front of the fire. Rama was standing on the

other side. Sita looked up at him. Janaka saw her behind the
sacred flames. She herself was glowing so radiantly that for a
moment he could not see the difference. This was more of
an inner experience for Janaka than something that his eyes
beheld. With Vasishta's consent, Rama stepped forward.
Vishwamitra and Shatananda presided over the wedding
ceremony. Janaka chanted the sacred mantras and sprinkled
the holy water over Sita. Janaka, through the hymns
chanted, offered the hand of Sita to Rama, proclaiming that
she would be the one to support him and help him uphold
dharma throughout his life. Rama extended his hand and
Janaka prayerfully placed the beautiful hands of his daughter
into the auspicious ones of Rama. When Rama's fingers
wrapped themselves around Sita's, she felt like it was raining
nectar on her. He held her with a sense of authority. She
felt that she belonged completely to him. They waited till
all the brothers were in their respective altars, holding the
hands of their wives. The four brothers circumambulated
the sacred fire together.

Sacred hymns from the Rig Veda solemnized the
commitment between husband and wife in seven aspects.
The couples took seven steps, called the *saptapadi*, together,
with *agni* (the sacred fire) as the witness.

The rishis and the priests chanted the ancient mantras
that were supposed to be chanted at this auspicious moment.
The songs of the Gandharvas could be heard even by mortal
ears on that day. The ethereal music added to the emotion
that filled the moment. Sunayana gave a beautiful carved
wooden box, inlaid with gold and containing the auspicious

sindoor, to Rama. He took the sindoor between his thumb and ring finger and anointed Sita's forehead. The moment his thumb touched her, she closed her eyes and, like a flash, she was pulled into another world, another state of consciousness. She saw the beautiful form of her lord, only it was far bigger, scaling all the worlds, and like a blue lotus in its softness, like a sapphire in its gloss and radiance, and like a dark raincloud in its freshness. His face shone like the full moon and his smile put the moonbeams to shame. His shoulders emanated the majesty of a lion and the sacred thread rested lightly on it. He had four hands holding the conch, the discus, a splendid lotus and the mace. And by his side stood his Maya Shakti, the primordial energy. Sita felt as if she was being washed by a scintillating wave of dynamic energy. She saw a glimpse of the radiant face of the Devi and instantly held her breath. At the same time, she also felt the touch of Rama's finger as it moved across her forehead. She felt his touch in every cell of her being. Her heart danced and the rest of her being watched the dance in stunned silence. Sita also saw a king with his wife, shining with the light of austere penance, receiving a boon from the lord. She did not recognize the lady, but the man had the energy of Dasharatha. She felt the light of the lord enter the king, with the intention of manifesting itself at the right time. Sita felt Sunayana's touch as she held her arms from behind her, and was brought back to the present.

The three brothers followed suit and applied sindoor to the foreheads of their wives. Grateful tears flowed from the eyes of Janaka, Sunayana, Khushadwaja and his wife.

Sita looked really grown-up to Sunayana. Her eyes were drinking in every small detail of the ceremony, especially the way Sita was looking, what she did, how she smiled and so on, and committing it to her memory.

She saw how happy Urmila looked and how much Lakshmana smiled at her. They would be happy together. She also noticed how both of them were stealing glances at Rama and Sita before turning their attention to the fire before them.

When all this was over, she would turn the pages of the book in her mind and relive these moments at a relaxed pace. Those moments passed like a dream, but it was the best dream Sunayana had ever had.

After the wedding, it was time for food. Sita had been instrumental in deciding the menu. She wanted laddoos, many types of laddoos—motichur, besan, dry-fruit laddoos—and also jalebis with rabri, milk cakes, malpua, sweet rotis, dal baati churma, kheer, soft plain chapattis, filled ones, badam rotis, cashew sweets, pumpkin halwa, varieties of rice cooked with abundant saffron, chana dal with lauki, stuffed parval, kadhi and many more treats. The guests returned to their camps with their hearts as full as their stomachs.

Everyone was full of praise for the wedding. It was as if they had had the darshan of a divine moment, not just attended a wedding. One of the sages remarked that Rama had shown his mastery over the three *gunas* with the wedding. Having destroyed Tataka, he won over *tamas* (inertia, ignorance and delusion). Having liberated Ahalya, he conquered *rajas* (desires, cravings and aversions) and uniting with Sita was his victory over *sattva* (absolute purity).

The young brides accompanied their husbands to their respective camps. Within the next few weeks, at an auspicious hour, the entourage would return to Ayodhya.

In the evening, all the four couples came to Janaka's palace to have dinner together. Dasharatha and other elders retired to their camp early. Rama and the brothers stayed back a little longer with their wives. All of Rama's brothers looked up to him with great love and respect. He was more like a father to them. They wanted to serve him in every way possible. This kind of devotion among brothers was a rare phenomenon, Janaka and Sunayana observed this in their attitudes.

After dinner, Sita was alone with Sunayana for some time while the others were busy chatting. 'My dearest child,' began Sunayana, 'the Devi has showered her blessings upon us. Rama is the perfect human being in more ways than one. Everything about him is perfect. Did you notice the way his brothers look up to him? Sita, until this morning, you were only my beautiful daughter. But now, you will be looked up to like a mother for all your younger sisters and Rama's brothers. Ayodhya is a big place. Things will be much more formal. There are three queen mothers there. Still, your sisters will look to you for guidance. They will follow you in everything they do. I don't have to tell you; I am sure you will be the perfect example. Still, for my sake, I want to share a few thoughts with you. A mother, Sita, has to be both gentle and assertive. You have to ensure harmony between the families of the four brothers. They may have diverse mindsets. You have to skilfully keep them all together. Your husband is the embodiment of dharma. He will impartially have to take everyone's opinions into consideration to make any decision. If you want to participate in the decision-making, then take the support of dharma. It is better to avoid putting any emotional pressure on Rama. Emotions may not always show you the right path to take. Maintain a respectful relationship with your mothers-in-law.

'Ayodhya is so big that you can easily create your own world within the palace. The palace assistants will be very curious. Be cautious and friendly. Try to avoid saying anything in front of them till you get a clear picture of how they are. It is good to avoid gossip as much as possible. Intrigue often accompanies royalty. While you should stay informed about whatever is happening with the subjects, give your opinions only if you are asked for them. The people will see you as their future queen. Try to connect with them. You can take up small projects for the benefit of the people in time.' She went up to her puja room and brought back a small parcel wrapped in red silk. She sat next to Sita and handed her the parcel. Sita carefully unwrapped it. Inside was a statue, a replica of her idol of Devi Parvati. 'This is for your puja, Sita. Light a lamp at her altar every day, offer some flowers, some fruits, incense, lights . . . You know all this, but I am just telling you . . .' said Sunayana, looking at her daughter with a tender smile.

Sita held the statue as if she were holding a newborn baby and gazed at the face of the Devi. The Devi, from a fragment of whose being countless Lakshmis, Umas and

Brahmanis emanate, filled her consciousness. She saw that the mere play of her eyebrows brought the cosmos into existence. Tears flowed from Sita's eyes and she rested her head on her mother's shoulders. Sunayana pulled her closer and held her as if she never wanted to let go. She could not hold the tears back any longer. She could not have been happier, but she would have to fill the vacuum that would be created in Mithila by Sita's absence with memories of her beloved daughter. The woodpecker was Sita's bird. The flowers were from Sita's plants. Everything in Mithila would speak to her of Sita. Every inch of the palace was filled with pleasant memories of Sita. Somehow, they would manage. Janaka and Sunayana would have each other's company to reminisce. Sita held the idol of the Devi close to her. She would always feel the comfort of being in her mother's home in the company of the Devi.

Janaka entered the chamber and joined the mother and daughter. He also had some advice for Sita. 'My child, all the sages and Guru Shatananda clearly say that Rama has come to earth for a divine purpose. While nothing can be more fulfilling than the constant company of divinity, the challenges to be faced may also be equally significant. Be strong, my child. Be his strength too. He loves you dearly. I can see it in his eyes. And come what may, have faith in him. That will be your greatest strength. Being the torchbearer of dharma for all of mankind is not an easy task. But if anyone on this planet can do it, it is Rama. He is certainly the highest among men. And you are his crowning jewel, the one whom he has placed in the lotus of his heart. You are blessed, Sita. And so are we all, to be a part of the magic that is unfolding on the planet now!' They could hear the pitter-patter of raindrops outside. Janaka moved to the window to look up at the night sky covered with rainclouds. 'Look, my dear ones,' said Janaka, 'the rains have started! The crystal-clear raindrops become turbid upon touching the earth, like the soul that is enveloped by maya upon its birth.'

Sunayana came to stand by Janaka and quietly watched the droplets as they embraced mother earth. 'These droplets, coming from all directions, collect in little pools, the way virtues collect in the heart of man during his life,' she observed. Sita added to what her mother said as she walked up and stood between them: 'The waters of these flowing streams will become still on merging with the ocean, just as the ego finds eternal rest upon merging with the lord!' Janaka and Sunayana both looked at each other and smiled. The three of them allowed the raindrops to fall on their faces and these droplets mixed with the tears of gratitude that flowed freely from their eyes.

Rama and his brothers, along with their wives, also came out to enjoy the rain. Bharata and Shatrugna, though they had come later, had also gone around the city of Mithila a little bit.

Bharata was a keen observer. He heard the sound made by the droplets as they touched the earth. He heard the sound they made when they fell upon the leaves of the trees and dripped down. Somewhere, the water collecting on the rooftops was falling like a small waterfall. And after every few minutes of pouring, there would be a short respite in which the frogs could be heard clearly. 'The frogs croak everywhere, like little boys of Mithila chanting the Vedas!' he observed. With Janaka being a very spiritual king, the study of the Vedas and the Upanishads flourished in Mithila.

Urmila added to the conversation: 'The trees will be clothed in fresh new leaves and look like the mind of the devotee after a glimpse of the lord!' Lakshmana turned pink and smiled to himself at her words. But the brothers and their wives all noticed his expression and their gentle laughter filled the air.

Rama again turned their attention to what was happening outside: 'Look at the travellers! They stop here and there in wonder, like the senses that become still when wisdom dawns!' Their minds too became still upon hearing his words. Having focused their attention on the scenery, he had guided them back within, to the space of the seer.

Janaka, Sunayana and Sita soon joined them. Sita and Urmila stepped out and stretched their hands out to catch the raindrops on their palms. It was such a joy to see the little drops falling on the leaves of fig trees and litchi trees, making a rushing noise while flowing over the roof—a noise that was so powerful yet soft. 'Look, Urmila,' said Sita, 'they have come from distant clouds, but you can still touch them. In a moment, you feel connected to the clouds and the sky. Through these little drops, we can live in the clouds, but let our minds not be cloudy!' pondered Sita.

The rain subsided and the stars came out into the night sky. The clouds had moved away, revealing these countless drops of light, as if a veil covering the sky had been removed.

Janaka and Sunayana stood gazing for a while into the infinite firmament along with the four brothers and their wives, all wrapped in a space of sweet love and silence.

The night sky in Ashoka Vatika also shone with a thousand stars and looked absolutely magical. These stars had existed for millions of years. They would have witnessed all the ups and downs of life. Sita wondered which star her destiny was written upon. Her star must definitely be watching her. Her star would know where Rama was and when he would reach the shores of Lanka. The stars twinkled back at Sita and she thought that they were telling her that the time was near! She smiled to herself at the thought and took courage again.

Rama and the brothers stayed in Mithila for several months after the wedding. The thought of Sita leaving would bring tears to the eyes of Janaka, Sunayana and the rest of Mithila. So Dasharatha promised Janaka that Rama and the brothers would stay back in Mithila till Janaka permitted them to leave.

It was a golden period for Mithila. Rama and the brothers witnessed every aspect of Mithila's culture. They were served new dishes every day. They visited many of the nearby sights. Bharata and Shatrugna and their respective wives went for a few days to Sankasya, where Kushadwaja ruled. In the evenings Rama, Sita, Lakshmana and Urmila would often go for a boat ride on the Kamala river. On full-moon nights, the rides were particularly romantic. They would sing songs, play instruments and have a picnic on the boat. On new moon nights, they would be able to see a galaxy of stars, and the sight was breathtaking. Sometimes, they would just sit in silence, listening to the sound of the water as it lapped against the sides of the boat.

On one full-moon night, while they were on the boat in Mithila, Sita's words flowed like poetry as she sang spontaneously. The words didn't rhyme, but the depth of her soul was expressed through them. Her music was free-flowing and ethereal, sometimes in verse, sometimes just a humming of the melody.

Is life a straight path?
A clear route, predictable?
The oars are in your hands
Only seemingly

Is life a winding road?
Full of uncertainty, perhaps mystical?
Nothing is in your hands
Only seemingly

The mind is your boat
To the moon and back
In the river of time, along stretches that are known
Turn by turn, up and down, into the unknown
Does it start at the end
Or does it end at the start?

Come home
Beyond the mind

Come home
Into the self
Where the river merges into the ocean
Where it knows it always belonged
Free from identities and notions
Reposing in who you are . . .

And as she sang the last line, she leaned back and rested against Rama's chest. He held her close to him and her mind froze. She held on to that moment as if it were forever. 'Sita,' said Rama, his voice full of love, 'Your words are brimming with wisdom, showing the seeker the path to liberation.'

'Being with nature is liberation, isn't it?' asked Sita.

'Being in your nature is liberation,' said Rama.

'Jijaji, Didi, I'd rather be here enjoying your company, listening to your songs, commenting on your conversations—whether or not I should—than be liberated!' said Urmila.

'Liberation is when you feel you are a part of the divine!' said Sita.

'I feel like I am a part of you, Didi!' replied Urmila.

'And a part of Lakshmana too,' added Sita with a smile as Urmila blushed. Her attention shifted to the water again.

Alongside the boat, a few leaves and twigs also floated on the river. Ducks, swans and other water birds swam along at a safe distance. They were often found closer to the banks. Sita was watching everything moving. The water, the banks: they looked like they were moving away while Sita was in the same place, still and unchanged.

In the river of time, so many events had passed, everything around her had changed, but Sita was the same, unaffected by everything. The water of the river was ever new, yet the river was ancient. The sunrise was new every day, yet the sun was ancient. Like that, the experiences that Sita went through each day were new, but a part of her felt eternal and unchanged. She was not as young as she was in Mithila, she was not as adorned as she was in Ayodhya, she was not as physically strong as she was while in the forest with Rama, but deep within, she was the same.

She had been carried across the ocean and held captive here. She waited for the moment when Rama would reach these shores. Normally, it is the river that flows towards the ocean. But here, it seemed that the ocean would come looking for the river. And every time they meet, the river becomes the ocean. From the moment Sita had met Rama, she constantly felt the vastness of his presence. And those who met her felt his energy and presence strongly through her.

14

The Shiva Principle

Rama would go for a stroll in the palace garden with Sita, excitedly pointing out some special bird or flower. Sita planted new varieties here and there, and monitored their growth carefully. She once planted a whole garden of sunflowers that grew over six feet tall, and large, round sunflowers bloomed. Many parrots flocked to that part of the garden. They would rest on the flowers as if sitting on a cushioned sofa. Sita loved these bright yellow, cheerful flowers. She pointed out the intricate details in the central part of the flower. Rama was also a keen observer. He asked her, 'Do you know what they do when the sun is hiding?' Sita had not noticed that. 'They turn to each other!' replied Rama. 'They draw their strength from each other. Having a good family, friends, neighbours and community is important. In tough times, they can turn to each other for support.'

Who could Sita turn to in Ashoka Vatika? Though the entire garden resonated with her longing, she yearned for a sign of someone, anyone, who could give her some news of her beloved.

Sita walked up to the stream and sat near the edge. She made a small Shiva Linga from the damp earth by the stream and decorated it with a few flowers. She would sit by the Shiva Linga with her eyes closed, imagining that she was with Rama while he was doing the Rudra Puja. This had been part of their morning routine in Ayodhya. While their family deity was Vishnu, Rama's ishta was Shiva.

The sage Vasishta had given a crystal-clear Spatika Linga to Rama for his daily puja. This Shiva Linga was kept in a small altar in their chamber in the palace of Ayodhya. Sita had kept the idol of Devi Parvati adjacent to the Shiva Linga. Every morning, she would prepare for the puja with great care.

She would mix some saffron and rose water with sandalwood to make the paste. She would carefully string various fragrant flowers together in new patterns each day to make garlands to offer to the deities.

A small lamp would be lit, and an incense cone kept nearby. She would prepare the prasad herself and wait for Rama to come and perform the puja. Some loose flowers would also be kept in a silver basket for Rama to use during the puja. She would wait for him to get ready and arrive. When Rama would enter, he would be in a different space. It was as if Shiva himself was coming to do the puja. Once he sat down, his eyes would remain half-open and silence and peace would fill the room. He would pick up a few loose flowers and place it on his own head. 'Only Shiva can worship Shiva,' he had told her. 'So you have to become Shiva before you can do the Shiva puja. A great principle of which everything is made: they called it Brahman. And when that Brahman becomes personal, it is called the Shiva Tattva: the innocent divinity that is in everything. In the trees, in the greenery, in the birds, even in the thieves and dacoits; everywhere, it is the same single principle.'

The priest would chant the ancient mantras honouring Rudra. The chants would end in a rhythmic *namo* that transported Sita into a meditative state.

'*Mana* is the mind moving outward. *Nama* is the mind going back to the source,' explained Rama.

'Then, the second part says, "*Chame, chame, chame, chame!*" This means, everything is in me,' continued Rama.

'I also feel that way, my lord—that everything is in you!' said Sita.

'But where are "you" to feel everything is in me, Sita? We are but one!'

Recollecting the wisdom shared by Rama, Sita performed her simple puja. Trijata saw her by the stream and sat at a respectful distance, observing Sita. When Sita placed some loose flowers on her own head and sat with her eyes half-open in meditation, she looked like Shiva herself. Trijata wondered if she should tell Sita that she looked like Shiva or Shakti. Towards the end of the puja, Sita sang as if in a trance. The music was not of the earth.

O Gangadhara!
The *gyan ganga* bounced on the earth

from your matted locks
Arrogance was washed off
The mind that was searching for the truth
Found solace
The mind that was searching for you
Found the self
And anchored itself there
Where is the difference between you and me?
This truth I realized
Saying 'you', the mind goes outward
Saying 'I', it goes inward
How many days will 'I' say 'you'?
O Beloved Lord, let me rejoice in the self!

When the puja was done, Sita got up, saw Trijata and, smiling, offered her a flower that had been offered to the Shiva Linga that she had made. She then submerged the Shiva Linga, along with the flowers, into the stream. 'Why did you feel the need to do that, Sita? This place would have become a temple for generations to come. Thousands would come to visit the Shiva Linga you made,' said Trijata.

'I made the Shiva Linga just for the puja, Trijata. Now the divine is back in my heart. The elements have returned to their source. When my lord, by his will, commands me to make the Shiva Linga, such a form will remain and uplift humanity for years to come,' replied Sita.

'I have seen many grand pujas of Lord Shiva before. My uncle is an ardent devotee himself. But I have never felt as moved as I was today. It felt like Kailash was here in this little garden!' said Trijata, sharing her experience with Sita.

'You know, the lord of Lanka once tried to uproot Mount Kailash. He was returning in the *pushpaka vimana* after defeating Kubera. However, he was unable to cross Mount Kailash. Nandi told him to change course and not disturb the lord. But he called Nandi a monkey and told him to get out of the way. So Nandi cursed him: his glory would meet its end at the hands of monkeys. Ravana was least bothered. He had already received a boon that no animal could ever destroy him. He did not heed Nandi's words and tried to uproot the mountain. The mountain shook, but Lord Shiva pushed it back down with his right toe. Ravana was stuck beneath the mountain and cried out in pain. His arrogance was crushed along with him and he sang in praise of the lord, asking for his mercy. He sings the Shiva Tandava Stotra even now at the altar. It is quite popular among the devotees of Shiva here. "*Kishora chandra shekhare, rati pratikshanam mama . . .*" he says. He really does adore him every moment.' Trijata felt that Ravana's devotion could not be disputed, but in her heart, she realized that something about it was amiss.

Sita mulled over this. 'Why would he sing rati pratikshanam mama? Perhaps the highest joy that he has experienced has only been that of physical union. "Rati" connotes lust more than love. The bliss of being in the self is described as *sahasrarati*. For one who has not experienced divine love, perhaps lust is the pinnacle of love. Yet, his devotion bore fruit because he offered the best of whatever he knew.' She just smiled at Trijata and walked on.

Trijata was also lost in her thoughts. In his arrogance, Ravana had tried to move the mountain just a few metres away and had utterly failed. And here was Sita, who had brought Lord Shiva himself to Ashoka Vatika simply by her devotion. His presence was palpable.

She asked Sita, 'Both Rama and Ravana are devotees of Lord Shiva! Whom will he favour? What is the difference in their devotion?' Though she knew there was an ocean of difference, she wanted to understand it better.

'Feeling the separation from the divine is the veil of maya,' said Sita. 'She is all-powerful. Maya Shakti is the adornment of the infinite consciousness.' She realized that Trijata was feeling a little lost, so she explained with an example.

'See, the snake is an ornament on Shiva's neck. But can you and I choose to wear it? Maya Shakti is akin to the snake. She adorns the lord but does not come in our grasp. Ravana's mind is clouded. He prides himself on being a devotee but does not recognize the divine as the prime mover! He is caught in the fangs of maya.'

Trijata nodded in agreement.

'My lord does not seek anything from Lord Shiva. There are no demands because there are no two! It is the infinity, the Shiva Tattva, that acts through him,' explained Sita.

'I felt that same infinity in you, Sita,' said Trijata as the realization of Sita's divinity filled her heart more deeply.

Sita's mind drifted to the forest, where they had had a very special visitor one day. Apparently, Devi Parvati wanted to test Rama and came to him in the guise of Sita. She followed him into the forest and tried to catch up. She managed this easily and was soon walking by his side. She even walked a little ahead of Rama. At this point, Rama stopped and with folded hands, bowed to the Devi and asked her, 'Mother, did you come alone? Where is Mahadev?'

The Devi asked him how he recognized her, to which Rama replied, 'Sita always follows me. I clear the path for her first.' At that, Devi Parvati couldn't hide her smile.

15

Absolute Comfort

Rama and his brothers returned to Ayodhya after celebrating Holi with their wives in Mithila. There was a grand celebration in Ayodhya and the mothers were eagerly waiting to meet their daughters-in-law. The girls had to get accustomed to many new ways. The food was different, the etiquette different, the rules of the palace were different, but the blessing was that in the six months they spent with their husbands in Mithila in the comfort of their own homes, the couples had come to know each other well. Ayodhya was a much larger empire and there were many more royal responsibilities. Rama and the brothers all diligently fulfilled the tasks that their father assigned to them. After the morning puja and breakfast, they would often head out of the palace for the day. There would be many people to meet and concerns to address. Sometimes they came back for lunch, some days they carried food with them and ate wherever they were. But they would have dinner together.

All the four brothers and their wives would spend time at dinner together talking about various subjects while having light-hearted fun. They never really discussed their work much during these evenings, but they would share stories of rishis, gods, asuras and so on, that they would come to know of during their travels.

Rama brought small gifts of various art and craft items that he found in the remote places that he visited across the kingdom. If Sita liked something or felt that she would like to promote the art form, he would buy the whole shop full of goods and bring the pieces to her. Sita would then make a list of all the people she could gift different pieces to and would go around giving them away while explaining the story behind each piece. She loved giving thoughtful gifts. While Rama was away, she kept herself busy with the garden, trying out new recipes, new art forms, a few projects to help people in need and so on. The sisters met regularly and had enough to chat and giggle about. Over a decade passed in the blink of an eye before the day arrived when Mother Kaikeyi claimed her boon from Dasharatha. The king had wanted to crown Rama and retire. But she had other plans. Influenced by her aide, she wanted her son Bharata to be crowned king instead, and for Rama to go into exile for fourteen years. Life was taking a completely different turn. It was very difficult to believe that Mother Kaikeyi was really asking for this because she adored Rama so much. Sita felt that there was more to this than met the eye. Kaushalya also felt the same way.

She was in Kaushalya's chamber when Rama arrived with the news. Kaushalya had been sharing her views on the

King Janaka holding the beautiful baby girl that
he found in the fields of Mithila

Sita and Urmila in the woods

Rama and Sita meet for the first time in the
gardens of the palace temple of Mithila

Ven	Sun Mer		(Ket)
	श्री राम Chaitra Shukla Navami Punarvasu Nakshatra Kataka Rashi		Lag Mon Jup
Mar			
(Rah)		(Sat)	

The auspicious horoscope of Sri Rama
(as per Kamba Ramayanam)

Sita with her mother, Sunayana, at the altar of
Devi Parvati

The ferryman washes the feet of Rama with great
devotion

Sita points out how the lotus has blossomed
along with the lily, thinking Rama's radiance to
be that of the sun's!

Sita offering kheer to Jatayu

Evening satsang with the rishis and their disciples
in Chitrakuta

Sita with Mata Anasuya in Chitrakuta

Rama lovingly braids Sita's hair with wild flowers

Sita in Ashoka Vatika

Sita performing Shiva puja in Ashoka Vatika as
Trijata watches on

Hanumana finds Sita in Ashoka Vatika and
shares Rama's message

Sita with Luv and Kush in Rishi Valmiki's ashram

Sita strolling in the forest with her young sons, Luv and Kush

kind of king Rama would be and what the responsibilities of a queen were. She, too, was aware of Rama's devotion to upholding dharma and had mentioned it. When Rama shared what had transpired between Kaikeyi and Dasharatha, it was an utter shock to them. One moment, he was about to be crowned king of Ayodhya, and the next, he was exiled. 'Pitaji has appointed me King of the Forests, Ma,' said Rama. He had a way of accepting any situation with genuine optimism. Lakshmana explained the details to them. Sita was visibly upset. She felt anger mounting at the thought of the injustice meted out to Rama. He had all the qualities of a great king and the people loved him. He had always been a perfect son. It was unbelievable that he was being sent into exile by his own family! Tears welled up in her eyes, but she saw the resolute look on Rama's face and held them back. Sita's heart was beating unbearably fast. The only thing playing on her mind was that Rama should allow her to accompany him. She didn't want him to think she was weak in any way. What would Mother Kaushalya say? Her permission was also necessary. She was already telling Rama about how delicate Sita was and how she wasn't fit for forest life. Further, she felt that it would be of great solace to her if at least Sita remained with her while Rama was away. Having heard her words, Rama too began advising her to stay back, describing in great detail the hardships of forest life. None of his words registered in Sita's mind. She was determined to be by Rama's side come what may.

She patiently waited for Rama to complete what he had
to say. As soon as he was done, she fell at Kaushalya's feet.
'Mother, what use is the lotus without the sun, a flower
without nectar, a river without banks or a body without
the soul? I have heard in detail the descriptions of all the
hardships that you foresee but I assure you that even a
moment of separation from my lord is far worse than any of
these difficulties. The birds and animals will be my family.
The flowers of the wild will add colour and fragrance
wherever we are. Sleeping on the earth, I will feel that I am
resting on my mother's lap. A hut of leaves in the company
of my lord will be far more comfortable than the heavenly
abode of gods. The majestic mountains all around will be
akin to the palaces of Ayodhya. As I gaze upon his lotus
feet that walk ahead of me, I will not feel any tiredness.
And, Mother, I will take care of my lord, make sure that
he eats, provide him comfort with my presence during the
long days.' Kaushalya's heart softened upon hearing Sita's
words and she felt her deep love for Rama. Lakshmana felt
terrible seeing Sita in this condition. He agreed with every
word she said, for he felt the same way.

'It is easy to say all this while we are in the comforts of the
palace, Sita. The forest is harsh. I still feel that it is better for
you to stay back in the palace. These fourteen years will pass
in the blink of an eye,' insisted Rama. Hearing his words,
her weakness was replaced with determination. She rose
from the feet of her mother-in-law and said confidently to
Rama, 'Lord, you forget that you are my greatest comfort!
I have promised to be by your side through everything that

you do. To care for you, to be your comfort, to share your life, to walk with you, is my dharma.' Sita walked towards the window as if the skies bore witness to her anguish. She remembered her father's advice: if she took the side of dharma, then Rama would surely agree with her. 'You cannot prevent me from upholding my dharma as your wife,' she continued. 'You, who are the embodiment of righteousness—I will not allow the world to say that your wife chose comfort over duty! Pray consider my request and permit me to go with you!'

Kaushalya saw that behind Sita's delicate frame, she was as determined as she was caring, strong as she was sensitive. She saw that her happiness was only in being by the side of her beloved husband. Being a loving wife herself, she understood Sita's sentiments. 'Let her go with you, Rama,' added Kaushalya. 'On the one hand, she is a princess who has been nourished like a flower-bearing creeper. But at the same time, the blessings of great warrior kings are with her. Her body may not be accustomed to hardships, but her mind is far stronger. Her commitment to you is unshakeable. A strong mind can easily carry a weaker body. But if you leave her here, she will lose the strength of her mind. And even a strong body cannot be sustained by a weak mind. It is your duty to care for her well-being and it is clear that both of you draw strength from each other's company.'

Sita was gladdened by Mother Kaushalya's words. Lakshmana looked hopeful too, and all three now awaited Rama's verdict. Rama looked at his mother and wife and rejoiced that they were a part of his life. Tears welled in his eyes, but they were tears of love, not of sorrow.

'Sita, we should leave soon. Let us take Mother's blessings and get ready to depart,' said Rama. 'Sita,' said Kaushalya, 'promise me that you will wear your jewellery, even though you may live like a hermit. You are my Lakshmi and must continue to be adorned.' Both Rama and Sita smiled and agreed wholeheartedly. It was a bittersweet moment for Kaushalya. She was happy that her son had agreed to take Sita with him, but the thought of the emptiness that she would have to live with created a heaviness in her heart.

Sita, on the other hand, felt almost liberated! A great fount of joy welled up in her and she was as eager to go as if they were embarking on an exciting adventure. All she wanted was to be by Rama's side. Nothing else mattered.

She had left behind the comforts of the palace and come to the forest to be with Rama, but yet again, she was moved away from the forest into a remote corner of another palace, and forced to live with unbearable pangs of separation. But there had been over thirteen-and-a-half years in between, where Rama's constant presence by her side had strengthened her will and filled her with courage. She had seen him vanquish many an asura, and had heard many a rishi say that he had taken birth to free her from the burden of these negative forces. Perhaps, in the case of Ravana, she was destined to play a role. She would become the reason for Rama to wage war upon Lanka, which had become the stronghold of the entire race of asuras, *danavas* and rakshasas. She knew he would come. It didn't matter which corner of the universe Ravana had brought her to, Rama would find her.

It was now Lakshmana's turn to convince Rama. He said nothing. He just fell at Rama's feet with tears flowing profusely from his eyes. He was choking when he tried to say anything. It was clear beyond doubt that for Lakshmana, they were inseparable. Rama lifted him up and hugged him dearly. 'I cannot imagine being away from you, Lakshmana, but if your mother needs you here, that is your primary duty,' said Rama.

It all depended on Sumitra now. For Lakshmana, Rama was his father, mother, brother, master . . . his everything. He fulfilled all relationships. He prayed with all his heart that Sumitra would not stop him. He went to her chamber and told her the entire story. Sumitra was shocked to hear the whole incident and felt like a doe surrounded by wildfire. She thought dearly of Rama and Sita and was distraught at Kaikeyi's behaviour. Sumitra was wise. She acknowledged the play of time and destiny and pulled herself together again. Lakshmana stood watching her every expression. He couldn't make out what she was going to say. What would be her verdict? He had never been so nervous in his whole life. Was she going to say yes or no?

'Son,' began Sumitra. Lakshmana's attention was on the next word before she could even speak it. 'Videha's daughter is your mother and Rama, who loves you in every way, is your father. Where Rama dwells is Ayodhya, not the other way around. Ayodhya is a place where there is no conflict, and such a place is only in the company of

Rama. If Rama and Sita are proceeding to the forests, then what work would you have here? Your duty is to be of use to them. Request your gentle brother that you may accompany him. Sita will understand how you feel. She will convince Rama to permit you to come.' Lakshmana was overjoyed at her words. They were sweeter than the taste of water to a parched throat. He fell at her feet, overwhelmed with gratitude. Sumitra pulled him up and embraced her dear son. She was proud of him and his devotion to Rama.

Lakshmana then went to his own chamber, where Urmila would be waiting for him. Having changed into simple forest attire, they went to Rama's chamber. Urmila saw Sita also dressed for the forest and threw her arms around her, distressed. Tears flowed from Sita's eyes upon seeing her little sister. Urmila shared with Sita the details of her conversation with Lakshmana. She would invoke Nidra Devi soon after they left for the forest because she wanted to be by their side for as long as possible.

Once ready, they went to meet Dasharatha, who felt the depth of sorrow at the moment. He wanted to convince Rama to stay but it was futile to do so, for Rama would honour his word to Kaikeyi come what may. Kaikeyi was in Dasharatha's chamber when they went there to take leave. She avoided looking directly at them. Sita sensed the phenomenal effort she was making to keep a stern and resolute face. She saw her stealing a look at Rama and struggling to stop the tears that were threatening to flow. She turned away when they sought her blessings to leave. Sita felt a lump in her throat. It was unclear if it was the pain of the forced rejection by a loving mother or a reflection of the pain that Kaikeyi was feeling but trying to hide. Having taken leave of the mothers and their guru, they left for the forest. Dasharatha ordered Sumantra, his minister, to escort them and to drive them to the edge of the forest. He did not want them to go on foot through the streets of Ayodhya. It would be unbearable for the people. As Rama moved out of the city, along with him went Dasharatha's will to live. He spent his last days pining for his son, and soon left his body.

The people of Ayodhya followed the chariot in hundreds. They had made up their mind to exile themselves along with the one who ruled their hearts. Rama was wondering what to do. In the middle of the night, he woke Sumantra and requested him to drive them away quickly. 'Drive in such a way that it is impossible for anyone to follow our tracks, dear Sumantra!' Rama told him. They rode all night till they reached the banks of the holy Ganga at Shringaverapura. The sacred river looked untouched by the world, though flowing amid it. They decided to take a dip in the river and refresh themselves.

Sita walked towards the river holding Rama's hand. The banks were a little slippery. When they came close to the river, she put just one toe in the water to check its temperature and quickly pulled it out. It was freezing. But she dared not say anything because she did not want Rama to think she was finding things difficult. 'Don't worry, Sita, just hold me and step forward,' said Rama. He had noticed her reaction to the freezing water and also realized that she put on a smile just for him, trying to hide her apprehension. He smiled to himself, held her forearms and gently pulled her into the water. Sita squeezed her eyes shut and braced herself for the cold, and went in. They were standing in waist-deep water. The Ganga felt different when they were standing on the banks. Now Sita could feel the current, as her body had somewhat adjusted to the temperature of the water. The coolness was almost pleasant. Now Rama wanted her to take a dip in the water. 'Just hold me, and when I go in, come with me!' said Rama with a big smile on his face. He was enjoying himself thoroughly. 'Take a deep breath in, and . . . now!' said Rama as he quickly submerged himself. Sita, in a hurry to follow him, closed her eyes, took a deep breath in, and plunged herself beneath the water. She was still holding on to his arms tightly. Now underwater, it was a whole new world. The coolness of the waters percolated throughout her body from head to toe. The water was everywhere and seemed boundless. She felt a sudden expansion and was transported to another realm. From beneath the holy river she had attained the heart of the ocean. Once again, she beheld her lord resting on Adi Sesha, the five-hooded serpent. He seemed to rise suddenly from his deep rest. The lord told her that the Sanat Kumaras, the great rishis and sons of Brahma, had come to visit him, and there seemed to be some disturbance. He left to see what was happening. Sita saw his guards, Jaya and Vijaya, clutching the feet of her lord, crying profusely. The sages, shining like four suns, were also bowing down to the lord. Jaya and Vijaya had angered the sages in their foolish pride and surely must have been cursed. 'We understand that they were only following your instructions, my lord,' said one of the four sages, 'but they need to do so with humility and not arrogance. As is your wish, we will definitely soften the curse, but having uttered it, they cannot escape it.' Sita's breath ran out and she emerged from the river to draw breath. The water was not freezing anymore. She enjoyed the pressure of the current on her body. She rejoiced in the coolness and felt refreshed. She drank to her heart's content and took a few more dips.

After bathing in the Ganga, Sita moulded a small Shiva Linga out of clay on the banks of the river, to which Rama performed the puja. Sita bowed down along with Rama and also prayed to the celestial river. 'O Mother, please grant my wish that after the specified time, I should return safely with my husband and his brother to worship you again before returning to Ayodhya.' She heard the benedictory voice of the river responding to her. 'O Vaidehi, who in the three worlds does not know your glory? Every power inherent in nature awaits your command. You have exalted me by addressing me so humbly and asking me for blessings! Every wish of your heart will be fulfilled, my dearest! You shall return safely with your beloved lord and his devoted brother. Your glory will be sung throughout the world for ages to come!' Sita was happy to hear the words of the sacred river, which also strengthened her hope that they would return safely.

Sita was now far away from the river, but she was close to the ocean, where all rivers merge. Yet, this ocean separated her from her lord, who was the ocean into which every stream of life merged. She was gazing at the little stream in front of her. It seemed to be dancing as it tumbled over little rocks and stones on its way. It never got tired of flowing. It was not flowing because somebody asked it to, but because that was in its nature. Though separate, this stream belonged to the ocean. Every drop flowing in it had emerged from the ocean and would eventually return to it. And along its journey, it was the reason for many flowers blossoming, many birds quenching their thirst, many hearts rejoicing in its beauty, many colourful fish swimming here and there; it was the longing of the stream to merge into the ocean that made it flow. Love was the basis of its existence. And between the longing and the love, life flourished. She wondered about all the activity that must be happening around Rama as he made his way towards the shores of Lanka. She wondered who his new devotees were, who now found purpose because they could serve him. Her memory drifted to the Nishada King Guha, whom she had never met or even heard of before, but who was full of devotion. It seemed like his love might have been one of the reasons they had to come to the forest. How else would they have been able to spend time together and partake of his offerings?

Guha had arrived with fruits, sweets and some snacks for them. After having had their breakfast, Rama requested Sumantra to return. It took a lot of convincing before the minister sadly agreed to leave. They then proceeded towards the river and asked a ferryman to take them across. The ferryman looked at Rama and said, 'Lord, if I must take you, there is a condition that you must accept.' Rama looked at him, bemused, but asked him to speak further. 'You must allow me to wash your feet thoroughly before you step into my boat.' This seemed like an unusual request, but even before Rama could ask him why, the boatman explained, 'They say that the dust of your feet changed a rock into a woman. If my boat changes into a hermit's wife, then my livelihood will be gone forever!' Sita could not suppress her giggle at this comparison. 'Dear lady, you laugh at my predicament, but this boat is all I have!' added the ferryman. For his sake, Rama allowed him to wash his feet. He filled his vessel with waters from the ever-pure Ganga and washed the feet of the lord carefully. He collected the water that was used for the washing and applied a few drops to his eyes too. Subsequently, they climbed into his boat and reached the other side. Rama wanted to give him something in return, so Sita offered her ring to Rama to give to the boatman. However, the boatman refused and told Rama, 'I have ferried you across this river today, but when the time comes, please be there to ferry me across the ocean of life, my lord! Make my final journey smooth!' They were astounded to see such profound faith and wisdom in a simple boatman.

This was the same request that Jaya and Vijaya had in her vision. 'Please be there to liberate us, my lord,' they had said this clutching his feet and never wanting to let go. The benevolent Hari had promised them that he would come.

He had then glanced at his Maya Shakti with a gentle nod. It was time for the *leela* to unfold and it was up to her to weave the story in the fabric of time and space.

These visions came like flashes to Sita, but she would forget about them almost instantly. She never discussed them or mulled over them while she was with Rama. Her mind was in the present moment and was focused on him and whatever was needed in the moment. Yet, the way she perceived Rama had transformed.

Guha would accompany them for a few days into the forest. 'You are one who is all-knowing, yet you allow me to show you the safe paths in this forest. I will come with you till we find the ideal place for your stay. I will help you build a hut with the appropriate raw materials and then I will return. Please permit me to do this, for it fulfils the purpose of my birth!' requested Guha ever so humbly. 'The devotee was fulfilled with an opportunity to serve the lord, who needed nothing. What could be offered to the one to whom the whole creation belonged? What place was appropriate for the one who was the substratum of the universe? What house could be built for the one in whom all the worlds were housed? Yet, there was inexplicable joy in these simple actions,' mused Sita.

As Guha led the way, they reached Prayag. 'This is the king of all holy places,' explained Guha. 'Lord Vishnu is worshipped here in the form of Bindumadhava.'

'I can imagine his palace here,' said Lakshmana. 'The confluence of Ganga and Yamuna form his throne and the eternal banyan tree looks like his royal umbrella.' Guha smiled and added, 'Seated here, the lord is busy fulfilling the desires of all who pray to him and freeing their minds from the shackles of bondage, like a lion who scatters a herd of wild elephants. People believe that just a dip in the confluence here is enough to wash away their sins.' 'If just one dip in these waters can wash away all sins, it is enough to show that sins are indeed superficial,' said Rama, 'and the consciousness is ever-pure and can never be sullied.'

Guha bowed to Rama upon hearing these words and said, 'The wisdom embodied by Ganga and the love that is the Yamuna flow together in you, my lord! Being in your presence is the same as a dip in these waters!' Lakshmana added, 'Don't forget Saraswati, Guha! She represents awareness. Only when the head and the heart are in harmony does true awareness dawn! The experience of divinity comes into our life. There are many who meet my brother, but only a few who perceive beyond the obvious. You are a gem among men, Guha!'

Guha was overwhelmed by Lakshmana's words and felt utterly content. They completed their prayers by the riverside and then called on Rishi Bharadwaja, whose ashram was between the forest and the nearby village.

The rishi welcomed them warmly and fed them the sweetest fruits and some fresh, hot food made in the ashram. The disciples of the rishi were eager to be the ones to get a chance to serve them. After lunch, they rested for a while and decided to go for a walk in the evening. The rishi walked alongside Rama. All the hundred-odd excited disciples walked behind them, trying to get as close to them as possible, but never ahead or even in line with the two of them. They were a young lot. It was quite chaotic, the way they moved, climbing over each other and finding gaps to squeeze themselves through to get ahead of each another. One young *sadhak* elbowed a boy next to him to get ahead. The ones at the back were walking left and right and changing their pace constantly to see if they could find a way to get to the front. Some young boys moved outside the group and ran ahead from the sides, trying to join back in the front. But they did so with big smiles on their faces. Sita walked behind the herd, along with Lakshmana. When they moved like this on the streets, villagers would come running out of their houses to catch a glimpse of them. The villagers would be tempted to follow them but were unsure if it was appropriate to do so. Sita and Lakshmana would enjoy watching the expressions on the faces of the villagers and the antics of the boys in front of them. The smiles, people waving, trying to get a glimpse of him, and the tears that flowed from their eyes after Rama moved ahead—it was wonderful to see it each and every time.

They stayed in the ashram that night. The next morning, the rishi suggested a possible route for them to follow. Four of his disciples escorted them to the banks of the Yamuna, whose waters were of the hue of Rama himself. After crossing the river, they walked through many villages, one after another. Everywhere, it was the same story. In a matter of minutes, the entire village would gather to catch a glimpse of them. The villagers would invite them lovingly to eat with them and rest in their homes. Sita would spend time with the women of the village. They would ask her questions about Rama, which she would answer happily. They would bring the children to be blessed by her. The little girls would sing songs and dance for her. Sita would be surrounded with their music and laughter. Rama would be with the men of the village. He was the king to them, wherever he went. They were curious to learn more about him. They would also share their concerns, to which Rama would suggest solutions. While they were roaming as homeless wanderers, every other home they visited became their own. Having rested in the villages for the night, they would set forth again with the rising sun. Rama walked in front. Sita followed him and was careful to step alongside his footprints, but never on them. Lakshmana walked farther to the right without disturbing the tracks of his brother and sister-in-law. Guha walked behind them.

The villagers treasured these footprints and gazed at them for hours. Those who missed meeting Rama were encouraged to have darshan of his footprints. And just their sight evoked tears of gratitude in their hearts. Proceeding in this manner, they reached the beautiful ashram of Rishi Valmiki.

Rishi Valmiki was overjoyed to receive them. 'Where do you advise me to stay in the forest, O, Rishi?' asked Rama. 'First, tell me a place where you are not, and then I can tell you where you should go!' replied the sage. Rama blushed a little. Lakshmana was happy with the sage's words. 'Lakshmana, who is the embodiment of Adi Sesha, agrees with my words,' observed Valmiki. Having said this, he advised them to stay in Chitrakuta, a region made lush by the river Mandakini and full of colourful birds and lions, deer and elephants. The great Rishi Atri also lived in one part of that forest, along with his wife Anasuya.

His disciples accompanied the brothers and Sita up to Chitrakuta. The site recommended by the rishi was picturesque. The land was situated by the river Payaswini and surrounded by a hundred varieties of wildflowers. 'Look at the giant beehives!' remarked Guha. 'Let me get some fresh honey for you.' So saying, he went off into the trees and returned shortly with fresh, clean honey in containers made of leaves stitched together. 'This is delicious honey, Guha!' exclaimed Rama. 'Yes, my lord—forest honey made of the nectar collected from all these wildflowers that blossom here,' said Guha. 'The flavour is quite exotic!' added Sita. 'And it is impossible to analyse what it is made up of, because no one knows how much nectar came from the purple jacaranda, or the yellow *champa*, or the white *sugandharaja*. No one knows how far the bee went each day to collect these little drops. If anyone tries to describe this honey, it is a futile exercise. But you can enjoy eating it, sense the taste, its sweetness, its texture, how it feels in the mouth, and then you don't feel like eating anything else after it!'

'So true!' remarked Lakshmana. 'What is the use of the analysis anyway? The bee has given it to you, now just enjoy the honey! What is the point of going into the details of the bee or the honey? We are just thankful for it and that is enough.'

'The bee may not even be alive anymore,' said Guha. 'Its life cycle is only two to three weeks!'

'This is why our seers said that we should taste the honey first before diving into one scripture or another,' said Rama. 'Just reading a little here and a little there and forming concepts about honey is not going to give you the experience of its taste.'

'So true, Bhaiya! See how those boys in the rishi's ashrams felt just from being in your presence! They all gulped the honey! They were gleaming and glowing in just two days!' said Lakshmana.

'Even the rishis themselves, Lakshmana!' added Sita. 'They, who are the embodiment of wisdom, looked as if that was the moment they had been waiting for all their lives!'

'Honey is honey for everybody,' added Rama, 'but how much honey can you have, how much can you store, how big is your container: this is where your effort can make a difference.'

'My lord, I have done nothing worthy to have enjoyed this supreme nectar. It is only your compassion and grace that has made it possible,' said Guha, as tears of love and gratitude flowed from his eyes.

Rama went up to him and embraced him. While Guha lost himself in the arms of his lord, Rama's eyes caught Sita's. Their eyes met, and that was nectar enough for Sita.

Guha approached the nearby Bhila and Kola tribes, and soon they gathered together to make a comfortable hut by the lake for the three of them to stay. These tribesmen appeared out of nowhere just at the right time. They left no stone unturned in making the house as comfortable as possible while being appropriate. The chief of the builders came to bow down to Rama after having completed his job. Rama looked into his eyes, smiled, blessed him and acknowledged in him the essence of Vishwakarma, the architect of the gods, who had himself come into the forests to build their abode.

The chiefs of the Bhilas and Kolas approached Rama and offered themselves in his service. The women told Sita to give them the list of things she needed; they would send them across to her every day. Throngs of hermits from the nearby regions flocked to the forest to pay their respects and have Rama's darshan. Her beloved was truly the king wherever he went. Sita felt assured that they would never lack company, and smiled to herself. He was already listening to all the people's concerns like a father and advising them on what to do. It was time for Guha to also return to his kingdom. He took a promise from Rama that he would visit him on the way back as well.

Sita was happy to finally have a place of their own to stay. Having changed homes every two days, the idea of staying in one place for at least a few weeks was comforting to her. And she made many new friends as soon as she arrived. Bluejays, cuckoos, parrots, chakravakas, *chakoras*, woodpeckers, hummingbirds, bulbuls, sparrows and many other birds flocked to that area of the forest. Seeing them, Sita rejoiced like a child. Rama had brought her a new flower almost five times that day itself. He was also excited to find them and brought them for her with childlike enthusiasm.

That evening, they sat by the river in silence while the moon rose over the peaks of the Vindhya ranges surrounding them. A cool breeze whispered the songs of the mountains. Rama, Sita and Lakshmana felt utterly at peace.

16

Devotion like a Diamond

Their hut in Chitrakuta was surrounded by many fig, jambu (black plum), mango and tamala (bay leaf) trees. In the middle, surrounded by these trees, stood a stately banyan that seemed like it had been an eternal part of creation. It had dark, dense foliage and tiny red fruits, and provided unwavering shade. Sita and Lakshmana thought that this would be a nice place to have their evening satsang. All the hermits who lived nearby would gather there, and they would speak on the Vedas, the Puranas and the Agamas. Rama loved listening to those stories and also had discussions on their deeper significance. Sita made a simple seat for Rama under the banyan tree. Rama saw the arrangements and approved of them. 'The aerial roots are the speciality of this tree! The roots are like consciousness; they are the unchanging foundation of life,' said Rama. 'And the branches, leaves and fruits are like the continuously changing appearance,' added Lakshmana.

Sita completed the conversation, saying, 'So stay rooted and keep smiling!'

She also planted many tulsi shrubs between the trees and their hut with the help of Lakshmana.

A few days after they had settled in Chitrakuta, in the early hours of dawn, Sita dreamt of an army that was advancing towards them. All the four units of horse, elephant, chariots and cavalry were present. Fully armed, they were approaching at a rapid pace. In her dream, while she surveyed the army, she caught sight of a flag with the symbol of the sun. A little taken aback, she searched for the one who was leading the army, and saw Bharata. She awoke that same instant and told Rama and Lakshmana about what she saw. Rama was happy at the thought of Bharata coming, even if it was just a dream. Lakshmana was a little apprehensive. 'Bhaiya, what need is there for an army to come and see you? You trust everybody, but I think this is a sign that we should be cautious,' said Lakshmana. 'It was only a dream, though it may well be a premonition. Let us wait and see, Lakshmana,' replied Rama.

The next day passed, with the three of them getting more accustomed to their new home. Nevertheless, Rama was already thinking about where to house Bharata if he did arrive, what food to offer him and so on. Late in the afternoon, the Bhila king came running to them with news of the advancing army. He told them that it looked like a sea of humans was marching in this direction. He had already told his warriors to arm themselves and to be prepared. They were on standby, ready for battle. No one could approach

Rama without fighting them first. And Lakshmana too prepared himself for the battle. 'I told you, Bhaiya! People have changed, circumstances have changed, only you remain the same. It is of no matter to me that Bharata is our own brother. Anyone who harbours ill intent towards you is my sworn enemy. Wasn't it enough for Ma Kaikeyi to send you into exile? Now she has sent her son to conquer us in the forest. She doesn't know that the entire army of Ayodhya cannot stand up to a single arrow of mine, let alone yours! Even if the gods were to take his side in the battle, I swear by you that I will leave no one alive!' Lakshmana's words were like sheer flames of fury. They fell like bolts of lightning on Sita's ears. Rama was taken aback by the intensity of his anger. Lakshmana raised his bow and clutched an arrow from his quiver. At this point, a voice from the heavens was heard, 'Dear child, they who act impulsively and regret later are anything but wise: so say the Vedas and the sages. Before you act, take a moment to judge the rightness of your action, taking all possibilities into account.'

The voice was ageless and calm, deep and profound. It shook Lakshmana completely and cooled him down.

'A few drops of lemon juice cannot sour the entire ocean, Lakshmana. Bharata is unshakeable in dharma, even if the abodes of Brahma, Vishnu and Mahesh are offered to him as temptation, let alone the kingdom of Ayodhya. Mount Meru will be blown away by a puff of the wind coming from the mouth of a mosquito before Bharata's ideals are shaken. I have full faith in him, Lakshmana. He is not one to be intoxicated by power,' said Rama.

The idea of a mosquito blowing away Mount Meru was absolutely ridiculous and even funny to Sita. But it highlighted how equally absurd it was to doubt Bharata. She witnessed how that statement changed Lakshmana's heart and softened him to a great extent. At least he agreed to wait and see how things would turn out.

The evening satsang had begun by the time Bharata reached their hermitage. Guha, who had accompanied and guided Bharata to Rama, pointed out the hermitage beyond the trees. Bharata could see them from behind the thickets even before Rama and Lakshmana could see him approaching. Rama and Sita, seated under the banyan tree, appeared like two shining suns. Lakshmana's lean silhouette standing by their side, holding his bow, was visible as well. There was a flutter in Bharata's heart. His pace quickened, he wanted to run, but his head pulled him back. What if Rama refused to see him after all that had happened? What if he believed that Bharata, who was at the residence of his maternal uncle while all these events had unfolded, was the one who wanted to usurp his throne? He shook himself out of his doubts and told himself that it didn't matter. He was just going to fall at his brother's feet and beg for forgiveness. He was going to do his best to set things right.

Sita saw Bharata coming and stood up. Rama turned to look in the same direction and he too stood up. He saw Bharata coming towards him and starting moving in his direction. Lakshmana too saw him approaching. His eyes narrowed and his hands held the bow tighter. He then saw Guha behind him. He wore a big smile. Lakshmana relaxed seeing his expression. The next moment, Bharata was prostrate on the ground before Rama. Rama pulled him up and embraced him, and tears of joy flowed from both brothers' eyes. Shatrugna stood behind Bharata, waiting for his turn to hug his dearest elder brother. Lakshmana's heart melted at this sight and he too moved towards them, and the four brothers stood close to each other, holding each other's hands, happy to be together again. Sita saw Guha escorting Rishi Vasishta and his wife Arundhati. She went forward to receive them. Rama joined her and they both took the blessings of the rishi and his wife. Arundhati embraced Sita and was happy to see that she looked well. She resolved to sit and talk to her at leisure. She wanted to share with her whatever she knew of living in the forest and how to manage the different situations that may come up. For now, she took her aside for a moment and told her, 'Sita, the three mothers will reach soon. Make sure you give equal attention to all three!' Sita nodded in agreement. She wondered: if the mothers were coming here, would the king come as well? But before she could ask anyone, she saw the queen mothers approaching.

One look at them and her heart missed a beat. She realized that the most untoward incident had come to pass. Clad in white, the queen mothers were fighting back their tears; tears of joy at seeing their sons together, and tears of sorrow at the thought of King Dasharatha. She turned to look at Rama. His eyes were fixed on the mothers. His pain was palpable. Sita felt his pain in her heart and tears formed in her eyes as well. Vasishta shared the news with Rama and Lakshmana, and guided them to offer the necessary oblations. Sita was hoping that her sisters might have come too, but it was evident that they had stayed back in Ayodhya. The army set up various camps all around the hill, and all those who had come retired to their respective shelters.

Sita recalled Arundhati's advice and did all she could to attend to the mothers equally. Kaushalya wanted to know all the details of their journey to the forest, which Sita narrated patiently. Kaushalya shared her woes about the passing of the king and the mood of the people of Ayodhya. Sumitra told her how Urmila had taken to painting the walls of her entire room with detailed images of the special moments in her life. Sita and Lakshmana featured prominently in those murals. And how, once she was done, she would go into yoga nidra, as planned with her husband. Kaikeyi was full of remorse and kept telling Sita how overwhelmed she was at the magnanimity she and Rama had shown. She wanted to somehow make it up to Sita. She was touched by Sita's warmth and hospitality towards her. Sita also ensured that the sage and his wife were duly taken care of, and that there was enough food provided to all the guests who had come.

Rama also went around meeting the queen mothers and the accompanying guests. Kaushalya told him, 'You know, Sita has been only with me the whole time. I know she thinks of me as her mother and feels comforted in my presence. It makes me very happy to have her around, but I will tell her to spend some time with Kaikeyi and

Sumitra too!' Rama agreed with her. When he met Sumitra along with Lakshmana, Sumitra said, 'Sita has taken such wonderful care of me. She has told me everything about your journey so far and also enquired about her sisters. But I think all her time would have been spent entirely with me. Kaushalya and Kaikeyi will want to meet her too. I will tell her.' Rama smiled at her words. He then went to meet Kaikeyi, while Lakshmana and Shatrugna stayed back with Sumitra for some more time. Kaikeyi burst out when Rama came to her, 'I thought I would never be able to speak to you again! Even if you forgave me, I would never be able to forgive myself. I was wondering what I would even say to you. But that darling wife of yours—she is just like you! She has patiently consoled me ever since our arrival and made me feel so honoured. She has no spite, not even a trace of doubt in her mind. She still treats me like her very own mother! I am sure Kaushalya and Sumitra must be wondering why Sita is spending all her time with me after all that I have done to you and to her!' Rama consoled her further but couldn't hide his smile thinking of Sita. Whomsoever he met that day, each one remarked how Sita had taken care of them so well. How did she manage to find the time? How did she manage their minds? It was all such a wonder!

Three days passed by in a flurry. During the first two days, everyone emerged from their grief at the loss of the king, and lightened up in the presence of Rama. In the evening satsang, the sages would speak on the eternal nature of the spirit. Listening to their words of wisdom was like applying balm to one's wounded heart. The days were packed with activity for Sita.

On the fourth day, Bharata approached the sages to seek their guidance and put forth the proposal for the future of Ayodhya. For three days, everyone had set aside their hopes for Rama's return to Ayodhya and were content to be in his presence. But the decision could not be postponed any longer. The city was waiting unguarded, and without a ruler in place. Sita did not share her views of the situation with anyone. She just heard everyone else out. Though she didn't think that Rama would change his mind, she was open to any decision as long as she would be going along with him. She felt compassion for Bharata and waited to hear what he would say with great interest.

Bharata, having sought the permission of the sages and of his brother, Rama, put forth three proposals with great humility and love.

First, Rama, Sita and Lakshmana return to Ayodhya, and Bharata and Shatrugna go into exile in their place. Sita couldn't help smile when she heard him say this. Bharata's demand was like that of an innocent child.

Or, if Rama must stay, then the others return and Bharata stay with him in exile. Sita herself did not approve of this one. If Rama stayed, they all stayed. As far as Sita was concerned, Bharata could also stay if Rama permitted him to do so.

Or the other three brothers remain in exile while Rama and Sita return to Ayodhya. She gently chuckled when she heard this. His proposals had only one basis: love.

Rama too could not hide his smile on hearing Bharata's proposals. They were the words of a devotee. However, none of the proposals were agreeable to Rama. Yet, he was overwhelmed by Bharata's love and wanted to find a resolution that would make him feel better too. Bharata had come prepared with all the materials needed for the coronation and was ready to perform the ceremony in the middle of the forest itself. He had brought along the entire army to witness the coronation and bring Rama back in full glory. While Rama was wondering what to tell him, a guard rushed in to announce the arrival of King Janaka. Rama sighed with relief. The sages were also pleased with the news. Janaka's wisdom was well-known. He would be the best person to resolve this dilemma. Sita's heart skipped with joy at the news. She shared a very close bond with her father and mother. Their company was probably the only comfort Sita missed once in a while.

Rama and Sita went ahead to receive Janaka. Sita rejoiced when she saw that Sunayana had accompanied him as well. They blessed the couple and embraced them. Janaka was alarmed to hear of the developments that had unfolded in Ayodhya in such rapid succession. Hearing that Bharata had proceeded to the forest to meet Rama, he too had set out for their abode.

Kaushalya welcomed Sunayana, and all the queen mothers went to her camp along with Sita. Having gone through all the formalities and courtesies, they sat down to speak their hearts to each other. On Janaka's arrival, the sages and the princes had unanimously chosen him to preside over the dialogue and to pronounce the verdict for what must be done.

Kaikeyi was not comfortable with the situation. She was not even sure how to face Sunayana. It was because of her that Sunayana's beloved daughter was now living in the forest. But Sunayana showed no sign of resentment towards her whatsoever. Kaikeyi decided that it was best to apologize to her in any case. 'I am deeply sorry that your child is going through this hardship because of me,' she began. 'Please, O queen of Ayodhya,' responded Sunayana, not wanting to make her feel worse, 'there is no need for you to explain yourself. The words of a mother can only be good, even if spoken in anger.' 'Only time will tell us of the yet unseen benefits to the world that these years in exile will yield, for I believe that Rama's destiny is one of greatness,' added Sunayana. 'You speak with such calmness and clarity, Sunayana. You have perceived the wisdom beyond these events,' said Sumitra. 'You are generous with your praise, O queen,' responded Sunayana. 'I am a simple woman of faith: faith in the higher power, faith that truth will prevail, and above all, faith in Rama.' 'O Queen of Mithila,' said Kaushalya, 'your husband is an ocean of wisdom. Still, do tell him of my humble request to give additional weightage to Bharata's condition. In the worst case, it would be best if he can accompany Rama to the forest and Lakshmana return to Ayodhya. My heart fears that something untoward will happen to Bharata if he returns without Rama.'

Sunayana was deeply touched by Kaushalya's big heart, her ability to not just accept the situation as it was, but also be deeply concerned for Bharata's welfare over her own son's. She bore no grudge whatsoever. Sumitra pointed out at this juncture that it was late in the night and that Sunayana might like to rest. Kaushalya insisted that Sita go to Sunayana's encampment and spend some time with her mother. But before leaving, she shared with the mothers the words of the great Sage Yagnavalkya. He had prophesied that Rama would complete the work of the gods while he lived in the forest and after the years of the exile, would rule Ayodhya unperturbed, with the gods, people and Nagas at peace under his sovereign rule.

Sunayana and Sita were happy to have some time together. Janaka also arrived in the camp shortly afterwards. Sita looked radiant even in the clothes of a hermit. 'How are you, my dear child?' enquired Janaka as he embraced his dearest daughter. Sita looked happy to him. She had shown Sunayana their simple forest dwelling. 'I was feeling a little sad that our little princess was living in a house without even a mirror for herself. But I realized how unnecessary my worry was!' said Sunayana. Janaka knew from Sunayana's smile that it was a pleasant realization. He played along and asked her why.

'Hmm . . . our daughter's image is so clearly seen in her husband's eyes that there is no need for a mirror, my lord!' At this, Sita blushed. They chatted for a while, after which Janaka had some words of advice for his daughter. 'My dear child, the gardens of Mithila and Ayodhya are orderly and have their own beauty. There is a certain discipline and predictability about them that is comforting. But the forest is chaotic. Uncertainty prevails at all times. This chaos can be blissful, but it can also pose challenges that will help bring out all your skills. Maintain your principles like the gardens of Mithila and be spontaneous in your actions like the trees of the forests. See what the moment needs and flow with it. If you notice, in just these past few days, everyone who came here had a heavy heart, but they have all been relieved of their burden by just being with Rama. The mind is like a complex forest and many creatures, small and big, leave their impressions on it. But all other footprints are wiped away when the elephant walks. In the same way, all other impressions are removed when the thought of Rama fills the mind. You have his constant company and that is the biggest comfort and blessing you have been bestowed with. By choosing to accompany him, you have upheld the honour of our race. We are proud of you.' Sita heard every word of his carefully, and secured it safely in her memory. Sunayana pointed out that it was late, and they escorted Sita back to her hermitage and walked back to their own.

The next day dawned with a prayer in the heart of every single person camped in Chitrakuta. Ganesha, Devi, Surya, Lord Shiva and Lord Vishnu, the family deities of the line of Raghus, were all invoked. After this, the different groups moved towards the banyan tree.

Janaka presided over the gathering. Sita had thought that she would sit with her mother and mothers-in-law. However, since Bharata's proposal concerned her as well, her father had indicated that she should take her seat by Rama's side. Bharata presented all his views with whatever support he could glean from Raja Dharma and the scriptures. However, at the end of it all, it was his devotion that shone clearly through his argument. Janaka acknowledged his state of being and expressed how this was a rare case where the decision was between dharma and bhakti. While all of creation is bound by dharma, the divine is bound only by devotion. So, according to Janaka, the scales tipped over to Bharata's side. The entire gathering, including Rama, smiled and accepted the verdict. Sita too felt overwhelmed by Bharata's devotion. She was looking at Rama, wondering what he was going to do now.

Bharata was relieved and amazed at his good fortune. He had not expected things to turn in his favour so easily. He looked at Rama with the utmost gratitude and love. Sita saw that Rama showed no sign of resentment that the verdict was in Bharata's favour. He only looked at Bharata with a smile and eyes full of love. He had set aside everything that he wanted or believed in to fulfil his brother's wish. Sita's attention turned to Bharata as he started speaking. Bharata was amazed at Rama's selflessness and bowing down to his brother, he said, 'My lord, your command is my wish! You know my heart better than I do myself. My wish is that I may live to fulfil your instructions.' Sita's smile became more evident on hearing Bharata's words. His lord was ready to fulfil his wishes and Bharat's only wish was to fulfil his lord's. Sita delighted on seeing the maturity of his devotion. She was also happy that Rama was now free to decide on the way forward. Janaka and the sages were once again taken by surprise at the turn of events. While the glory of Bharata reached its pinnacle, they all realized, with a prick of sadness, that Rama was now likely to stay in exile.

'Bharata, you are the embodiment of dharma, upheld by pure love. For your sake, I accept the kingship of Ayodhya,' said Rama. Sita's eyes widened in surprise and she looked keenly at Rama's face to try and discern what he really had in mind. While to all other others, it seemed that once again, the tides had turned, Sita waited patiently for what the coming moment would unfold. The entire gathering caught its breath and a smile found its way to their faces. Bharata could not believe what he was hearing. He said, 'Lord, shall I bring forth the materials for the coronation, then?' 'At the appropriate time, Bharata. For these fourteen years, take care of Ayodhya for me. I entrust you with that responsibility. Having fulfilled our father's command, I will return and take my place on the throne.' Sita felt almost relieved on hearing his words. Rama was not one to disregard a vow given by his father. He was free to fulfil it now. At the same time, the kingship that was a burden to Bharata earlier was now the blessing that Rama bestowed on him. Sita turned her attention to Bharata, who seemed to have accepted Rama's instructions, but he still seemed somewhat unsettled. He was mentally trying to find a solution to a problem that loomed over him. But since Sita did not know what it was, she waited for him to express himself.

It turned out that he needed a token, something to symbolize Rama's presence. He asked Rama for his wooden sandals to take back with him. He would place the sandals on the throne and serve the city on Rama's behalf. Sita's throat choked with emotion when she heard his request. Rama removed his sandals; Bharata took them, placed them upon his head and circumambulated Rama and Sita thrice. She felt a motherly love gushing out of her for Bharata and blessed him with all her heart. The entire gathering stood up and tears of joy flowed uninterrupted from every pair of eyes. Even the sages Vasishta, Jabali, Vishwamitra and Atri were deeply moved and their hearts were full. The gods in the heavens rejoiced at Bharata's devotion, which made this moment eternal. Rama advised Bharata to take the guidance of Sage Atri and deposit the waters from all the sacred rivers, which were brought for Rama's coronation in the forest, and oceans wherever he instructed. The rishi showed Bharata a sacred well that he had dug up earlier and told him to pour all the waters into it. He named it Bharatakupa.

Now that the matter was settled, it was time for everyone to return to their respective places. With heavy hearts, one by one, they all took their leave, bestowing blessings in abundance upon Rama, Sita and Lakshmana, who shone like the embodiments of wisdom, love and dispassion.

Once everyone had left, the silence was like a solid presence in the hermitage. Dark rain clouds gathered in the sky and the winds blew stronger. It was early evening when the rain started. The winds bent even the large trunks of the ancient trees. Thousands of leaves rustled and sounded like a waterfall. The river flowing in front of their hut was covered with mist and seemed more like an ocean. The water swelled here and there, trying to contain the downpour. The roll of thunder declared the authority of nature for all to hear. The bolts of lightning lit up the heavens for all to see—but only for a fraction of a moment. Standing on the porch of her little hut, Sita watched the storm in all its terrifying beauty. She felt one with the wind and the waves, the trees and the leaves. A branch here and there would surrender to the wind and let go. Freed from its bondage to the tree, it was carried far away into unknown regions of the hills. Along with it went all the tiny seeds encapsulated in the little fruits that stayed connected to the branch. They would begin a new life nourished by the earth, at the place where the wind would carry them. The storm was nature's dance of power—a glimpse of her magnificence. Till a few hours back, storms had been raging in the hearts and minds of all the people who had been there. New pathways had come forth, new ideas nourished by ancient values had been sown in the fertile minds of people, new paradigms for trust among royalty had been created in the calm amid the storm. And yet, the parting had been another tidal wave of emotions. The clearness in the mind could be experienced between two storms. Now their minds were quiet, but the storm was raging outside. Rama was standing a few feet away, also watching the storm. The intensity of nature reflected the intensity of his love. She saw a tear form in the corner of his eye and flow down his cheek. Her eyes too filled with tears on seeing him. 'The experience of divinity could not be more personal than this,' thought Sita. Rama was her husband, but he was also mother, father, friend, child, master, lord: he fulfilled all her relationships, yet was much greater than all of them. It was an ancient love.

Tears of longing—love mixed with pangs of separation—filled Sita's eyes as she watched the moon rise in the eastern sky. There was no storm in Ashoka Vatika at this moment, outside or inside. Sita's mind was a silent witness. Her heart was like the serene lake in which the reflection of the moon could be seen undistorted. Without the lake, the moon would not have been visible to those whose eyes were focused on the ground. The rakshasa women could not but cool themselves in the radiance of this moon amid them. When their mind was focused on her, they would soften. When the memory of their terrifying king would surface, they would also turn monstrous. Their mind was like water. It changed shape readily based on the qualities of the person that filled it. They were unlike Bharata, who was steadfast. There was no place for anything or anyone else in his mind. Fortunately for them, their minds had at least experienced the contrast and coolness of Sita's presence in their lives, where previously those minds had had room only for the lord of Lanka.

17

The Hand of Maya

The brothers were either in the company of devoted hermits or fighting asuras. Sita was an equanimous witness to both. When the number of visitors to their hermitage in Chitrakuta rose beyond their capacity, they moved from there with the guidance of Sage Atri, whose ashram was on the outer periphery of Chitrakuta. That whole area was lush and prosperous, with abundant water and vegetation, thanks to the river Mandakini. It was the sage's wife, Sati Anasuya, at whose bidding the river changed her course to flow through Chitrakuta, which was otherwise suffering from drought and starvation. Sati Anasuya was respected and honoured immensely, even by the devas and devis. Her devotion to her husband was the source of her immense inner strength. She was perfect herself and saw no fault in others. Her eyes were focused only on the positive aspect of every person or situation and, with her attention, that positivity grew. She had no complaints and made no excuses. She was happy to see Sita and spend time with her. She had fed all three of them lovingly. Both the rishi and his wife kept looking at Rama with so much adoration and love. While the sage was in conversation with Rama and Lakshmana, Anasuya took Sita inside to speak to her. She checked her hands and the soles of Sita's feet. She inspected her elbows and ankles for dryness. 'You have to take care of yourself better, my child!' said Anasuya. 'Here, keep this ointment and apply a little bit of it on your face, arms and feet daily. It will keep your skin soft, nourished and youthful.' Sita accepted the box of the soft, fragrant, creamy ointment with a smile. Anasuya then took out her comb, sat Sita down in front of her and combed her long hair. Sita's hair was luxurious and silky. It was also quite thick and Anasuya couldn't hold all of it in one hand. She divided her hair into two parts and started combing it part by part. She gently removed the few knots that had formed and then braided her hair. Sita was reminded of Sunayana. 'Sita,' said Anasuya, 'you represent the true strength of a woman. Her caring attitude, softness in approach, the ability to keep harmony in the family, her skill of compromise, the innate quality of putting others before herself: these virtues make her a powerhouse. The happiness of the entire family depends on her. If she is a slave of her thoughts, emotions and feelings, life is bound to be miserable. But if the basis of her life is one-pointed commitment, then such a woman is more powerful than time itself. There is no weapon in the three worlds more potent than the words of a chaste wife. The power of her virtue can turn a blade of grass into a bolt of lightning.

Her presence is like the purifying fire. I don't need to tell you all this, but I speak for the benefit of humanity. For generations to come, the glory of Rama and you, Sita, will be sung. And along with those verses, these few words of advice will also be remembered. They say that the strings in the garland also become fragrant because of the company of the flowers. By your presence, you have immortalized these moments in our life.' She finished braiding her hair and decorated it with forest flowers.

Sita was overwhelmed by Anasuya's humility and love. 'Mother, it is my greatest honour to receive your guidance and wisdom,' said Sita. 'Your blessings are like a sheath of protection around me. By throwing light on the true wealth of a woman, you have also shown how she is complete in herself. One who rules the mind, rules the world. The power of her chastity becomes her impenetrable armour.'

It was time to take her leave. Sita bowed and touched Anasuya's feet. Anasuya held her with both arms and embraced her dearly. She opened a small wooden chest in her room and took out a pair of golden bangles. She took Sita's hands in her own and, like a mother adorning her daughter, she slipped the bangles over Sita's wrists.

When they returned to their own kutir, Rama inspected Sita's braids carefully. He was trying to examine how Anasuya had exquisitely placed the flowers, and yet the braid was also neat. 'Do you mind if I remove your braid and make it again?' asked Rama. 'I like the way the sage's wife has styled your hair. I want to learn it too.' Sita agreed happily. She sat down in front of him and he carefully removed the flowers and unloosed her long hair. He gently combed her lovely locks again. The touch of his fingers on her hair gave rise to waves of joy and contentment in Sita. She could not have been happier. The company of her beloved was her absolute comfort. When he was done, he carefully examined his workmanship, pulled her closer towards himself by her braids and held her close to his chest, enveloped in his arms. She was precious beyond measure. He loved her more than life itself. His world was filled with many responsibilities, but she was his joy. Her presence was the only comfort that he sought.

Within a few days, they left their ashram by the Payaswini and headed in the direction suggested by Maharishi Atri. They visited the hermitage of many sages en route and Rama freed the region of the demons who were troubling them. The Sage Sharabhanga waited just to have their darshan and left his body by his own will, invoking a yogic fire. This was a different experience for Sita because there was no sorrow associated with his death. He cast off his body like he would his used clothes. His eternal spirit shone much stronger than his form. They met another sage whose devotion was of a different flavour. Though he was in the world, Sage Sutikshna's being was in another realm. When they approached his hermitage, they saw him dancing, singing and swaying around in no particular direction. Rama hid behind a tree along with Sita and Lakshmana and they watched him from afar. Suddenly, he just sat in the middle of the path and went into a kind of trance. After a long while, Rama went up to him and tried to wake him, but he did not rise. 'He has my image fixed so firmly in his heart that he is unaware of the world outside. I am here, standing in front of him, but he is not opening his eyes!' said Rama. Sita laughed and told Rama, 'Maybe you should change your form in his mind! He may not be so immersed then . . .' Perhaps Sita's words manifested because the sage opened his eyes at that moment and fell at their feet.

Sage Sutikshna accompanied them to the hermitage of Sage Agastya and for that entire journey, he did not want to close his eyes at all, even to get some sleep! Sage Agastya welcomed them lovingly. There were many who saw Rama as an extraordinary prince who captured their hearts. They naturally loved him and wanted to follow him, not really knowing why. However, in the company of the saints, there was no hiding the deeper truth. They saw beyond the obvious. Rama would bow down to them as a king honouring the wise. They would bless him. Yet, they would sing his praises, unable to contain their devotion, and state that this was the very day they were waiting for. They saw infinity beyond his form, they saw wisdom in his every act. For them, he was the personification of love and divinity. He was Lord Vishnu himself, who had come upon the earth to re-establish dharma. Sita thoroughly enjoyed listening to their praise and prophecies while they spoke about Rama. When they turned to her, she would turn pink and look down shyly, smiling. It was a similar experience for Sita in Rishi Agastya's ashram too. While Rama and Lakshmana were in discussion with the sage, Sita had a chance to spend time with Lopamudra, the sage's wife. She was a very strong and vibrant person. She was straightforward and spoke bluntly. She knew a lot about plants and herbs, especially those that were useful for forest life.

They had been living on frugal meals of fruits and vegetable roots. Lopamudra taught her some tricks to add spice and bring some variety to these basic meals. She also told her of plants and roots with medicinal properties, and gave her a pouch of herbal medicines that she should keep with her. 'They are making plans for fighting and destroying rakshasas. For sure, they will come back home with a cut or two,' said Lopamudra, advising Sita. 'These herbs will be useful at that time. They will ease the pain and heal the wounds quickly.'

'Mother', said Sita, 'is it right that we enter their territories and homes, and destroy them when they haven't done us any harm? Living as ascetics should in the forest, is it right for us to harm them?'

Lopamudra smiled. Only a person with an all-encompassing sense of belonging could even think the way Sita did. She accepted asuras the way they were and was concerned for their well-being. This was the attitude of a mother. 'Sita,' said Lopamudra, 'the earth belongs to no one. In fact, we belong to her. You cannot claim a right on any part of her if you violate the laws of nature and dharma. And Rama is a king, wherever he may be. All living beings are his responsibility. To uphold dharma is his purpose. All that he does is his own leela.' She paused, holding Sita's chin in her long fingers. Looking deeply into her eyes, she said, 'But remember this, child: you are his joy.'

Sita blushed and her cheeks turned from pink to red. Her eyelashes felt heavier and longer, and her lips broke into a sweet smile. Sita enjoyed the love and attention of the sage's wife. It was good to have the company of a woman who was both motherly and strong. When it was time to leave, Lopamudra embraced Sita warmly, and some of her strength and wisdom became a part of Sita.

The sage had guided them to go to Panchavati and stay there for some time. As usual, Rama walked in front, Sita followed closely behind and Lakshmana walked behind them both. En route, they were waylaid by the asura Viradha. The brothers effortlessly slew the asura. Even as he breathed his last, a radiant celestial emerged from him, and thanked Rama for liberating him from the demonic body that he had been caged within for so many years. The being took their blessings and rose to the heavens. Rama's leela became even more evident. The rishis were happy that their prayers and penance could now proceed without further interruptions.

One day, they decided to rest awhile by the shade of a tree. Lakshmana found some ripe mangoes on the nearby trees, which they ate for lunch. The cool water from the adjacent stream quenched their thirst. Sita said, 'My lord, a mango will always be a mango, though its size, colour and sweetness may vary. An apple will also remain an apple, though there are so many varieties of apples. In the same way, do asuras have to remain asuras throughout their lives?'

Rama smiled at her and said, 'Being an asura is not just by birth, Sita. When the mind clings constantly to the negative, is caught up within the six-fold enemies and deluded, the "asuri" tendencies develop. A "sur" is a harmonious note. "Asur" is that which is not harmonious with nature. Their ignorance forms a veil over their being and they are caught in darkness. For the seed to sprout, the husk must break open. Like that, this veil of ignorance must be destroyed for their true nature to shine through.'

'How is it that they are so powerful even if they are deluded?' asked Sita. 'Their delusion is not the source of their power, Sita! It is the self that resides beyond the veil that empowers them. That self is unconditional. These asuras were not always asuras. Many have even been celestials in their past, just like the one you met now. Their past merits make them powerful and their foolishness pushes them into living a life of ignorance,' replied Rama. 'But is destroying them the only way to free them?' asked Sita. 'The spirit is eternal, Sita. Only the body is destroyed. A mango is different from an apple. But the water element in a mango is the same as the water element in an apple. At that level, you see that all of creation is connected. As you go deeper, it is just the play of one consciousness in many names and forms. Within the consciousness, the interplay of time and forms gives rise to this leela. When you recognize this truth and are established in the self, negative tendencies cannot come near you.' One glance at her beloved's lotus face and demonic tendencies were sure to dissolve, just as the shadow disappeared when you faced the light. Sita understood what

Rama tried to explain to her, but beyond that she had absolute faith in him. Once in a while, it was nice to engage in conversation, but like a lily blossom soaking in the rays of the moon, Sita's being emanated happiness and peace from simply soaking in Rama's presence. She thought that the rishis must also feel like as she did. They had access to all the knowledge in the world, but their joy at seeing Rama was indescribable. They waited for him as if it was the fruit of all their penance.

Lopamudra knew Rama's purpose. The rishi and his wife had welcomed them with all due respect and love. They worshipped her lord, but they also played their role and advised him, and gave the knowledge of divine weaponry that they foresaw he would require.

Rishi Agastya guided them to make their new hermitage in Panchavati, in the Dandakaranya forest. Once based there, Rama would free the area from the rakshasa hordes that roamed the forests. On the way to Panchavati, they met Jatayu, the great vulture, who became a good friend. They built a simple thatched hut by the banks of the Godavari river and settled down there. It was here that Shurpanaka saw the two brothers and became infatuated with them. Shurpanaka was the younger sister of Ravana. She was a shape-shifter. Along with her brothers, Khara and Dushana, she created havoc in these parts of the forest. Whatever is beautiful, the discontented and insecure mind seeks to possess immediately. Shurpanaka disguised herself as a pretty forest damsel and approached Rama shyly. Rama was sitting by himself outside the kutir. Sita saw her coming from where she was inside the kutir and intuitively hid herself. She saw Shurpanaka say something to Rama. He was looking at her with a gentle smile but declining her request. Lakshmana was standing a few feet away, alert and curious about the visitor and the conversation. He was taken aback when he saw Rama pointing in his direction! Sita was watching apprehensively. Something was not right about her. From her walk and expressions, from her very presence, Sita sensed her state of mind, though she could not hear their conversation. She saw her going back and forth between the brothers, becoming more and more impatient each time. She was casting hateful looks towards the hut. Sita was still inside watching her when suddenly, her eyes met Shurpanaka's. She instantly returned to her demonic form. It was as if the cover of maya disintegrated when her mind focused on Sita. 'You are the reason they reject me!' she growled and started racing towards the hut. In the blink of an eye, Lakshmana caught up with her and cut off her nose and ears. She vowed revenge and disappeared.

'She wanted bhaiya to marry her! She said she is the sister of the most powerful asura king in the world. It seems she lost her heart to bhaiya in the first instant she set her eyes on him. She claims that her brother has gifted her this part of the forest. So whatever is here, naturally becomes her property,' explained Lakshmana. Turning to Rama, he added, 'Bhaiya, why did you have to point her to me? You could have just told her "no" and sent her away!' 'She would have never accepted a "no" from me Lakshmana! I thought you would be more convincing. She did mention to me how she found both of us exceptionally handsome. In fact, the best among men she has seen! She said her powerful asura brothers would make us kings. Now since you have cut off her nose, let us see what the asura brothers are going to do with us!'

They knew that trouble would come soon. Within three days, her cousins Khara, Dhushana and Trishira turned up in the forest with 14,000 asuras. They made blood-curdling noises, howled and hooted eerily, and screamed and screeched in a terrifying manner. The forest animals were visibly distressed and retracted into their hiding places with fear. There was a chill in the atmosphere. Rama told Lakshmana to quickly take Sita to the safety of a nearby mountain cave and stand guard. He would handle this lot of asuras himself. From where Sita and Lakshmana were standing, they could see the sky darkening as the asuras encircled their hut. Rama was standing alone in the centre of the circle. He seemed like a lion on a mountaintop, looking up at an immense mob of crows. Lakshmana and Sita were waiting for the asuras to attack, but they just hung around doing nothing. 'What is happening, Lakshmana?' asked Sita, a little perplexed. 'Their heart does not want to wield weapons against Bhaiya. They are struck by his peaceful presence and beauty,' said Lakshmana with a smile. 'I have seen this happen every time, Bhabhi. These asuras are nothing new. The leaders will probably send a messenger now.' They saw one asura approach Rama. There was some dialogue, after which the asura flew back. They started a wildfire all around the hermitage. The fire consumed everything in its path and formed a circle around the hut. Sita prayed that it would not spread any further, because she had planted many tulsi shrubs around the hermitage. And so it happened that the fire simply dissipated and died.

Normally, Sita never ventured to see what the asuras looked like or how the conflict was progressing. She would just stay inside, praying with all her heart to the Devi, for she was the one who bestowed victory. The first time she saw an asura, she was taken aback by how frightful they looked. But eventually, she accepted that this was their natural appearance, and their fierce forms did not leave any further impressions on her mind. Behind all their grim looks and terrifying accessories were highly deluded and insecure minds full of fear. But today, Sita couldn't take her eyes off the battle. She could not see the individual asuras, but the contrast of Rama's radiance and their collective darkness was stark and riveting. She saw Rama's silhouette aiming a single arrow and letting it loose. Within minutes, she saw the skies clearing up as the asuras fell to the ground on their own, like a shower of black snow. And, just like that, the battle was over. Simple as it was, it was stunning to watch. She had never seen Rama in a fight before, and she was awed by his magnificence on the field.

Lakshmana and Sita proceeded back to the hut. Lakshmana was beaming. 'Bhaiya, what did you do to them? What arrow did you fire?' asked Lakshmana, eager to know his brother's battle strategy. Rama smiled and told him it was all a play of Maya Shakti. 'They saw me in each other and started fighting amongst themselves! I did not have to do anything,' he said, underplaying the unbelievable victory. 'Bhaiya, by your grace, they have only seen Rama in their last hour! Each one of them faced Rama and died at the hands of Rama! Though they fought each other, the arrow behind their arrows was yours!' These asuras, having lived in darkness all their lives, left their body with their minds fixed on Rama while fighting him. This was such a paradox! There were many who did penance all their lives in the hope that they would remember the divine at the time of their passing and attain higher realms thereon. And here, these asuras were inadvertently getting that very opportunity.

Sita wondered: though their bodies had fallen for the time being, what impressions would be left on their minds? Would they be reborn as asuras or as some higher souls? Would they ever experience devotion? Certainly there was something better waiting for them, having met their end with their minds filled with Rama. These asuras were the chosen ones.

Once Khara, Dhushana and Trishira were defeated, it remained peaceful in the hermitage until the day when the golden deer arrived. Sita saw the deer and was filled with the cheerful fancy to pet and play with it. But it eluded her. It was unlike other deer, which usually sought to be close to Sita. She requested Rama to catch it for her. How could he refuse her anything? He followed the golden deer into the distance, and soon it fell prey to Rama's arrow and transformed into a demon. 'Sitaaaaaa! Lakshmanaaaa!' Rama's voice echoed with great pain and calamity. It sent a shiver down Sita's spine. Lakshmana looked alarmed. His heart missed a beat. 'Go, Lakshmana! Hurry! Something is wrong!' exclaimed Sita.

Lakshmana's hands were already holding the bow firmly, but his intuition told him that he should stay put. 'Something tells me I should not leave you alone here, Bhabhi. There is some trickery afoot. Nothing could have happened to Bhaiya. I am sure he will return soon,' said Lakshmana, a little wary of the situation. 'I will be fine, Lakshmana. What if he really needs you? We cannot take that risk! Please leave immediately!' implored Sita. Lakshmana was torn between her emotions and his intuition. He too wanted to go and make sure that all was fine, but Rama had told him to stand guard over Sita till he returned. He did not want to disobey him. He told Sita so! But Sita was overcome by fear and insecurity. In that state, she was least bothered about her own safety. She only wanted to be sure that Rama was absolutely fine. In her desperation, she told Lakshmana in a voice that was full of pained authority, 'If it is really true that you see your Bhaiya and me as one, if you really respect me as your mother, then honour my command and go find Rama this moment!'

Sita never demanded proof of anybody's love, let alone Lakshmana's. She was unconditional. Lakshmana knew this very well. So hearing her speak like this pierced Lakshmana's heart. He unwillingly agreed. He drew a line outside the hermitage with the tip of his arrow and said, 'Bhabhi, please do not step outside this line. You will be safe within this boundary.' Sita agreed and he left. How she wished she had not been tempted by the golden deer! The object of beauty may be outside, but the one who experiences that beauty is within. The deer was outside, but the feeling of beauty was in Sita's heart. She did not need to possess the deer at all. But in a moment of spontaneous desire, she sought to hold the deer close. Now, with her eyes closed, she just prayed for Rama's safety.

At this moment, she heard the voice of a hermit saying, '*Bhavati bhiksham dehi*.' He was asking for alms. It was nothing unusual; several hermits visited them day in and day out. And honouring them was their dharma. She took some fruits and stepped out of the hut to offer them to the hermit. He was standing several feet away from the hut. Though he looked like a typical hermit, there was something disturbing about his presence and oddly familiar. Sita felt uneasy. Nevertheless, she invited him to come forth to receive her offering. The hermit attempted to take a step forward, but quickly pulled himself back. Perhaps he felt the presence of the boundary created by Lakshmana. Why would it stop a hermit? Perhaps, Lakshmana was just being overprotective. The hermit appeared deeply offended. He said, 'I am a hermit, O lady, not a beggar! It is respectful that you come forth where I am to offer me the food, and not ask me to come and receive it from you!'

Now Sita was in a fix. She did not want to cross the line that Lakshmana had drawn for her, so she took a few steps forward and requested the hermit to take a few steps too. 'I should never have asked you for alms! It is better to go hungry than to engage with women who have no knowledge of dharma! Your husband will be demerited for your behaviour. I am leaving,' said the hermit angrily. Sita really did not want to turn a hermit away like this. But there was a strong inner voice that told her that something was not right and that she should not step out. But Rama would never refuse a hermit's request for alms. Where was Rama now? Had Lakshmana found him? Her mind was clouded with concern when the hermit's voice pierced through, impelling her to act. She sighed heavily and stepped across Lakshmana's line.

Things were a blur after that. The hermit dematerialized and in his place stood Ravana. He forced her to mount the pushpaka vimana, his flying chariot, which he had usurped from Kubera, the lord of wealth, after defeating him in battle. In a matter of moments they were high up in the sky, thousands of metres away from the hut. Sita screamed out to Rama but her voice was heard only by the clouds, or so she thought. She felt a ray of hope when she suddenly saw the great vulture Jatayu challenging Ravana. But he was no match for the rakshasa king. Ravana cut off his wings and wounded him perilously. Sita felt awful for Jatayu. She prayed with all her heart for him. Her helplessness grew with every inch that the vimana flew further from her lord. She could feel the unrest in the forest. She could feel the agitation in the wind that blew past her anguished face. There was a tightness and a sense of contraction in all of nature because of the strength of the connection it felt with Sita. She held on firmly to the image of Rama in her mind with the conviction that he would find her, come what may.

She noticed that Ravana was headed in the southern direction. They were flying over a range of hills which caught her attention. She instinctively removed some of her jewellery and quietly tossed it into the hills below in the hope that when Rama came in search of her, it would reassure him that he was on the right path. Soon, the land below disappeared and they were flying above the vast, endless ocean. All that she could see was the boundless blue below and the infinite blue above, as she moved into a trance-like state. She saw the cosmic form of Lord Vishnu amid the ocean. He was surrounded by all the gods. They were asking for his help. Mother Earth was also present and wanted to be relieved of the burden she was carrying. The lord heard them all and turned his eyes to look at his Shakti. Sita felt the eyes of the lord penetrate her being and she came to her senses with a jolt. Perhaps this was part of a bigger plan, her role in Rama's divine purpose. She prayed to the Devi to be by her side throughout this time and protect her. With tears streaming down her face, she resigned herself to the moment.

18

The Winds of Change

Sita was sustained by her love for Rama in the silent core
of her heart. This silence was broken for a moment by a
few excited rakshasa women approaching her with golden
trays filled with numerous objects covered with fine silk.
Murmuring amongst themselves, they placed these trays in
front of Sita one after another. They were intricately carved
and ornate trays studded with precious gems of all hues.
The silks covering them were flowy, soft and in various
vibrant colours. Sita watched them in silence without
batting an eyelid. One of the rakshasa women removed
the covers on all the trays with much flourish. The most
exquisite jewellery was neatly arranged in every tray. They
were not piled up or placed in a random manner; they were
handpicked, matched with each other and placed together
in a thoughtful and orderly fashion. Other trays had a
selection of silk garments to go with the jewellery. 'Our
king feels that a princess must live and dress like a princess.

He has sent this for you to choose from so that you may adorn yourself as you please.'

Sita closed her eyes and turned her face in another direction. 'Please tell your king that I do not accept anything from those who do not bow in reverence to my lord. You may take them away,' replied Sita. 'You foolish mortal! You dare to spurn the gifts bestowed upon you by the lord of the three worlds? If not for his compassion, I would have ended your life this moment for your audacity,' replied an enraged rakshasi. Sita was unmoved by her threats and just kept a distant silence. Another rakshasi tried reasoning with Sita, 'Why don't you understand, Sita? If he learns that you rejected his carefully chosen gifts, he may become angry and take your life. What use would that be to you or to your husband whom you await against all odds? Please our king now and your life may be spared!' 'Why are you begging her?' asked another rakshasi. 'Our lord wants her adorned. Let us adorn her by force. Who cares what she likes?!' and she stepped forward to grab Sita. 'Don't touch her!' came the stern voice of Trijata. 'Follow the instructions given by the king. Nothing more. I will not allow any of you to touch a hair on her head. She is the prized jewel of the king placed under my protection.' Sita was grateful for her intervention. But Trijata was worried. She approached Sita and told her in a troubled voice. 'He will come here soon, Sita. When the moon rises to the zenith, he plans to come and meet you. I am praying for you with all my heart. But I am worried for you. May the Divine Mother and Lord Shiva be by your side.'

The moon always reminded Sita of Rama. But now, with every passing moment, as it rose higher in the sky, a quiet dread filled her heart. As she sat with her eyes tightly closed, she heard the frightfully rhythmic footsteps of Ravana approaching. As usual, he was followed by his listless troupe of women. He came to a halt a few feet away from Sita and saw that his gifts remained untouched. Sita's eyes were closed. She refused to even look at him. She prayed with all her heart for the strength to pull through these moments. As the women watched, Ravana praised Sita's beauty without any shame or sensitivity. He thought his words flowed like nectar, but they were more like drops of venom for Sita. Ironically, they were like drops of venom for the other women there too, for Ravana had never uttered such words for them. He was the only one who enjoyed the sound of his musings.

He went on and on until Sita had had enough. The blue flame of anger shot out like bolts of lightning as Sita rebuked Ravana, saying, 'Do not expect a lotus to blossom by the light of a firefly! The sun will soon rise upon Lanka, and there will be light everywhere.' Those were the harshest words that could come out of Sita. Ravana took a moment to digest what she had said. This was the first time she had spoken to him. But she had likened him to a firefly and called Rama the sun! The insult was grave. His arrogance burnt him like a volcanic fire and he raised his sword to behead her. He raced at her like a madman. Sita gently picked up a blade of grass and placed it between them.

Mandodari saw what Sita did. She instantly intervened and held Ravana's raised hand and stopped him from taking the next step forward with all the strength that she could muster. 'Raising your hand against a woman is not worthy of the lord of Lanka. Drop your weapon, my lord,' urged Mandodari. She pacified him in many ways. The other women dared not speak or move. They were stunned for no one would dare to approach or speak to Ravana when he was in that mood. Sita watched her in silence too. She felt compassion rising in her heart for Mandodari. She admired Mandodari's courage in speaking up in front of this monster. She too was fearless.

Ravana was shouting uncontrollably and gave Sita one month's time to reconsider and come around. He ordered the rakshasi guards to intimidate her in every way possible. He was not going to let Mandodari come in his way again. In a fit of rage he walked away, followed by his mindless and intoxicated band of women. Only Mandodari stayed back. 'The lord of Lanka is blind to the power of chastity, Sita. He thought he was going to take your life, but he would never have been able to cross the blade of grass that you placed in front of you. Nevertheless, I do fear for your life. You have weakened physically to a great extent due to lack of food and nourishment. Yet you shine with the light of your penance. But for how long? Lanka is not easy to find, let alone enter, for even the gods. One month will pass in the wink of an eye and death will be upon you. If your body does not discard you, the lord of Lanka surely will. Choose wisely, Sita, for you are still young. The world will not blame you for saving yourself.'

With these words, the queen left the garden. Sita burst out sobbing as soon as she left. Her will to survive was declining rapidly. She cried piteously. Her emotions were a mix of fear, relief and her longing for Rama. The rakshasis left her alone that night. She again and again told herself that she did not wish to live any longer. But there was an inner voice that assured her that Rama would come soon. As her emotions settled, she drifted off to sleep. In her dream, she was riding a white horse, though she was still wearing her forest clothes. There were two young boys, twins, who rode along with her. They kept telling her to go faster and faster, laughing and giggling with joy as the wind blew against their faces, their shoulder-length hair flowing and bouncing behind them. The horse entered the main hall of a palace. The boys disappeared and Sita saw herself dressed like a bride. She walked forward shyly and garlanded her lord, who stood tall among other kings, radiant beyond measure. The moment she looked into his eyes, they were back in the ocean of milk where a saint with the face of a monkey was in great pain. In his anguish, he told the lord that only when he too was separated from his beloved, would he understand the saint's plight . . . And at that moment, only monkeys would come forward to help him.

Just then, Sita awoke to the sound of gentle rustling in the leaves of the simsupa tree. She looked around and saw Trijata patiently waiting and watching over her. It seemed as if she wanted to say something, but was waiting for Sita's permission to speak. 'What is it, Trijata? There is something on your mind,' said Sita. 'Yes, Sita! I had the most unusual dream, but I believe it is a foreboding of the coming of the lord! I saw a vanara burning down the whole city of Lanka. I saw legions of the Lankan army dissipating like waves receding into the ocean. I saw Ravana mounted on a donkey riding south. The entire city of Lanka was calling out the name of Rama, accompanied by drumbeats. I tell you, this truth will come to pass in a few days. The time has come, Sita! I can feel it! I will proclaim it to all, so those who can may seek protection at the feet of Lord Rama!' Trijata was very excited. Sita's anticipation was also kindled. She couldn't help smiling at Trijata's optimism. Trijata was happy to have brought a smile to Sita's face. 'You are tired, Sita. Rest now. We can talk tomorrow.' Saying this, she ordered all the other rakshasis to stand guard at a distance and leave Sita alone for the night. Trijata turned to leave, but hesitated. 'What is it, Trijata?' asked Sita. 'I noticed the blade of grass too, Sita. What kind of protection was that?' 'I prayed to Sati Anasuya, Trijata,' replied Sita. 'She had told me that the power of a woman's chastity can turn a blade of grass into a bolt of lightning.' Trijata, having heard Sita, gently bowed her head in reverence and returned to her quarters.

Sita was happy to be left alone. Once again, there was a rustle in the trees. It was not unusual to hear a few sounds here and there at night in the garden, but Sita felt a new presence. For some reason, it filled her with joy. She thought that perhaps she felt this way because she had been dreaming and thinking of Rama, but the presence grew stronger. She looked up into the branches of the simsupa tree and her eyes caught sight of a tiny vanara. The words of the saint in her dream, and those of Trijata, rang in her mind. As she gazed further at the little animal, she felt like she saw an orb of light that was gently pulsating and growing stronger. As the light grew bigger, it started resonating with a very pleasing sound. A sound that was dearer to her than life itself. The vibration of the sacred sound of her lord's name, Rama, was gradually filling her mind and the space around her, as it continued to emanate from that tiny vanara. 'His entire being is filled with Rama! But does he know me?' she wondered. The vanara gently approached her and bowed at her feet. In its feeble voice, it said, 'Jai Sri Rama!' The words soothed Sita's being like water to a parched desert nomad, and her eyes opened wide in amazement. This vanara could talk! 'Who are you, child?' exclaimed Sita, her life force seeping back into her. 'I am Hanuman, dear Mother, son of Vayu, the Wind God, servant of Sri Rama!'

Sita felt a sudden jolt of strength in herself and further enquired, 'Hanuman, how did you reach this place? It is filled with rakshasa guards. It is unsafe for a tiny vanara like you. You must leave soon. But please tell me, what news do you have of my lord?' The vanara jumped off the tree branch and suddenly his size increased to that of an adult human in a fraction of a moment. 'I am not a tiny vanara, Mother. That was just a guise for me to search for you, unseen by these guards,' explained Hanuman. Sita could see him better now, but she was a little wary of shapeshifters. A doubt arose in her mind: was he yet another asura sent by Ravana to trick her again? He had a form that was half-human and half-monkey—just like the saint in her dream. But how would Ravana have known what came to her in her dream? Had he dreamt of such vanaras too?

Hanuman sensed that Sita was going back into her shell. He felt he had to reassure her of his intent. The lord had anticipated this situation and given Hanuman his ring for this very reason. 'Mother, please be assured that I speak the truth,' said Hanuman, as he took out the ring and handed it to Sita as proof. She quickly took the ring in her hands and held it as if it gave her life. Its very touch was like a shower of nectar for Sita. She closed her eyes and felt the cool touch of the ring in her palms. A pleasant sensation went through her body, her breath stopped, and she heard her lord's voice in her mind.

Beloved Sita,

The waves in the ocean rise again and again,
Longing to merge with the moon,
The seeds on the branches of the cotton tree
Long for the wind to carry them to freedom,
The delicate hibiscus shines a bright red
As it yearns to share its nectar with the world,
The entire planet rotates on its axis
As every part of it longs to meet the sun,
The river flows ceaselessly

As it longs to dissolve in the ocean,

The rain clouds gather here and there

To quench the earth's thirst,

A soul seeks a human body

As it longs to become one with infinity,

A newborn cries with its first breath

As it longs to once again be with its mother,

A lover pens poetry of endless love

Until he is reunited with his beloved,

The divine manifests himself in human form

As he longs to behold tears of blissful devotion,

Yet all of this longing put together cannot come close to the magnitude of pain that this separation from you has caused me.

With every passing moment, I move closer and closer to you,

You who are always a part of me.

Your Rama

Rama's eyes opened with a start in the same instant that Sita heard the last of his voice resound in her being. 'Sita has been found, Lakshmana,' he said with a joyful surge of energy. Sita's trust in Hanuman was complete now, and she longed to hear the news of her lord. 'My lord was aware of the importance of winning your trust, Mother,' said Hanuman. 'He understands your situation. So he told me of an incident that no one but you and he are aware of. He said that after the battle with the brothers of Shurpanaka, he knew that the time was near for the ultimate battle with the rakshasas. He asked you to abide by the fire till the destruction was complete. The world knows not that you are beyond its reach. Yet you experience everything as if it is real. Like the light that passes through the crystal reflects all the colours in their pure, undistorted form yet leaves no stain on the crystal, in the same way, the pure form of energy that you are, you experience and express all the emotions to their fullest, but they leave no impression on you.' Sita felt completely relaxed upon hearing the words of Hanuman. 'Tell me, son, how does my lord manage his days?' asked Sita with tears welling up in her eyes again. 'What are the brothers eating? Please do tell me how you met him, how you found me and when the lord himself will arrive!'

'Yes, Mother! It was easy for me to recognize you because I have seen this same yearning and pain in the lord's eyes. All that is beautiful reminds him of you. While you are surrounded by the fire of negativity, his heart burns in the scorching fire of separation. Even the light of the moon is unbearable for him. At his command, vanara troops have been sent to every corner of the planet, in all directions, by King Sugriva, in search of you, Mother. King Sugriva is the son of Surya. Most of the vanara leaders are sons of the devas and possess extraordinary strength, skill and valour. It is my greatest good fortune to be the one to have found you,' replied Hanuman. 'The golden deer was the demon Maricha, Ravana's uncle. When the lord and Lakshmana returned to the hut and were not able to find you, they were both shattered. They went out searching every nook and corner of the forest, and chanced upon Jatayu fallen on the ground.'

Tears of sadness flowed from Sita's eyes. 'I feel bad for Jatayu, Hanuman. He was such a dear friend. He lost his life trying to save me,' she said. Hanuman replied, 'He lived the life of a true warrior and fought for dharma. He showed Ravana that Rama is not alone. He showed him that his love for Lord Rama is far stronger than the fear of Ravana's powers! He did not give his life in vain. He breathed his last in the arms of the lord after telling him of your abduction at the hands of Ravana. His soul is at peace now, Mother!' 'The lord and Lakshmana then proceeded in the southern direction and entered Kishkinda. There, as they were walking near the Rishyamukha hills, Sugriva saw them and sent me to learn their identity. That was the sacred day when I first met the lord. My heart knew instantly that serving him was the purpose of my very existence. Having heard what happened, I took them with me to Sugriva and a bond of friendship was forged between them. Sugriva is the heir of the Sun. His brother Vali was the son of Indra. However, Sugriva lived in hiding in the forests, out of fear of Vali, who had wronged him in many ways. With the lord by his side, Sugriva challenged Vali to a fight, and while the duel was going on, the lord, while standing behind a tree, shot his arrow which has never missed its mark, and Vali fell to the ground. Vali was taken by surprise. He wondered why Rama would choose to kill him surreptitiously. He thought it was a breach of dharma.

Rama explained to him clearly that the laws of humans do not apply to vanaras. They live by the laws of the forest. Rama is the king of the forests too. It is his duty to uphold dharma everywhere. What he meted out to Vali was punishment for his wrongdoing. Rama had done his duty by punishing Vali and Vali was liberated, having met his end at the hands of Rama. There was no question of a battle between them. While it was clear that Rama's actions were according to those prescribed by the shastras, Rama's very presence purified Vali's heart. He realized his mistake. He was humbled and was able to surrender. In his last moments, when he felt that all was lost for him, he saw the lord by his side, and that was enough. Before he departed, he sought Rama's blessings and protection for his valiant son Angada. That young vanara is a gem. Sugriva was then crowned the ruler of Kishkinda and eventually sent out the vanara troops in search of you. Angada, Nala, Neela, Jambavan and I went in the southern direction with our army. All of us reached the shores of the ocean but were unsure as to how we should proceed any further. Many of us leap well, but to jump all the way across the ocean was unthinkable. But Jambavan was very optimistic. He encouraged me to find a way. He reminded me of the blessings of all the devas that I had received as a child that were meant to come to my aid when it was really needed. And it was the right time now. Further, I felt it was my responsibility to find you regardless of the obstacles. I simply took the name of the lord to invoke the strength and skills that were needed and jumped across the ocean. In spite of several obstacles on the path, I reached here safely,' said Hanuman, describing all the events that transpired: all this while Sita waited. 'You jumped across the ocean, Hanuman?' repeated Sita in wide-eyed wonder. She could not even see the other side. How could anyone jump so far? Hanuman replied as if he had read her mind, 'The lord's name is my mantra, Mother! When this small mantra is enough to help you cross over the ocean of life, then crossing this limited ocean is no big feat! Anyhow, now that I have found you, I must teach a lesson to that wicked rakshasa king before I leave. Mother, is there anything you would like me to tell the lord when I return?'

'No, Hanuman. The lord knows my heart. But the world may demand proof. So I will also tell you of another incident which only my lord and I witnessed.'

Sita's mind drifted to that beautiful day in Panchavati. The weather was cool and pleasant. Rama had gone to the forest but had not returned by his usual time. Sita was wondering what was taking him so long, and stepped out of the hut to see if he was perhaps anywhere nearby. Having looked around for a few minutes, she caught sight of him sitting by the river, bent over something. Whatever he was doing consumed all of his attention. He was completely engrossed in it. Although Sita was curious, she did not want to disturb him. She went back inside and continued with her work in the kitchen. After a while, she heard him approaching the hut. He was trying to walk in quietly, as if he wanted to surprise her. Sita also played along and pretended that she did not realize that he had come in.

However, she could not help smiling to herself. He came and stood just one foot behind her, and the fragrance in the room was overwhelming. Was it jasmine or champa, or the sugandharaja? It even had a tinge of forest lily . . . so many fragrances at the same time! She closed her eyes as she breathed them all in deeply. She opened her eyes and turned around with a smile, eager to see what Rama had brought with him. He had a childlike gleam in his eyes. He had his palms held together, and as Sita turned, he gently parted his hands to reveal a string of wildflowers. There were many different flowers in diverse colours strung together in an intricate flow. It was beautiful to see.

'Will you sit down, Sita?' said Rama in a gentle voice. He was not sure if she was free now or had to complete her cooking. But Sita was more or less done, and she was happy to oblige. He took out a wooden comb that he had fashioned out of the fallen branch of a fig tree, and gently combed her hair. He then carefully braided her lovely, silky locks with the flowers that he had brought. Sita sat in silence, enjoying the gentle touch of Rama's hands on her hair. Rama was totally absorbed in making the perfect braid. When he was done, he pushed her braid forward and turned her around to admire his workmanship. He looked into her eyes and told her in his soft and deep voice, 'Sita, these flowers looked beautiful when I saw them in the forest, and while I was stringing them together. But when I look into your eyes, everything else fades against your beauty. There is nothing else that I can see.' Sita blushed and felt her cheeks turn pink. The moment was so complete, and there was no plan for the next one. So, with no particular intention, they started strolling together towards the riverbank. There, they sat by a rock and watched the flowing waters. All the searching in the forest for flowers must have tired Rama, for he quickly went off to sleep with his head in her lap. She sat without moving an inch.

Sita rejoiced in the details of the memory of this event in her mind, but shared it in just one line with Hanuman. She said, 'One day, the lord was resting his head in my lap by the river. At this time, a crow flew dangerously close, diving towards my feet, and bit my toe. It was painful, but I did not flinch nor cry. My lord was sleeping deeply. He rarely slept much and I did not want to disturb him. I was not even bothered about the crow. I somehow swallowed the pain and sat immobile. My lord woke up after a few minutes, refreshed and relaxed, and was taken by surprise to see my bleeding toe. Before I could even explain, he plucked a blade of grass, invoked the Brahmastra and set it upon the culprit. Within a few minutes, the crow came back and fell at my feet, seeking forgiveness and refuge. I looked at the wily bird and felt only compassion. Rama saw the look in my eyes and relented. The blade of grass blinded one of his eyes and spared him. The crow turned into a celestial. It was Jayantha, the son of Indra, who in his foolishness had thought to test the powers of the lord by committing such a meaningless yet hurtful act. Remind my lord of this incident and also give him this,' said Sita, as she handed him her beautiful round hairpin, her *chudamani*. Hanuman received the ornament with humility and grace, and secured it carefully. He bowed to Sita and took her blessings. 'You have my protection, Hanuman. No weapon, nor harsh words, nor earth nor fire, nor water nor wind, will hurt you while you have the sacred name of the lord in your heart. Go forth now and bring my lord here soon!'

Hanuman leapt into the trees, went to another part of the garden, far from where Sita was, and created havoc. He uprooted the trees there, ate up all the mangoes, and threw the seeds on the heads of the guards. Soon, he was throwing the guards themselves around like seeds. A battalion entered the garden to imprison the vanara but they all met with the same fate. News of the rebel vanara reached Sita's enclosure too. The rakshasi guards were alarmed because Trijata's description of her dream was still clear in their minds. The Vanara was unstoppable. Soon, word reached them that Akshay Kumar, the son of the lord of Lanka, had met his end at the hands of this intruder. His elder son, Indrajit, was now on his way. Indrajit was known in all the three worlds for his valour. He received this name after defeating Indra, the king of the gods, in battle. Sita prayed to the Divine Mother to protect Hanuman. Soon, word reached Sita that Indrajit had released the Brahmastra against Hanuman. However, it had bound him and caused no other harm. Hanuman was now being led to the main hall to face the king. He had anyway wanted to give a message to the lord of Lanka. Sita smiled to herself, reflecting on Hanuman's skill and intelligence. An hour or so passed after which the hoarse laughter of the rakshasi guards caught her attention. Their joy did not bode well with Sita. Apparently, they were tying a cloth soaked in oil to the tail of the incorrigible vanara, and soon he would be set on fire. They were laughing at what they imagined to be the plight of the vanara. Sita was disturbed at the news and prayed to Agni, the God of Fire, to leave Hanuman unscathed.

As evening flowed into night, the sky began to take on an eerie red glow. Distant screams from the city could be heard even in this remote corner of the garden. The rakshasi guards abandoned Sita and ran away, deeply troubled. Sita was not sure what was happening when, out of nowhere, Hanuman jumped down in front of her with a burning tail. Sita was alarmed at the sight. 'The city of Lanka is on fire, Mother! Those who see the light will come to know of the lord's coming. Those whose mind is focused on the ashes will stay here and meet the same end. Mother, come with me! I cannot bear to leave you here with these demons!' said Hanuman. 'Not now, Hanuman. The glory of my lord will be known to the world only when he defeats Ravana himself,' insisted Sita. 'Bless me, Mother! I will return soon following my lord!' Hanuman kneeled in front of her and Sita raised her hand in blessing. He leapt up into the sky the next moment and was gone. The ocean was waiting to serve the lord's devotee by putting off the flames. But her children in the skies held themselves back from showering the city.

The fire of hunger may be satisfied by food. The fire of enquiry may be cooled by wisdom. The fire of desire may be quenched by faith. But the fire of longing is eternal in the soul. Sita saw smoke from the burning city rising up into the sky. The flames would consume everything in their path. The fire within her, fuelled by the separation from her beloved, had consumed all other emotions, even fear, and had kept her going. 'What is it that even fire can't touch?' reflected Sita, 'fire itself, and space.' Her faith was the fire within that kept her going.

The rakshasi guards who returned the next day looked upon Sita with fear. Word had spread like wildfire that the lady imprisoned in the garden had brought this misfortune upon the golden city. 'Why does the king not send her away? Are there not enough women of beauty among the celestials? Why does he seek the favours of a mere mortal?' said a faceless voice among the people. 'I am not certain she is ordinary, for no simple woman can withstand the lord of Lanka the way she has,' said another voice in the crowd.

Trijata shared these growing concerns of the people with Sita. She had no misgivings about them. But they suffered for the choices their king made with regard to her. It was now a matter of days before her lord would come. 'How will he cross the ocean, though? His devotee took his name and came across. But what will my beloved do?' thought Sita, as she resolved with renewed courage to wait some more.

19

The March of Truth

'Rama has arrived at the opposite shore with an army of vanaras,' exclaimed Trijata. 'News is that they are building a bridge across the ocean! A young vanara named Nala is connecting great stones and uprooted mountains effortlessly and making the bund. My father has joined him, Sita!'

Sita felt jubilant . . . Trijata's father Vibhishana joining Rama was a significant turn of events. Now there was someone with her beloved who could share the details of the enemy, who knew the strengths and weaknesses of Lanka inside out.

Within a few days, Vibhishana had sent a message to Ravana on Rama's behalf. Rama had invited Ravana, in the capacity of being the most learned brahmin in their vicinity, to conduct a Shiva puja before they started building the bridge. Ravana's dharma and personal commitment to his ishta (personal deity), Lord Shiva, did not allow him to refuse an invitation to conduct a puja for Him. Ravana accepted.

At the time of the puja, Trijata came running to Sita in excitement. 'Sita, we are going to the other shore! Prepare yourself!' Sita couldn't believe what she was hearing. She asked Trijata for the details. It all sounded too simple and too good to be true. Trijata explained what had transpired when Ravana reached the opposite shore, where Rama and his vanara retinue were waiting. Ravana had realized that Rama couldn't conduct the puja, saying, 'You are incomplete without your wife. Her presence here is a must.'

Rama promptly responded, saying, 'It is the duty of the pandit to fulfil the requirements for the puja. Do what you must to perform your duties.'

Ravana had the option of making an idol of Sita and proceeding with the puja, but he was a perfectionist, especially when it came to the Shiva puja. He told Rama that he would send for his wife on the condition that Rama send her back to Lanka after the puja, and duly battle Ravana for her freedom.

Sita arrived with Trijata in the pushpaka vimana and hand-moulded the Shiva Linga from the mud that lay by the ocean. It seemed as if the mud was waiting to be given a divine shape by her hands. All the preparations for the yagna were made and the puja happened very smoothly. Having Sita beside him was such a fulfilling feeling for Rama. His attention was only on her. The thought that she would have to leave shortly was unbearably painful. As his mind dwelt on these thoughts, the sound of Ravana's voice as he chanted the ancient verses fell on Rama's ears and transformed the pain into anger. But as his attention shifted to the chants, he experienced the benevolent and peaceful Shiva tattva and his emotions settled down. Sita was keenly aware of the battle of emotions within Rama and took refuge in the Shiva tattva too. At the end of the puja, as was custom, Rama and Sita bowed to Ravana to take his blessings. '*Vijayi bhava*,' said Ravana to Rama. He blessed him with victory unflinchingly. Now it was Rama's turn to give *dakshina*, or the dues to the pandit, for having conducted the puja. Ravana breathed deeply and told him, 'There is nothing on this plane that you can give me which I don't already possess.' And in his mind he found himself saying to Rama, 'But at the moment when my life leaves this body, be there to take me across.' Rama heard him fully and accepted. The puja was an equally intense experience for Ravana. He could not take his eyes off Rama. He wanted to do everything to the best of his ability. The vibrations from the mantras were amplified greatly. He felt a serenity within which was unlike anything he had felt before. He attributed the peace to his ishta, Lord Shiva, and allowed himself to be in that space for the duration of the puja. When it was over and Rama and Sita stood up together, his heart felt like it was being torn apart. Emotions rose within and almost weakened him. They fell at his feet and he involuntarily blessed them. He would leave with Sita as his prisoner now. But he wanted to take Rama with him. He felt if he stayed even a minute longer, he wouldn't be able to leave without him. He turned away abruptly, mounted his pushpaka vimana with Trijata, with Sita following, and they returned to Ashoka Vatika in no time. For Sita, it all felt like a dream. Tears flowed freely from her eyes but she felt a new strength within.

Rama and his army would march across the ocean soon. There was apprehension in the air in Lanka. 'There are crores of vanaras on the bridge, Sita,' said Trijata. 'I don't even know where they are going to stand once they reach the shores of Lanka! The vanaras themselves amount to the size of an ocean! It is a matter of hours now before Rama reaches the city. The time has come, Sita! The time has come . . .' Her senses were sharper than ever before. Hours passed by like eons. And then, it happened. Like a bolt of lightning, a surge of energy passed through Sita. Every cell in her body thrilled with the knowledge of what had come to pass. Rama had set his feet on the island of Lanka. The earth had faithfully carried the message to Sita that very instant. A new strength filled her.

'They are here, Sita!' exclaimed Trijata as she came running to update Sita with the latest developments. She said it had looked like two suns rising on Mount Suvela when the two brothers climbed her peak to see the glorious city of Lanka. 'I am sure they would have marvelled at the beauty of the city, crafted by the master architect of the gods, Vishwakarma himself. You haven't seen the city yourself, Sita, though you have been here for months now. You have such a keen eye for beauty. You would have appreciated his skill. Queen Mandodari's father, Mayan, arrived today as well. He has voiced his concerns to the lord of Lanka in the council today. He has declared without mincing his words that the hour of reckoning is at hand. He shared that Sugriva is the son of Surya, Angada is Indra himself, Neela is the son of Agni (the God of Fire), Hanuman is the son of the Wind God, and the wise ones say that he is Lord Rudra himself, who has come in this form just to serve his beloved Lord Vishnu in the form of Rama. Jambavan, the king of all bears, who can tell the past, present and future by his wisdom, and who has lived since the days of the churning of the ocean, also accompanies them along with many other vanaras, who are said to be the devas themselves, born in this garb to support and fight as part of Rama's army. Mayan advised Ravana to return you to Rama and save the city from certain destruction, but Ravana paid no heed to his advice. War is upon us and it will be one that is remembered for time immemorial. While Rama and Lakshmana stood above Mount Suvela to survey the city, the lord of Lanka emerged into the pavilion on the topmost spire of his palace to survey the Vanara army. The two leaders of their respective armies were standing miles apart, and looked like two magnificent pillars of power and enormous energy. Rama was surrounded by an aura of pure and radiant golden light that seemed to encompass everything around him, while Ravana's presence was like a burning blue thundercloud holding a million bolts of lightning within it.'

It was clear that Trijata was mesmerized by the unprecedented nature of whatever she had witnessed. Though it spelt doom for Lanka, she was still in amazement at the thought of what was unfolding around her. She would tell Sita everything and be her eyes and ears. Trijata's sister Kala and one of the other rakshasi guards ran into the enclosure with some news. 'Trijata, you have to hear this! After you left the vantage point, we witnessed the most unbelievable incident! The vanara king Sugriva, with one mighty leap, scaled the distance from the top of the Suvela mountain all the way up to the king's palace, and landed just a few feet away from the lord of Lanka. They fought terribly; the vanara king took hold of the crown jewels, and jumped back to the feet of Rama. Eagles would be jealous of the speed with which he leapt back and forth! I have never seen anything like this before, Trijata!' Kala was speaking only in exclamations. It seemed as if every day was going to be filled with one unimaginable story or another. Sita was listening to everything carefully, absorbing every detail. 'Soon after this they descended the mountain, and the vanara armies dispersed. They have now begun the siege of the city. Hanuman and Sugriva are at the western gate with their army, while Angada is at the south, Neela is at the eastern gate, and the brothers are at the northern gate.' Trijata said, 'Night has fallen now. Let us see what dawn brings.'

Trijata returned mid-morning the next day. Sita was anxious to know of the fresh developments. 'They have sent Angada, the son of Vali, as an emissary. When he entered the city the citizens fled from him, thinking that he was the one who had earlier burnt the city down. As he walked through the streets fearlessly, mothers wished for such courage for their sons. Ravana tried to lure him with riches and comforts to join his army instead—and reminded him that Vali was Ravana's friend—but Angada scoffed at his attempt. That young vanara is audacious. With the pride of being Rama's emissary, he made himself a seat higher than Ravana's by coiling his tail beneath himself. He told the lord of Lanka that one who relied on the intelligence gained purely through one's senses is a pitiable fool. He who thinks that he can fathom the ways of the divine with his limited intellect is deluded. He who has no access to his intuitive intelligence has no eyes for the truth. Ravana saw Rama as a mere mortal and called the vanaras monkeys. He refused to see the divine forces that have come marching to his doors. In Angada's eyes, Ravana is already defeated. He told him so and left the assembly like a lion among bleating sheep.'

'What now, Trijata?' asked Sita. 'Well, they will surely form a battle strategy and meet on the field. Sword will meet sword. The hearts of the warriors will recede into their caves for there is no place for feelings on the battlefield. Arrows will separate souls from their bodies. Elephants, horses, chariots and cavalry will march forth in Ravana's army, while Rama's army has only vanaras on foot. Many vanaras will likely die fighting for Rama. The rakshasas will certainly die fighting against Rama. Whatever be the reason, Rama will be the last impression on their mind, and this alone is enough for them to attain a higher birth in their next lifetime,' said Trijata. Sita sighed heavily.

Like a distant rumble of thunderclouds, the roll of the battle drums could be heard faintly even in Ashoka Vatika, which was far removed from the scene of war. The sounds of battle were coming forth from all sides, pervading the city of Lanka. Even the birds in Ashoka Vatika had stopped chirping and kept an eerie silence. In the silence, the sound of various conches could be heard.

'Prahasta will lead the army today. He is the commander-in-chief of Ravana's army and a formidable rakshasa,' said Trijata. 'The vanara army have uprooted most of the nearby hills and filled up the moats around the city with them. The moats previously filled with lotuses ebbed and flowed into the ocean. The swans have flown away to safer havens. The creatures from the hills are also fleeing to safety, running helter-skelter, not knowing which direction to take, for the armies are stretched across all sides as far as the eyes can see. This war is like a great deluge itself, Sita. There is one Ravana and one Rama, and the world is divided between them. Time will devour thousands of lives from both sides in the coming few days. It is a rare time on the planet that leaders of such stature are born. Many battles have been fought on this planet, but few to match the magnificence that we see today.'

Sita thought of the word 'magnificent'. It suited Rama well. Whatever he did, be it a celebration or a war, it was all magnificent. He never seemed to do anything in small measure. He might start something humbly, but it eventually ended up being grand.

The rakshasas had refined weaponry. The vanaras fought with stones, tree trunks and bare hands. The trumpeting elephants, the stomping and rearing of neighing horses, the sound of the chariot wheels, the heavy ornaments worn by the rakshasas that clanked against each other, the conches and drums, all together created an orchestra of raw strength and formidable power playing out on the field amid the rising dust from many thousand pairs of feet.

While the dance of the deluge was happening on the shores of Lanka, silence enveloped Ashoka Vatika. From time to time, Trijata would update Sita of the happenings. Sita would listen, but was not really keen on knowing what was happening. The gory details of war did not interest her. But she wanted to make sure that Rama and Lakshmana were safe. She was also particularly concerned about Hanuman. She did not know who the others were, but she prayed to the Divine Mother for all.

A guard came running to Trijata with the news that Ravana himself would be entering the field, even though it was just the first day! The guard said, 'The Lankan army has been crushed and defeated and, in some parts, is not even traceable. Prahasta, who had the strength of all the divine weapons, was defeated by a vanara with branches. The lord of Lanka has worn his impenetrable armour, picked up his bow—whose twang is the song of the God of Death—taken several other weapons of mass destruction and mounted his chariot. Standing under the pearl-studded umbrella in his chariot, his flag, with the symbol of the veena, surrounded by thousands of foot soldiers, he looked like Mount Meru surrounded by the seven seas, moving forward at a steady pace.'

'What a contrast!' thought Sita. Perhaps one whose mind is in harmony irrespective of the situation is the one who can conquer death. However, at this moment, Ravana's mind was certainly scattered and in shock at the developments. Still, he was a formidable enemy and Sita was nervous.

A few hours passed, after which Trijata received some news. Hanuman and Lakshmana had vigorously fought Ravana, but had become tired. Ravana had thrown a spear given to him by Brahma at Lakshmana. However, it only rendered him unconscious. Apparently, Ravana had tried to capture him but was unable to lift his body from the ground. Hanuman had appeared on the scene from nowhere and had quickly taken him away like a mother carrying a child. Rama entered the field himself after this, and destroyed Ravana's chariot, weapons, flag, crown, and his pride. Seeing him standing on the earth with neither weapons nor the will to fight, Rama had advised Ravana to take some time to reconsider fighting him, and if he still wanted to continue, he could rest and return to the battlefield the next day.

Sita was thrilled at the news. But Ravana had been given a second chance. It was not over just yet. Hours passed by and the sky was filled with the stars again. Even though innumerable vanaras and rakshasas had gathered under this very sky, they still paled in comparison to the countless stars above. Sita imagined the view of the earth from these stars. From such a great height, even the mountains would look like a tiny speck. Would the dust rising from the battlefield be even visible? Not really. It would all look the same. The sun would still rise and set, and the earth would continue to rotate as always. Her lord was the one who ruled over these multiple universes.

And as the sun rose, dynamic activity would spring up in every corner of the planet wherever it shone. To what degree would the activity on the battlefield compare in magnitude to all that was going on every moment in the entire creation? And her lord was the basis of all the happenings, everywhere. These thoughts caressed her mind like soft ocean waves that touch one's feet and recede, leaving a cool feeling of respite. And in spite of the storm brewing around her, she drifted off to sleep. She might have slept for a little over an hour when she started hearing drumbeats, loud clanging noises, trumpets and trombones playing resounding notes. It was as if their only purpose was to create sounds of discord. And the noise just grew louder and louder! It was like a midnight celebration of rakshasa children who had been let loose and were now making a racket. The intensity of the sound went up and down—perhaps as the players grew tired or out of breath, and then with some fresh burst of energy, they all went at their instruments yet again. But suddenly it all stopped. The planned effort to play such chaotic music at this unearthly hour kindled Sita's curiosity. But she was glad it was over.

Morning came and the rakshasi guards looked rejuvenated. Something was afoot. But they never spoke to Sita the whole day. Trijata also did not come to give her any news. Sita was watching the fish jumping in and out of the water in the nearby stream. When they were in the water, waiting to jump, their attention was on the sky. When they had jumped into the air, their attention was on getting back into the water, their source of life. Their minds moved back and forth between the sky and the water, in rotation . . . What would it take to have one-pointed focus and attention, irrespective of where you were or what you were doing? Could such a quality of attention be practised? Or would it only come from love? She felt fortunate because her mind effortlessly dwelt entirely on Rama. Even when she wasn't thinking of him, he was the very basis of her existence.

She walked towards another part of the garden where she saw a chameleon on a low tree branch. Its colour changed from a muddy brown to a greenish tinge as it moved from the trunk into the branches full of leaves. The transformation happened effortlessly. She wondered what the true colours of the chameleon were, or even if there were such a thing. If it were to look at its own reflection in the stream, what colour would it retain or take on? This little lizard was an ideal example of effortless adaptation to one's surroundings. However, while one's outer expressions could be adapted, one's core values could not change according to one's circumstances. If one's morals changed as per one's convenience, that was the sign of a weak mind full of cravings and aversions. Sita reflected on all her family members and admired each one for their steadfastness and commitment to dharma. She too was doing her best to uphold her dharma given the situation she was faced with.

While she stood pondering, she heard someone approaching. There were several confident footsteps and someone who was resisting coming here. 'Sita! Look who is here to meet you!' Sita heard the gruff and deep voice of Ravana calling out her name and shuddered. She turned to see who it was and was utterly shocked by the sight confronting her. Ravana's guards were dragging her father towards where she was. Her heart was struck by misery and tears filled her eyes. She wanted to run to her father's side but the sight of the monstrous guards surrounding him held her back. 'Leave him alone!' she implored. Ravana laughed without restraint and seemed to thoroughly enjoy the pain he was inflicting upon both father and daughter. 'How did they get you, Father?!' asked Sita in a strained voice, tears streaming down her face. 'Did you think that monkey was the only one who could fly across the ocean? My rakshasas are in Ayodhya even as we speak. I thought you might want to have a glimpse of your father, though. So we brought him here. Let him also see for himself how careless his son-in-law has been with his daughter, leaving her alone and unguarded in the forest!' said Ravana, laughing again to himself. His joy seemed inappropriate. He laughed at the plight of others, and laughed alone. 'Look at you, my dear! I didn't expect to send you from Mithila to see you like this. I wish I had never lived to see this day,' said a distraught Janaka as he broke down sobbing. Sita's heart broke and her strength began to fail her. 'I cannot bear this anymore, Sita! I had told Ravana that he must shun the thought of making you his queen, but having seen your pitiful condition, I feel that one may not be at fault if one surrenders and adapts to such a terrible circumstance. Ravana's power is undisputed, and you will finally receive the protection and respect that you deserve. Enough of waiting for Rama, Sita. He is not going to reach this part of Lanka. Save yourself! Save your father, and protect your lineage. This is your duty,' said Janaka.

Sita could not believe what she was hearing. She never thought that she would hear such words from her father, who was the epitome of right conduct and far more courageous than he seemed to be now. She was reminded of the chameleon on the tree branch. Her heart told her that something was not right. Still, she was shaken. 'Looks like your daughter doesn't really listen to you, O King of Mithila,' said Ravana, as he raised his sword. 'Lord!' cried a guard as he came in running at that very moment, 'Lord, that which should not be has come to pass! Kumbhakarna is no more!'

Ravana was stunned and immobile. The sword dropped from his hands, his knees gave way and he placed his head on the ground in deep anguish. It was as if he had been drained of all his life force. It was clear that tears were silently flowing from his eyes. The asura who held the chains that bound Janaka dropped them as well. Janaka himself became disinterested in Sita, and was fixated instead on Ravana. The lord of Lanka rose and walked away from the garden amid an eerie silence. Janaka followed him quietly without even casting another glance at Sita. What was wrong with him? Something was greatly amiss. While Sita stood with a confused look in her eyes, Trijata walked up behind her. 'That was not your father Sita. It was Marutha, who is an expert at creating illusions.' Sita turned to look at her in wonder. Appearances could be so deceptive. For a moment she had believed her eyes and ears, and felt deep misery too. But her heart saw beyond her senses.

Sita felt relieved, but she saw tears in Trijata's eyes. 'What happened, Trijata?' enquired Sita with concern in her voice. 'My uncle Kumbhakarna was vanquished by Lord Rama today, in one of the most fierce battles that the world has ever seen. He was one of the greatest rakshasas that ever lived. All the music you heard in the middle of the night was Ravana's attempt to rouse him from his deep slumber. He would sleep for six months in a year. He too had advised Ravana that what he had done was wrong, and that he should return you with dignity and respect. He chided Ravana for sending my father out of the kingdom. But Ravana ignored his advice and goaded him to fight. Before he died, he asked Rama for a boon . . .' and Trijata could speak no more as her throat choked and tears gushed from her eyes.

Sita made her sit down and allowed her emotions to pour out. Once she settled down, she spoke again. 'My uncle shared with Lord Rama that Ravana will seek to take Vibhishana's life. He told him that Ravana's mind was lost to the darkness and filled with negativity. And he requested the lord to protect my father. He said that my father is the saving grace of the lineage for he alone stood up for dharma.' Tears filled Sita's eyes too as she shared Trijata's sorrow. 'Be wary of Ravana's tricks and illusions, Sita,' said Trijata. 'While his warriors are on the field fighting a real battle, he is here trying to trick you into submission. He knows that if you break down and accept him, the battle is won. You are the centre, Sita. He thinks he has imprisoned you, but he is the one whose mind is without freedom. He cannot even come near you, even though you are unarmed and in his captivity. While you stand untouched in this garden, the side of truth will stand victorious on the battlefield. I will do whatever I can to protect you, Sita. My uncle will not have given his life in vain.' Kumbhakarna had died fighting for Ravana. But Trijata felt Kumbhakarna's life's fulfilment was in protecting Sita. It seemed quite contradictory. Though Kumbhakarna played his part fully, there was no enmity in his heart for Rama. He fought Rama with all his strength, knowing that this battle would glorify the lord. Nevertheless, Sita was relieved that at the end of the day, her lord was safe. Tomorrow would be yet another day.

20

Fleeting Clouds, Clear Skies

Sita dreamt of the ocean that night. Suddenly, she saw a huge wave rising in the distance, like a giant wall of water and it was approaching her with a steadfast focus. She searched immediately for Rama and saw him also looking at the same wave. She was not worried anymore. Rough or smooth patches, as long as he was with her, she had nothing to fear. She felt utterly safe and serene. She looked up again and the giant wave was no more. In the distant sky, she saw Garuda flying in circles. She could hear his shrill call all the way down to where she stood.

She woke up with a comforting feeling. Her dream seemed like a good omen. However, she did not show any outward sign of the pleasantness she felt because the rest of Lanka was still in mourning. She went for her customary walk around the garden when she noticed someone looking at her from afar. It was Queen Mandodari. Though she stood at a distance, Sita could sense her sorrow. She pretended as if she did not realize that she was being watched, and allowed the queen her space to mourn. After a few minutes, she was no longer there and had perhaps returned to her quarters.

The day went by without any major incident in Ashoka Vatika. However, closer to sunset, she heard a familiar piercing shrill sound from the sky above. She looked up and saw Garuda encircling a particular area which was likely somewhere on the battlefield. He swooped down at full speed and was soon out of sight. Moments later, he rose to the skies again and disappeared into the distance. Sita now waited for Trijata to come and give her news. It was night when she finally came and told her what had happened. Indrajit, the son of Ravana, had bound Rama and Lakshmana with the Nagapasha, the arrow of the serpents, and they had both become unconscious. Then Garuda, the celestial vehicle of Lord Vishnu, appeared out of nowhere and the snakes withdrew instantly. Rama and Lakshmana were revived, along with thousands of vanaras, who were all affected by the Nagapasha. Sita sighed heavily with relief. It was not the end but for the moment, things seemed fine. Sita did not get much sleep that night. The aerial roots of the banyan tree in the garden seemed like snakes to her. Her lord would have to win over illusions as much as the real rakshasas. One could not fight what was not there. Yet one could not win by ignoring it. Victory was in seeking the truth rather than fighting the illusion. The skill was in identifying the illusion and dropping it. The senses alone could not see through this web. Sita prayed to the Divine Mother Maya Shakti herself, to dispel this darkness.

The skies were grey and a kind of bleakness continued to hover even after the sun had risen the next day. Sita spent the day in prayer. There was a great apprehension in her heart. There was unrest in the subtle. Trijata arrived close to sunset but refused to look up. With a lot of difficulty, she told Sita that Lakshmana had fallen to the Brahmastra fired by Indrajit.

Sita went blank. This was not possible. The war and its outcome was meaningless without Lakshmana. She did not want to know more. Her conversation was only with the Divine Mother now. With all the strength of intention that Sita could muster, she willed life for Lakshmana. She was in a state of deep meditation through the night. When she returned to her conscious state, she became aware of her body and surroundings, and slowly opened her eyes. She naturally looked up into the sky that was nearing dawn, when she saw a hill flying between the clouds. She could not help but smile. In her heart, she knew it must certainly be Hanuman who was carrying that hill at this hour. In any case, something fortuitous was about to occur.

In about an hour's time, Trijata came to her with the full story. Hanuman had uprooted and brought the Gandhamadhana mountain from the Himalayas to bring the *sanjeevani* herb to revive Lakshmana. His mission was successful. Sita had seen him flying back with the mountain to its original place in the Himalayas.

The events grew more miraculous with each passing day and glorified the power of faith in the divine. Nothing was impossible for a devotee with one-pointed focus and devotion to the lord.

While Trijata and Sita were conversing, they were momentarily distracted by a buzzing bee nearby. They both watched the bee hovering in the air above them. 'This bee seems more interested in us than in the exquisite flowers here, Trijata,' said Sita with a smile. 'I think the sight of you is sweeter than the nectar obtained from the rarest of flowers, Sita,' replied Trijata. 'That bee is not what it appears to be. It is my father.' Sita turned to look at the bee with renewed interest. 'He has come here to ensure that you are fine. Who knows what tricks the Lankan king has played in these early hours?' The bee left and was out of sight in an instant, and soon, so was Trijata, as she went to collect more news from the battlefield. As the day moved into night, Trijata returned to Sita and announced, 'Indrajit, the valiant son of the lord of Lanka, attained liberation at the hands of Lakshmana today. It is heard that Lord Rama attributed the victory to my father, without whose help it would have been nearly impossible to defeat him. Indrajit knew whom he was fighting, Sita. He told Ravana too, but as usual, his ears were deaf to any wisdom. I feel bad for the queen. She is a good lady but now truly alone in her sorrow.'

They were silent for a few moments. Then Trijata continued, 'Ravana has summoned the Moola Bala army. The most powerful rakshasas from all directions have arrived on the shores of Lanka. They have marched across the ocean without the need of any bridge. Many of them still remain on the waters because there isn't enough land in Lanka for them to stand on. The time has come, Sita. They have all arrived here like moths to a flame. In a matter of a few hours, the earth will be cleansed of the race of asuras.'

Ravana himself had entered the battlefield, and fought with Lakshmana and Hanuman, while Rama fought the rakshasa army. Trijata, overwhelmed with gratitude, told Sita, 'Today that younger brother of Lord Rama took the force of Ravana's Mayastra upon himself and saved my father's life. He was prepared to give his life for my father. That incredible vanara Hanuman brought the medicine hill all the way to Lanka, and saved Lakshmana again. Malayavan, Ravana's chief adviser, says that Hanuman must be the fourth god after the great trinity.'

Another day went by. It was likely to be the final day of battle. Sita was restless. She noticed that nuts were slipping from the forefingers of squirrels as they tried running around with them to find a comfortable place to sit and nibble on them. Honeybees seemed indecisive about which flower they should drink the nectar from. The wind was blowing from different directions, carrying a new fragrance with it each time. Sita sat down, then got up; she tried walking, going up to the streams, then to the ponds, finally walking by the deer and the peacocks, but her mind could not achieve repose. Nothing interested her. She finally accepted the restlessness that had enveloped her and surrendered to it completely. As the hours passed, she became tired of all the walking around and sat down under her simsupa tree. She placed her hands fondly on the earth and felt the presence of a mother. She sensed the same anticipation in her as well. The entire planet seemed to be pulsating with expectation. All energies were singularly focused on one event, whose result was eagerly awaited by even the gods. She told the earth, 'You will know it when it comes to pass. Will you please tell me too?' She felt as if the earth embraced her with all her love.

Another half hour or so later, Sita felt a sudden relaxation in the earth beneath her. Something stirred in the air around her. It was as if an unseen heaviness was lifted from space itself. It was as if the entire planet had been a tightly clenched fist which was now utterly relaxed, with palms wide open to the sky, holding all of infinity upon it. It was finally over. Her heart felt light and tears of gratitude flowed from her eyes. Every cell of her body was celebrating. It was just a matter of time before her lord would send for her. She washed her face one last time in the cool waters of the stream at Ashoka Vatika. She gave a final, fond glance at the colourful fish and thanked them for their company all these months. She met every deer and peacock, she visited all the plants and flowers, she expressed gratitude to all the squirrels and birds who brought her nuts and fruits every single day. There was an unspoken communication between her and the trees. She looked at the simsupa tree with particular fondness. It had been her constant companion and source of shelter and support.

While she was affectionately saying her goodbyes to all her friends and loved ones in the garden, Trijata arrived with the news. 'The war is over, Sita. The lord has sent these new garments and jewellery for you. Please get ready soon and let us go!' said Trijata with a smile. Sita took her new clothes and opened the jewellery pouch with much elation. It had all the pieces she had thrown into the forest, hoping that Rama might find them. The chudamani she had given to Hanuman was also there. She changed quickly and adorned herself. Trijata saw Sita dressed in clothes deserving of her stature for the first time. Though she still exuded the same inner strength and radiance as before, her outer appearance finally reflected the true quality of her being. For just a moment, it took Trijata's breath away to see Sita like this. She asked her to be seated inside the palanquin so that they could take her with all due respect and decorum. Sita offered to walk. She was not keen to use anything that belonged to Ravana for her comfort. Trijata sensed her resistance and said, 'This palanquin has been sent for you by my father, Sita. He is the new lord of Lanka.' Sita was glad to hear that and grateful for Trijata's care and sensitivity. She got into the palanquin and left Ashoka Vatika.

The moment they exited the garden and entered the city, they were thronged on either side by thousands of vanaras shouting, 'Jai Shri Rama! Sita Rama! Jai Shri Rama!' The line of vanaras extended as far as the eyes could see. Their voices echoed in the clouds and mixed into the waves. The atmosphere was electrifying. The joy was unbounded. The relief was nothing short of a taste of liberation. Sita felt her cheeks turn pink. Her heart beat faster, and there were butterflies in her stomach. She felt like jumping out of the palanquin and running into her lord's arms as fast as her legs could carry her. But she had to sit still and move through this endless, jubilant crowd. She had learnt infinite patience in the past few months. The palanquin finally came to a halt and they placed it on the ground. Sita's excitement mounted again. She delicately parted the curtains and stepped out. Thousands of voices roared to the heavens shouting, 'Sita Mata *ki Jai*! (Victory to Mother Sita!)' She looked straight in front of her. There was a clear passage of about a hundred feet, and standing at the end of it was her lord Rama. And in that most auspicious moment, their eyes met once again like the confluence of two oceans. The rest of the world dissolved instantaneously. While they stood separately, their spirits felt united as one. Sita was no longer conscious of her body, and stood still as a statue with her eyes locked with her lord's. Lakshmana and Hanuman were standing next to Rama, and were overjoyed to see Sita. Tears flowed unstoppably from their eyes. They were about to step forward to escort her to Rama when he gently stopped them.

'Sita must first prove her purity to the world,' said Rama, in a voice that was soft yet matter-of-fact. All the cheering lulled into a stunned silence. No one could believe what they were hearing.

'She will walk through fire to come to me.' Rama's words were definite. The fire of doubt destroys the joy in any relationship. There may have been a few who did not believe it was even possible for a delicate woman to withstand Ravana and keep her purity. Perhaps Rama, who knew the minds of all, reflected this doubt. But by questioning Sita in a public gathering, amidst thousands, he had already lit the fire of humiliation.

Sita did not once question or doubt Rama's words or actions. If Hanuman could jump over the ocean and fly, carrying mountains, with Rama in his heart, she could certainly walk through fire. She did not even think this much. She looked at Lakshmana and mentally commanded him to bring a few dry sticks and other materials that had the ability to ignite. Heartbroken and unable to comprehend what was going on, Lakshmana looked back and forth between his brother and sister-in-law. But he saw only an unshakeable resoluteness on both faces. Unwillingly, with tears flowing constantly, he gathered the sticks and placed them at Sita's feet, and lit the fire with an arrow from his quiver. The entire gathering was filled with disbelief and remorse. Only Rama, Sita and Hanuman did not seem perturbed. Hanuman felt fortunate that the lord had shared the secret of fire with him when he left to search for Sita. Else he too would not have been able to cope with this moment. Lakshmana was yet unaware of this secret, and this was the most severe test of his faith in his lord and brother. The flames grew in size and formed a wall between Rama and Sita. Sita prayerfully stepped into it and all of creation held its breath. The flames turned a translucent blue as she stepped forward into them. Blue was the colour of the purest of fires. The light from the flames expanded to fill the entire visible space, and for a moment, nothing else could be seen. When everyone opened their eyes again, the flames were gone and Sita stood gleaming and glowing, more radiant than ever. Along with her was Agni, the God of Fire. It was not common for the celestials to appear in a form perceivable by the senses, but this occasion was no ordinary one either.

O Lord! What fire is there that can purify its own source?
What flame is there that can be purer than the flame of
    chastity?
What light is there that shines brighter than the light of
    Sita's pure love?

She has restored the glory of the fire element by infusing it with her effulgent presence. It is with humility and great honour that I escort Sita to you!' said the deva in his ethereal voice. As Sita came forward and stood beside Rama, she looked like a golden lily standing beside a blue lotus.

21

Scene of Contentment

The celestials offered their prayers to them one by one, followed by the vanara king and Vibhishana. Now that the mission of being in exile for fourteen years was nearing completion, Rama wanted to urgently go back to Ayodhya. He had promised Bharata that he would return not a day later. If he delayed, Bharata would give up his life. Rama was concerned about the time it would take to reach Ayodhya. Vibhishana brought forth the pushpaka vimana and requested Rama to mount the aerial vehicle that would fly them to Ayodhya. The vehicle was filled with jewels, ornaments and new clothes. Rama expressed his deep gratitude to the vanara army as he distributed the gifts among them and bid them farewell. Sugriva, Angada, Nala, Neela, Jambavan, Hanuman and Vibhishana had no heart for parting with the lord so soon. They all looked like they would break down in tears if Rama did not allow them to come along. Sita saw their expressions and felt a deep motherly affection for all of them. She was relieved when Rama consented to take them along with him to Ayodhya.

On the way back, Rama pointed out the places where he had fought Kumbhakarna and Ravana, where Lakshmana had fought Indrajit, the bridge they had built, all the places in the forest where they had halted in their search for Sita, and so on. They stopped for a short while at the hermitage of Rishi Agastya. They shared various incidents from the battlefield with him over a quick meal, and after taking his blessings, continued their journey. They stopped to pay their respects at the various ashrams, including Chitrakuta, and then finally reached the ashram of Rishi Bharadwaja. They again bathed in the confluence at Prayag, and here, having decided to spend the night at the ashram, Rama sent Hanuman ahead of him to give the message to Bharata of their return to Ayodhya. Guha joined them in the ashram with great happiness. As promised, he rowed Rama, Sita and Lakshmana across the Ganga on his boat, while the pushpaka vimana was flown to the opposite bank to await them there.

Sita spent some time at the river by herself. She recollected her conversation with the goddess of the river, and her prayer to her when they had come here fourteen years ago. She felt grateful for all the blessings that she had received, which had helped them return safely after all the trials and tribulations.

As she sat on a rock with her feet in the water, watching the river flow, she pondered on how everything that had happened now felt like a dream. The river of time continues to flow, carrying everything from the past, present and future as an offering to the mighty ocean.

'Sita, where are you? Shall we go?' called out Rama. She quickly got up from the riverside and walked back to where Rama, Lakshmana and Guha were waiting along with Rishi Bharadwaja. They took leave of the rishi and stepped into Guha's boat. The Nishada king picked up the oars and rowed as fast as he could so that Rama could continue his journey to Ayodhya at the earliest. In his heart, he wanted to extend his time with the lord as much as he could. Still, he was a devotee, and what the lord wanted was more important than what he wanted for himself.

Though Rama was keen to reach Ayodhya quickly, he made time for many people along the way. He reached wherever he had to at the appropriate moment. He was always there at the right time, or perhaps time was right there with him. Like the Ganga that had been eternally flowing yet had remained the same, Rama was continuously moving with time, yet his presence was the same. Much had transpired since they had crossed this river, yet it felt like nothing had changed. Sita reached down from the boat to touch the water. She enjoyed the coolness of the river on her fingertips. The only sound was of the oars moving through the water as Guha rowed at a steady pace. The silence had solidified and Sita felt like she could almost touch it. All thoughts stopped flowing as she watched the moving water. As the silence became deeper, her lord's presence became stronger and more expanded. Rama looked at her with his large, gentle, dark eyes, and she was filled with blissful modesty. Rama looked at Guha with his doe eyes, and he was filled with gratitude and devotion. He turned towards his dear brother, and between them was a sense of absolute comfort and oneness. He turned to the skies. It felt as if the entire world of the gods were waiting for this moment, and bowed in deep reverence and offered salutations to Rama. The gentle, rocking movement of the boat across the river was like the harmonious flow of musical notes in a love song. And when the song concluded, they reached the shores of time; their exile was complete. They had returned to the spot where, years ago, the disconsolate minister Sumantra had bid them farewell. They mounted the pushpaka vimana again and soon reached Ayodhya.

From that moment onwards, it was only an experience of love in all its different flavours. Bharata and Shatrugna, along with Vasishta and the other sages, the three mothers, and Hanuman, stood waiting with the people of the entire city. The men had run to the city gates, leaving all their work. The women had come running without informing their husbands or family, without a care for how they looked. The children came running along with all their friends without having told their parents or teachers. Perhaps they saw their other family members in different parts of the crowd. But today, it didn't matter. Rama bowed to the sages first and met everyone turn by turn. He walked through the street, meeting every single person who had come to receive him. Later, they would excitedly share with each other, 'Rama looked at me', 'He smiled at me', 'He waved at me', 'He raised one eyebrow and asked me how I was', 'He wanted to know if I was happy', 'He raised his arms and blessed me', 'He patted me on the back', 'He touched my head with his fingertips', 'After all these years he still remembered me.' This was the song on everyone's lips.

They finally reached the palace and stepped into the rooms that had been prepared for them. The sages had wanted them to freshen up, get dressed and come to meet them. Rama sat down and requested Sita to remove all the knots in his matted hair. This would be quite a task because Rama had such lustrous, thick hair. She carefully combed out his hair but was surprised to see how smoothly it unloosened. Though it had been matted for very long, it was not entangled. Rama too was like that. He felt like he belonged to everybody yet was attached to no one. 'Except maybe me,' thought Sita, 'and Lakshmana and Hanuman and Bharata also . . .' And slowly the list kept growing until she gave up. The truth was that he was attached to none because he did not see anyone as separate from him. They were all a part of him. There was no other.

Once she was done combing his hair, he went to bathe. Sita too went to ready herself. She quickly got ready and was particularly keen to meet Urmila. She hadn't come into the crowd to receive them. They hadn't seen her in the palace either. Sita was aching to see her sister. She went to Urmila's chamber and found Lakshmana sitting by her side, still in his forest attire, holding Urmila's hand in his own with tears flowing from his eyes, as she lay sleeping. Urmila looked the same. Time had not touched her. Sita glanced around the room and saw the walls painted with images of

Lakshmana, and of some precious memories from their days together in Mithila. 'Lakshmana, wake her up!' urged Sita. 'Your debt is paid well. Thank Nidra Devi now.' Lakshmana heard her words, folded his hands together and prayed. He placed his hands on Urmila's head and bent forward closer to her face and gently called out to her. 'Urmila. Wake up. I have come,' said Lakshmana in an endearing voice, brimming with love. A tear from his eye fell onto hers, and rolled down the side of her face towards her right ear. She gently moved her eyelids and stirred. She opened her eyes and looked at Lakshmana like an infant waking up to its mother's eyes. A moment later she had thrown her arms around him in jubilation. He held her, too, as if he would never let her go again. She saw Sita and was at a loss to describe her happiness. When the surge of joy in the room settled, Sita told both husband and wife to get themselves tidied up and ready for the sages.

It was good to be back. The sages had announced the date for the Pattabhisheka, the coronation. Her father and mother would also be arriving soon. Sage Vasishta had given instructions and sent the vanaras to different corners of the kingdom to procure the various items required for the ceremony. Kaushalya had selected several pieces of delicate and ornate jewellery to adorn Sita with. Sunayana had arrived, bringing with her a beautiful, handwoven, soft, pure golden tissue sari, with sparkles of deep blue here and there. The sari had a peacock-blue blouse with intricate gold embroidery. Sita would wear it for the coronation. Sunayana helped her match the jewellery with her sari. She made Sita wear her earrings, nose pin, bangles, neckpieces, waist belt, finger rings, armlets, anklets, and finally placed the magnificent crown on her head.

Urmila arrived in the room, ready to escort Sita to the royal hall along with her mother. Together they walked, feeling close to each other. They entered the hall and Sita climbed up the steps to the throne, bowed to the sages, her father, and then sat down beside her lord. She was the majestic queen, resplendent with the light of a thousand rising suns, pure and divine. Rama was already there, wearing radiant yellow silk garments and a greenish-blue upper garment. The throne was encrusted with freshly cut rubies all over. Hanuman was at their feet, guarding the throne. Angada held the royal sword. Bharata held the royal white pearl-studded umbrella. Lakshmana and Shatrugna stood on either side, fanning them with white cowries. The Brahmins recited the Vedas, the kinneras in the garb of humans played the drums, and the Gandharvas sang melodiously. Conches were blown. Sage Vasishta walked up to them with the sacred vessel of auspicious water from the seven oceans and the seven sacred rivers, and poured it upon them through a sieve that transformed the potent water into countless little droplets that rained like pearls on Rama and Sita. It looked like an auspicious shower of the sacred Ganga on an emerald mountain with red hibiscus flowers in full bloom. All the elders and the mothers, followed by the neighbouring kings, showered them in turn. All those who were witnessing this sacred moment sprinkled themselves with the water that flowed from the crystal platform on which the throne was placed, and felt purified for lifetimes. The moment was eternal and remains the most auspicious impression in the hearts of many a devotee.

Urmila was in Sita's room, talking to her till late in the night on the day after the coronation. Rama was still busy talking to Vibhishana, Sugriva and the others. Lakshmana was fast asleep. Even as the coronation was being completed, he had started yawning and his eyes were closing. Sita noticed his condition and thought he might end up sleeping while he was still standing. After all, it had been fourteen years since he had slept! She quickly pointed it out to Rama, who smilingly excused him from the hall and told him to go and rest. It was the next day and he was still sleeping! Urmila had sat by his side, admiring how he looked as he slept. She was simply overjoyed to have him back. She also ached to be with Sita and hear everything from her. Lakshmana had shared some of the details with Urmila the night they had arrived, but she had not had much time with her sister.

'You know, Didi, Lakshmana was telling me about how Rama became so angry when the ocean did not respond to his request for a path across to Lanka. He had patiently waited for three days. But on the fourth day, there was no more time to waste. In his anger he announced that he would dry up the entire ocean, and stepped forward into the water.' Urmila's eyes were wide with amazement at the thought of Rama drying up an entire ocean in his anger. She had never imagined such prowess, though she knew he was special. In fact, life in the forest had now unveiled many dimensions to the brothers that had otherwise remained hidden.

Urmila continued, 'The water started evaporating all around him because of the scorching heat emanating from his being. Soon, the creatures in the water started feeling uncomfortable and began to suffocate. They started praying to Rama. Seeing their plight, Rama stopped himself. But here is the part that touched me the most. In order to restore the waters, Bhaiya willed that all the tears of longing and love shed by you should fill the ocean. He said that your tears were the only substance powerful enough to assuage the heat of his anger! Did you even know this?'

In fact, this was a new story for Sita. And both sisters agreed that it was very romantic too. 'But Didi, it troubles me to think that you cried so much that Bhaiya could restore an ocean with it!' said Urmila, hugging Sita with tears in her eyes. Sita hugged her back and felt more like a mother to Urmila than a sister. Urmila returned to her room soon after and Sita was by herself.

Now that Ravana was gone, would truth and justice prevail upon the planet once again? Would there be happiness and prosperity everywhere now? Perhaps it would be that way for at least some time. Contemplating the dual nature of the world, Sita drifted off into sleep before Rama returned.

22

The Forest of Fulfilment

Sita was racing on the white horse in the forest with the wind blowing in her face. She wore a big smile as she rode with two excited boys sitting in front of her on the horse. Their enthusiasm was contagious as they shouted, 'Faster, Ma, faster!' The one right in front was holding on to the base of the horse's neck for support. The one in the middle held on to his brother for part of the time. But as the horse gathered speed, he wanted to hold his mother and the easiest thing for him to clutch was Sita's hair, which he held on to tightly. It was quite painful for Sita. 'Ow,' said Sita in her sleep, as she woke up to see a tiny palm wrapped around her hair, clutching it tightly. She looked lovingly at the face of her son who was fast asleep, and gently freed her hair from his tiny fingers. She turned to the other side and saw his brother also sleeping peacefully. Dawn was about to break. The curtain of darkness that nature provides the earth with was gently being drawn away. The planet would soon rise from its peaceful inner state with a gentle smile and gradually move into a state of vibrance and dynamism. She was listening patiently for the first sound of chirping from the birds outside her window. The golden light of the sun made its way into her room and caressed the faces of the sleeping children. They looked utterly content and blissful. Motherly affection flowed in her heart and poured out of her being. She gently played with the curls in their hair and marvelled at their tiny hands and feet. They made her feel full and complete. She recollected the verses of the ancient scriptures that spoke of a fullness that is born out of fullness. The mother and the child were a perfect example of this. She smiled to herself and rose to get herself ready before the babies awoke.

She stepped out of their modest hut in the ashram of Rishi Valmiki. When they were in Chitrakuta amidst the beauty of nature, she had thought it would be wonderful to be able to bring up her children in such an intimate atmosphere, in the company of saints, away from the complexities and intrigue of the cities. Her gentle thought had manifested. She had been here for a little over a year-and-a-half now. To her right was a creeper with exquisite purple flowers that had grown to almost cover the roof of her hut. The flower petals were scattered here and there on the mud floor and had formed an intricate pattern on the ground. To her left was the small herb and vegetable garden she had created for the boys. She had shown them how to plant tulsi, ginger, turmeric, coriander, palak and chillies. They would water them with their tiny hands each day and check how much further they had grown. The coriander leaves were maturing and the first few leaves with the zig-zag edges had sprung forth. Sita was sure the boys would notice the change in the shape of the leaves. There would be cause for some excitement today. She noticed her pet squirrels looking expectantly at her from the branch of the parijata tree that grew adjacent to this patch of plants. They had their bushy tails up in the air and their black, sparkling, beady eyes were transfixed on her. She smiled and went inside to get a few nuts for them. They were not domesticated and ate sufficiently from all the trees in the forest. But the attention they got from Sita was special for them. The boys would be asleep for at least another hour. Nevertheless, one of the ashram girls came by to keep a watch over the children while Sita went to the nearby stream to bathe and complete her morning sandhyavandan. She returned quickly, only to shortly return to the stream with the children. This time, it would take much longer because the boys loved to play in the water. The same activities that became chores for adults were endlessly playful for children. Bathing was a game, changing clothes was a game, eating was a game, even going to sleep was a game. Their company helped Sita continue to see life as a game and keep her spirits high, even though the pain of her longing was ever so deep.

The twins were in her womb when she had come to the ashram. The rishi had found her fast asleep under the shade of a tree at the crack of dawn. He had recognized her instantly and requested her to come to the ashram with him. 'You are to be revered like a mother, Sita, yet you are also like a daughter to me. Please give me the opportunity to take care of you. You will always have a home here.' Sita was grateful for his invitation and followed him to the ashram. She requested the rishi to keep her identity a secret to avoid unnecessary gossip. So all the ashram residents addressed her as Vandevi—the Goddess of the Woods. She naturally became the centre of attention in the ashram. Everybody loved her company, especially the young girls who lived there. They waited for any opportunity to do something for or with her. The older residents noticed the gentle affection and reverence that the rishi showed towards her, and adjusted their behaviour towards Sita accordingly. In time, they all formed their own personal bond with her. For the disciples of the rishi, who were advanced seekers, the radiance of Sita's face and the serenity in her presence were the fruit of incomparable penance and showed the refinement of her consciousness. For the disciples who took greater interest in serving the rishi and attending to his needs, her presence effortlessly strengthened their faith in the higher power and brought a lightness to their hearts as they went about their work.

Sita was very hard-working too. She helped with many of the ashram activities. She attended to the food, supplies and cows, ensured proper attire and grooming of the young girls, and along with all this, she brought up her two little bundles of joy.

Their eyes were just like Rama's. She would feel awashed with love whenever he looked at her. Now she had two such pairs of eyes that were looking to her for most part of the day. Even if she had had to come away from Rama, the Divine Mother had given her the support of the children to fill her heart. 'But it must be so difficult for Rama,' pondered Sita. Though he was in the palace, he was alone and missed her. 'But then,' thought Sita, 'Rama was always alone, because when you came in his presence, you dissolved and there was only ever him.' She smiled to herself at this thought. Nevertheless, Rama's heart did indeed ache for Sita. He knew that he had become a father because Sita was well into her pregnancy when she had left for the forest, but he did not know that she had birthed twin boys.

She could hear the voices of the twins inside the hut. They normally rested for sometime in the afternoon too. Somehow, when one awoke, the other would also wake up immediately after. It was interesting to consider that they also moved into deeper states of consciousness, like the deep sleep state and the dream state, together. As soon as they got up, their eyes searched for Sita. She went up to them, lifted them up, and seated them on either side of her lap. With her arms around them, she told them to open their palms and look into them. The day would begin with a prayer acknowledging the presence of the Divine Mother in their palms. She told them it would bring them 'palm power'. They chanted along with her in their sweet baby voices and, once done, playfully placed their palms on their faces the way Sita did. But after this point, they thought it was time for a game of hide-and-seek. They would run to hide before Sita removed her palms from her face, and though she knew each time exactly where they were both hiding, she would have to pretend to search for them everywhere. And when she would finally 'find' them, they would both convulse with laughter and excitement.

After one or two rounds, Sita would let the ashram girls continue playing with them so she could proceed to the kitchen to oversee the food preparations. Dalia khichdi was on the menu today. There was also a spicy version with some vegetables and a sweet version with jaggery. The kids liked the sweet version. Sita brought back two wooden bowls of the porridge for the boys. When they sat down to eat, they saw the single tulsi leaf that was placed on top and promptly ate that first. Their food always had a tulsi leaf on top. They liked the leaf and the story around it. It was part of Sita's daily routine to tell them their favourite story of Hanuman and the tulsi leaf. She cleared her throat and began, 'It was a beautiful day. The whole city of Ayodhya was still in a mood of celebration after the coronation of King Rama. People could not stop smiling with joy and the stories of his valour were told and retold by the elders and enacted by the children in every home.'

Sita's heart was brimming with joy as she told Rama, 'I want to cook and feed Hanuman myself today. He has done so much for us!' Sita had exceptional culinary skills and was quite confident of her abilities too. 'Are you sure, Sita? Do you really think you can feed Hanuman?' enquired Rama. 'Why, of course!' said Sita, and set off in great excitement to the kitchen. Lunchtime arrived and a fresh banana leaf was laid. Hanuman sat down to eat and Sita started serving. Everything was tasty and Sita was eager to serve second helpings. Hanuman relished the food and ate and ate, and asked for more, and then some more and even more, but he was still hungry. Sita rushed to cook again, and kept serving one dish after another. At some point, she became exhausted. She recollected Rama's mysterious words to her and went to him for help. Rama smiled as he heard Sita and went into their garden. He came back with a fresh tulsi leaf and told her to place it upon what she served next. She took the leaf and went straight to the kitchen, where a cup of kheer was ready to be served. She gently placed the tulsi leaf on it and took it to Hanuman. Hanuman graciously accepted the bowl from her and ate the leaf first. 'Hmm . . . I feel so full. I cannot eat one morsel more! Thank you for the delicious meal, Mother!' said Hanuman. 'And that is the story of Hanuman and the tulsi leaf!' Sita exclaimed to the twins.

'Thank you for the delicious meal, Mother!' said the kids in chorus, pretending to be Hanuman. They had also just finished eating their breakfast, along with the story.

'So what do we learn from this story?' asked Sita. 'When you offer food to the divine and then eat it, it becomes prasad,' said one. 'And prasad makes you happy and full!' added the other.

Sita smiled and got up to wash the bowls. She remembered her mother, who would never let her and Urmila eat till the food was offered. Sunayana would never make small talk or gossip while cooking. She would instead be chanting 'Om Namah Shivaya' and encourage the cooking staff to also do the same. 'We must be attentive to the food while we are cooking. Our minds cannot go here and there,' she would say. 'You may not even remember if you added salt or not otherwise!'

Sita remembered how, during their time in exile, there were many occasions when they would have to cook and eat food without any salt. The first time she had to serve Rama food with no salt in it, she had felt very apologetic. But Rama had eaten everything as if it was the most deliciously cooked meal he had ever had! When she told him that she had cooked without any salt, he had said in the most matter-of-fact way, 'Sita, what makes the food tasty is the fact that you have made it, not the salt or the spices.' He never let Sita feel any lack at all. And in turn, not just while cooking the food but in every aspect of her life, Sita was grateful for Rama's presence and considered her body, breath, emotions and time itself, as prasad (a gift from the divine).

Time went by very quickly with the kids around. One day they came up to Sita and told her, 'Ma, Gurudev (Rishi Valmiki) says that Lord Vishnu himself has come to this planet now as King Rama of Ayodhya.' Sita smiled and asked, 'What else did he say?'

'He said that he has written the story of Rama's life and has called it Ramayana. He said he will teach it to us!' 'Oh, that's wonderful, children!' replied Sita joyously. 'Ma, if Rama is Vishnu, then Sita must be Devi Lakshmi, isn't it?' 'Perhaps,' replied Sita with a half-smile. 'So wherever

Sita would be, mountains of gold and ornaments must be surrounding her, isn't it?' Sita laughed at this and said, 'Sita has the mountain of joy and abundance, and the ornaments of golden boys like you!' 'But we belong to you, Ma!' said one of the twins. 'Of course, my dears!' replied Sita, 'And we all belong to Sita! Having good people around you for company is a great wealth. And having a master is the greatest wealth—like the two of you have Gurudev in your lives!' She further explained, 'There are many types of wealth, my dears. Courage is wealth, good luck is wealth, wisdom is wealth, the feeling of contentment and abundance is wealth. Sita represents all kinds of wealth that unite the hearts and minds of people.' 'And what does Sita like, Ma?' 'She loves plants, the gentle forest animals, the birds, the squirrels, she loves to shake the trees' branches after the rain and allow the little droplets to settle on her hair like translucent pearls. She likes to sing, she likes to cook, she likes to tell stories.' 'Ma,' interrupted one of the boys, 'Sita is just like you . . . she loves everything that you love!' 'That means Sita will love us too!' added the other excitedly. Sita fondly hugged them both, and held back the tears that were waiting to flow from her eyes.

The twins were born in the ashram, and Rishi Valmiki had chosen the names Luv and Kush for them. While they were babies, they had filled Sita's day and kept her busy. Now they were growing up. They had started asking questions and forming opinions too. They had apparently asked the rishi why they didn't have a father. One of the disciples told Sita of the conversation. The rishi had told them that their mother was both father and mother to them. He had said that she was very special and complete in herself, and that they were very lucky to be her children. While they were inquisitive, they had deep reverence for Gurudev and his words were final. Sita was grateful to him for his loving care and protection of her two precious sons.

23

Beyond Stories

Rishi Valmiki had started telling the boys the story of the Ramayana. Every day, they would return from their classes with great enthusiasm to share the stories they heard that day with Sita. One day, they returned looking very upset. She had an inkling why, but she waited for them to bring it up themselves. They were feeling bad about Mother Kaikeyi asking Rama to go into exile for fourteen years. 'How could she be so cruel, Ma?' asked Luv. There were tears streaming from their eyes. They could not accept that anyone could be so harsh with Rama and Sita. 'Hmm . . . come here, my dears! Sit with me. You know, while Rama and Sita were in Chitrakuta during their exile, a parrot became friends with Sita. Sita also loved playing with it and lightly asked Rama for a name for the parrot. And Rama said, "Let us name her Kaikeyi." Sita was surprised at Rama's choice. But Rama continued, "This parrot simply imitates and repeats whatever we ask her to. Mother Kaikeyi was a parrot in the hands of the gods. But she loves us so much that even a harsh word from her could only bring us glory in the end.'" The smiles returned to their faces and they felt better now. They hugged their mother and went off to play.

Not a day went by without some or other discussion about an aspect of Rama's story. Sita would give them a new insight and help them go beyond the event and absorb the wisdom behind it. They had reached the part where the battle had begun. Here, Sita herself came to know more details when she heard the boys narrating them. So much had happened on the field while she was waiting in Ashoka Vatika. 'Ma, if the asuras were so evil, how did they become so powerful? If they were a burden to Mother Earth, why did she nourish them?' asked Kush one day. 'For a mother, all her children are the same, Kush. Her love is unconditional. The wind, the rain, the sun, the moon, they treat all beings with equal love. A tulsi plant gets the same nourishment as a weed growing near it. The mother does not differentiate. That is why she is a mother.' 'Then what makes them different, Ma?' asked Luv. 'Their karma. Their values. For as long as you don't recognize the divinity permeating through every aspect and taking care of this whole creation, you keep thinking that you are the doer. And if you are the doer, then you will reap the consequences of your actions too!' The boys were listening to her carefully. Their intellect was sharp and refined. Their spirit of enquiry was growing day by day.

As the years passed, the boys grew in valour as much as they grew centred in their wisdom. Their grasp was extraordinary and their skill in action unparalleled. Their devotion to the guru was unshakeable. They learnt many things from their mother too. She would tell them never to use 'shastras' as a 'shastra': knowledge as a weapon. She had told them of a scholar named Bandi who had come to Mithila to debate and defeat opponents. The problem was that whoever lost to him had to willingly sacrifice their life. Many challenged him and gave up their lives after losing to him. And when he became far too arrogant and was ready to declare himself an unmatched scholar, a young boy of exceptional radiance, with eight deformities in the body, arrived in the kingdom. His name was Ashtavakra. He defeated Bandi, and allowed him to live. He advised him never to take the life of another being, especially at the hands of knowledge, for it was a gross misuse of the very spirit of enquiry that we are all bestowed with. He encouraged King Janaka to also set rules that would protect the innocent scholars who sought refuge in his land. While Bandi had misused knowledge and defeated many, the boys were now being told the story of the battle with Indrajit, who defeated even the gods with the strength of his weapons and magical prowess.

'Ma,' said Kush, 'Gurudev says that Rama is God. Then how did he become unconscious when the Nagapasha bound him? If he is God, he should not be bound by any actions or their consequences, let alone the Nagapasha!' Sita smiled at him and said, 'Yes, Kush, but did the rishi tell you what happened after they were bound?' 'Yes Ma, he told us how Garuda came and freed them from the clutches of the snakes,' replied Luv. Sita continued, 'You know, after this incident, even Garuda had the same question as you. He could not understand why he had to free the lord, who was all-powerful. He was just his devotee. How could he be more powerful than his lord? This question was eating him up and he approached Brahma to help him out of his predicament. Brahma sent him to Shiva, who then sent him to Kaka Bhushundi.' 'Kaka Bhushundi? A crow? The king of all birds went to a crow to get an answer?' asked Kush in surprise. 'That is it, Kush! When you think you are somebody, either great or not so great, when you consider yourself as separate from the divine, then you get caught in maya. That is what happened to Garuda. When the king of birds was in the presence of the crow, he felt like a nobody. The crow was so full of devotion that in his presence, you could only feel the divine. Garuda also melted in devotion and his doubts vanished even before the crow said anything. Nevertheless, Kaka Bhushundi told him a very beautiful story. Kaka Bhushundi loved to be in the company of baby Rama. He would perch himself on a nearby tree branch and watch all his childish sports. He saw Rama laugh, run, sometimes fall and even cry. Little Rama would play with his toys and brothers like any other child. Kaka Bhushundi was expecting to see miracles, something extraordinary, but everything seemed normal. He was a little disappointed. One day, the little baby Rama had a small piece of cake in his hands and was relishing it by himself in the garden. The cake looked tempting and the crow snatched the piece from the hands of the child. Rama got upset and started chasing the crow. The crow flew away but he saw the child following him and catching up very quickly. He flew higher and higher, but the child kept pace. He kept going and entered different and higher realms, but he saw the child still following him. He was not even getting tired. The crow traversed all the seven celestial realms with the piece of cake and could not rest for a moment with the child still on its tail. He finally returned to the garden in Ayodhya and surrendered the piece of cake to the child. The child was happy as soon as he got back his cake. He chased away the crow and happily went back to playing as if nothing unusual had happened. The child had no clue of his capabilities. He had given chase across unreachable worlds so effortlessly, all for a piece of cake! Kaka Bhushundi was now satisfied and amazed! If the lord chose to be human, then that was the rule of the game. Still, it is not really possible to hide the divinity that shines forth from him in everything that he does!'

'Wow, Ma! That was such an amazing story! Who told it to you, Ma?' asked Luv. 'Mother Kaushalya,' pat came the reply. The boys' eyes grew wide and they asked Sita, 'You knew her?!' She quickly changed the topic and said, 'Enough now, boys! It's getting late for dinner. I have to go to the kitchen. You go and play,' and she ushered them out quickly before they could enquire any further.

However, the boys did not forget this. Later that night, Luv asked again, 'Ma, does Mother Kaushalya know that Rama is God?' 'I think she has some idea,' replied Sita. 'One day, when Rama was about one-and-a-half years old, Mother Kaushalya had put him to sleep in the cradle, tucked him in nicely and then come to the puja room to do her daily prayers. She is an ardent devotee of Lord Vishnu and prayed to him incessantly for his darshan. But when she entered the puja room, she saw the baby sitting near the bowl of laddoos, and putting them into his mouth one by one. He looked very happy with all the sweets neatly arranged in the bowls in front of him. Mother Kaushalya was surprised at how he could have come here so quickly. He had been left fast asleep just moments ago. How did he get down from the cradle without any help and reach the puja room even before she did? She wanted to make sure that the cradle hadn't fallen or broken in the process, and rushed back to the nursery. When she reached back, she was totally bewildered, because the baby was still sleeping comfortably in the cradle. She ran back to the puja room and this time, the baby was smiling at her with the sweets smeared all over his hands and face. She thought she was imagining things and looked up at the idol of Lord Vishnu in wonder, and back at her baby. For an instant, she caught a glimpse of the entire creation with multiple universes, the infinite expanse within the little baby. In her heart, she had been given a glimpse of his divinity on that day.'

The boys were listening to every detail with keen interest. They especially enjoyed these childhood stories of Rama. 'Ma, Gurudev hasn't written about many of the stories that you tell us,' said Kush. 'That's good, isn't it? You get new stories then. Otherwise you would have to listen to the same story again and again!' said Sita.

'True, Ma,' said Kush, 'But I can listen to these stories many times and I don't think I would ever be bored of them!' Sita smiled fondly at him. 'Ma,' said Luv, 'Does Devi Sita also know that Rama is God?'

'Yes,' replied Sita. 'Does she know that she is also God?' continued Luv. Sita started laughing and said, 'Sita is not separate from Rama, my dear. She is a part of that same divinity. In fact, you too are a part of the divine!' Luv pretended to be a powerful god and said, 'Kush Bhaiya, can you see the glow around me?' Kush pretended to cover his eyes to protect them from the light emanating from Luv. Sita had a good laugh. A few minutes later, Kush posed another question. The children had many questions. Sita patiently answered them and encouraged their curiosity. 'Ma,' said Kush, 'Gurudev mentioned that people used to say that Hanuman was even more powerful than Rama. But Rama is God. How could Hanuman be more powerful?'

Sita smiled at his question. 'You know, Hanuman's relationship with Rama is very special. His devotion is iconic. One day, Rama asked him, "What is it like to be Hanuman? I would really like to know!" And Hanuman said, "When I am in the body consciousness, I am your servant. As the individual soul, I am a part of you. As the Supreme Self, there is no difference between us. I was able to jump across the entire ocean just by taking your name, Rama. You know, when the vanaras built the bridge across the ocean, they whispered your name and threw the stones into the ocean, and they floated upon the surface. Just whispering your name with faith is powerful, Rama." I will tell both of you a very interesting incident that took place after the coronation. But first, you must both lie down. You can sleep as you listen to the story. It is quite late into the night now.' 'Yes, Ma, we will sleep, but please tell us the story!' requested the boys. They readied themselves to sleep and spread the mat of kusha grass on the floor. They placed a wooden plank for Sita to use as a headrest. They dimmed the light in the lamp and were all set for their bedtime story.

'So,' began Sita, 'One of the kings who came to visit Rama after the coronation did not pay his respects to Rishi Vishwamitra and bowed only to Rama. The sage got angry and ordered Rama to take the king's life. Now, Rama could not disobey the words of his guru. The king fled and found Hanuman meditating by the banks of the Sarayu and asked for refuge. "In the name of Rama, protect me, O great Hanuman!" pleaded the king. Hanuman could never refuse anyone who asked for anything in the name of Rama. So he promised the king his protection. Soon, he was faced with Rama himself. He was in a dilemma. Hanuman would not fight Rama, but he had vowed to protect the king in his very name. As Rama stood with his bow strung and arrow ready to fly, Hanuman stood between him and the king. He closed his eyes and started chanting the name of Rama. Everyone who gathered around could not believe what they were seeing. Rama himself was shocked at the turn of events but he could not refute the wishes of his guru. So, he let loose the arrow. However, the arrow burnt down and turned to ashes when it approached Hanuman. This was perhaps the first "Ramabaan", arrow of Rama, that did not find its mark. Rama's arrow was ineffective where Hanuman was concerned. Rama took the second arrow, but Rishi Vasishta arrived in time and stopped him. He told Vishwamitra to let go of his anger and order Rama to stop. Everyone was utterly relieved!'

'Does this mean that Rama's name is more powerful than him, Ma?' asked Luv. 'Perhaps,' replied Sita. 'The name is subtler than the form, Luv. The subtle is always more powerful than the gross. The creation we see is like the tip of the iceberg. The unseen aspect, the subtler dimensions, govern creation in a much bigger way. Now both of you say your prayers and go to sleep.'

The boys fell asleep shortly. But Sita was still wide awake. She strolled outside and sat on the porch of her hut, watching the stars. They appeared to be like shining pearls in the sky. Her mind wandered back to Ayodhya, to the moment when she had gifted the beautiful pearl necklace to Hanuman after the coronation. Instead of wearing it, he started breaking it open as if looking for something. When asked what he was doing, Hanuman had replied that he was searching to see if the pearls contained Rama and Sita within them. Trust him to think like that! Some of the gathered kings had laughed at Hanuman and scoffed at him. How could he imagine Rama and Sita to be inside pearls? He had replied that it is possible, because he felt their presence in every cell of his being. They laughed at him even more and commented on the futility of giving a pearl necklace to a 'monkey'. Sita felt protective of Hanuman and didn't want the others to speak like this. But Hanuman's devotion was so strong that everyone in the hall that day were given a vision of Rama and Sita within the being of Hanuman. It was an ethereal experience. Rama, as a child, had shown his mother how all of creation was contained in him and Hanuman had shown everyone how the divine resides in the heart of the devotee. Sita's heart searched both inside and out for Rama. He was closer than the closest yet farther than the farthest at this moment. The longing was her connection with him. She knew for sure that Rama was also thinking about her that very moment.

She went to sleep with the same longing in her heart. She dreamt of the white horse again. But this time, the horse was running by itself. It was well-decorated, like a royal horse, but no one was riding it.

24

The Sacred Secret

Rishi Valmiki called for Sita. She immediately went to the Rishi's kutir. He asked her to sit down and said, 'My dear, the time has now come for you to return to Ayodhya, to meet your husband again. I would like you to perform a puja which will take a few days. We will have to travel to a place where two rivers meet.' Sita bowed to him and returned to her room to pack and prepare. 'Ma, Gurudev has told us that we are travelling tomorrow. He said we have to collect lotuses for you everyday too!' announced Luv, as he excitedly entered the room. 'And I told him that I give my word that I will make sure all the lotuses you need are there every day!' said Kush. Sita smiled. Her young boy was sounding so grown-up. He was already giving people his word and taking responsibilities!

The puja would take up most of the day for Sita and she barely got time for anything else. The boys were busy searching for lotuses for most of the day. Many times, they would be asleep by the time she returned. Days went by and she noticed that the boys had become quite busy and preoccupied. She did not have time to discuss anything with them but was happy to see that they were keeping busy and looking healthy. Finally, one day, she completed the puja and returned to her room. She saw Gurudev walking back with her sons and waited for them patiently. They came running to her when they saw her. They bowed to her and were happy that her puja was completed successfully. 'Ma! Guess whom we met today!' said Luv with great excitement. 'We met God, Ma!' said Kush. Sita looked at them curiously. 'We met His brothers first, along with His favourite devotee, and finally Him!' added Kush. Now Sita's heart was beating faster. 'Whom did you meet, boys?' she asked eagerly. 'You may not believe us, Ma, but we met Lord Rama himself!' announced Kush. 'He came to fight us, but Gurudev prevented the battle!' 'Fight you? Why would he ever do that?' questioned Sita, impatient to know the details.

'Tell your mother the full story, boys,' implored Rishi Valmiki.

'Ma, while you were busy in your puja, we were wandering around this area and saw a well-decorated white horse. It was the horse of the *ashwamedha yagna* that Lord Rama wanted to perform. There was a challenge to any Kshatriya that was attached to the horse,' said Kush. 'And a true Kshatriya never walks away from a challenge,' added Luv. 'Of course, the horse was very comfortable in our company, but the warriors soon came to fight us. They were no match for us. Then the valiant Shatrugna came, and we defeated him. Bharata and Lakshmana followed Shatrugna but were defeated too. Hanuman had also come and we simply bound him tightly with his own tail. He was very friendly with us, Ma. We also shared our lunch with him. He was just watching us fight. It seemed as though he was enjoying the whole spectacle!'

'And then?' asked Sita expectantly. 'Then the lord of Ayodhya himself came, Ma.' Tears were forming in Sita's eyes. 'What did he say?' she asked in a voice that reflected both pain and joy simultaneously. 'He said he came to fight with the ones responsible for injuring his brothers and warriors, but he did not feel like fighting us after he came face to face with us.' Sita smiled in relief. 'But we told him that we were not going to surrender the horse.' Sita raised her eyebrows in alarm. 'And Hanuman was just watching?' asked Sita. 'Yes, Ma! He was untouched by whatever was happening though he was fully involved and listening to every bit of our conversation! In any case, before we could actually begin the fight, Gurudev arrived.' Sita looked at the rishi with hands folded in gratitude. He had averted disaster. 'On his instructions, we returned the horse and asked for forgiveness.' Sita was utterly relieved. 'What did he say to you?' she enquired. 'I feel he really liked us, Ma!' said Kush. 'He said we were remarkable warriors and that, as a reward, we could ask for anything from him.' 'Then? What did you ask for?' said Sita eager to know every detail of what had happened. Kush's eyebrows furrowed and he looked as if he was trying to face something he did not want to.

'Ma, we told him that we wanted answers.' Sita's heart missed a beat and she looked at the rishi for confirmation. The rishi gently nodded. The boys knew what had happened to Sita, but it seemed that they still did not know that she *was* Sita. Tears had started pouring from Luv's eyes. 'Ma, we could not bear to hear what happened to Sita. It is just not fair. Sending away Devi Sita to the forest because of the words of a washerman and his doubting mind was just unacceptable,' said Luv.

'Gurudev told us everything while you were busy in the puja, Ma,' said Kush.

Now Sita could not stop the tears that were flowing profusely from her eyes too. 'So we asked the lord of Ayodhya about this. We wanted justice for Sita.'

'You know, Ma, the king's eyes were full of tears when we asked him about Sita. I tell you, he misses her a lot. We could see it in his eyes,' said Kush. Just this much was enough for Sita. She felt so grateful for the love of her lord. 'He explained many things about Raja Dharma and why it was necessary,' continued Kush, 'but what made us feel better was just knowing how much he loved Sita. Seeing his tears flow and the softness with which he spoke to us of her, we felt reassured that whatever he had done must have been because the circumstances were such.'

'Did you take his blessings, children?' asked Sita, with her voice choking intermittently. 'Yes, Ma, we touched his feet and he embraced us warmly. He said that for some unknown reason, he felt great affection and love towards us.' Kush was smiling when he said this. 'We also felt very special, Ma,' said Luv. 'When he hugged us, we forgot everything else. It was like being enveloped by light itself. We felt so complete, Ma.'

'He is bound by the people of Ayodhya, Ma,' said Kush, with a sense of purpose in his voice. 'But we have decided that their eyes must be opened. Gurudev says that we must travel there and sing the Ramayana to everyone so that they know the whole truth about Rama and Sita.'

'Perhaps it is time that the boys also know the complete truth, my dear,' said the rishi to Sita. She acknowledged his guidance and held the boys close to her, but words would not come out. Only tears flowed. She looked back to the rishi for help.

'My dearest boys, it is time you knew the truth about your mother,' said the rishi in his deep voice. Luv and Kush braced themselves with eagerness. They knew their mother was someone special. They were sensitive and trusted her so completely that they never asked her about their father. They knew that she would tell them of her own accord when the time was right. Nevertheless, their heart ached to know. 'Your mother is the daughter of the King of Mithila, the wife of the lord of Ayodhya, the mother of two brilliant and valiant sons named Luv and Kush; she is the epitome of patience, endurance, courage, compassion, love and wisdom. She is the daughter of the earth, a goddess walking on this planet. Your mother is Sita.' The boys were listening to every word that Gurudev spoke with absolute attention. Sita stood holding them both and her gentle clasp gave them strength and assurance. Emotions rose like tidal waves in the hearts of the boys. 'And you, Luv and Kush, are the sons of Rama,' said Gurudev, with finality in his voice. Hearing this, a surge of enormous strength swept through the boys. It was as if a tiny flower on the tallest branch of an enormous parijata tree suddenly felt within it the strength of the trunk and the stability of its deep roots. They felt at home.

25

Depth of the Consciousness

It had been several days since the boys had left for Ayodhya. Sita was nervous about her children and apprehensive about the outcome. She was unsure about how the people of Ayodhya would react, but she had faith in the words of the rishi.

It was late afternoon and she thought she would lie down for a few minutes to rest. She spread the kusha mat on the floor and lay on her side, close to its edge. There was a small mud bowl with water nearby in which one lotus flower was kept. She pulled the bowl closer to her and was just looking at the lotus. The water in the bowl stirred when she moved it and a few droplets perched themselves atop the petals of the flower. The droplets slid down the petal slowly and soon became one with the water in the pot. The petals were dry, though they were surrounded by water, and the water remained the same, though in the company of the lotus. So many events had passed in Sita's life like these little droplets.

Though the world viewed Sita through the spectrum of these events, she was untouched by any of them, like the petal itself. Eventually, these events merged with the pool of memories that become etched upon the walls of time. The event was over, the memories remained for a while, circumstances changed, the one who had experienced them remained. The petals remained untouched by the water, but not by time. They would soon return to their source—fire with fire, air with air, water with water, earth with earth—and the space that they occupied within would once again belong to the larger, infinite, unbounded space. The unseen spark of divinity that moved the elements together into a lotus, holding it as a flower, infusing it with its life force, began to let go, only to come together again as yet another flower, fresh and beautiful. This dance of the unmanifest continued, the pulsating rhythm of consciousness keeping life ever-new.

Sita turned and lay down on her back, and felt the touch of the earth beneath her. As her awareness stayed with that sensation, she felt as if the earth below was melting away and beckoning her into its heart. Sita let go and felt as if she was going deeper and deeper beneath the surface. She was moving faster and faster while feeling lighter and lighter. She merged into a serene, loving, nectarine light, full of bliss. She remained there for a while and rested. Anyone who saw her would have said she was fast asleep.

Sita awoke after a few minutes, feeling rejuvenated. She went out for a stroll in the direction of the pathway that led towards Ayodhya. Even as she stood watching, she saw the rishi and her sons on their way back. The boys broke into a run as soon as they saw her and flew into her arms.

'Ma, we have come to take you to Ayodhya! Our father has asked us to bring you!' said the boys in a chorus. 'Why did he not come along? Nor anyone from the family?' thought Sita. Perhaps things did not go as smoothly as one would have desired, but Sita did not ask. It was already a very difficult situation for the boys to handle. The rishi arrived in the meantime. 'The people of Ayodhya wanted you to personally come and state that these are indeed the children of Rama,' said the rishi. 'Of course, it was the people of Ayodhya again,' thought Sita. She wondered why the word of the rishi was not enough. What is it that would satisfy the people? In reality, people's opinions flowed like an ever-changing river. And often, they assembled into a mob mentality, taking the singular form of a mountain. One just had to accommodate their needs from moment to moment.

'I will wait for the appropriate day, and then we will go to Ayodhya, Sita,' said the rishi. Sita nodded in agreement. She sensed mixed feelings in her sons.

And then the day arrived when they left the ashram, accompanied by Rishi Valmiki. Sita was finally returning to Ayodhya. She looked back at the kutir where she had spent close to twelve years. She would probably never return. They had said their goodbyes to the ashram residents. Many tears flowed, especially from the younger children and girls in the ashram. They were all exceptionally fond of Vandevi.

The boys were deeply sensitive to their mother's feelings. From the time they had come to know who she really was, they had grown up overnight. They imbibed the patience that Sita embodied. The questions they had about Rama's decisions simply dissolved as they experienced the oneness between their mother and father. They would try to understand the nuances of Raja Dharma that brought about this circumstance and pacify the questions arising in their evolving intellect. But in their hearts, there was only love. They felt very protective of their mother but they also felt her magnificent strength. She was always pleasant, patient and positive. She never complained about anybody or any circumstance. She never spoke a single harsh word. She was multi-talented, skilled, knowledgeable, wise, and yet so natural and all-inclusive. She always insisted on the importance of caring, sharing and friendliness. She would say that these were essential human values. They had thought of her as a delicate, soft, sweet mother, but they had also awakened to the knowledge that these gentle values were in fact the foundation of great strength that had stood the test of time. The world around the boys had turned topsy-turvy in the past few weeks. But they felt secure in the company of their mother.

They entered the city without much pomp or show, and reached the king's durbar. When Sita entered, every single person in the hall rose to their feet. In her simple forest attire, she glowed more radiantly than those adorned with the most brilliant jewels. She was shining with the power of her penance and austerity. She purified the space by her very presence. All eyes were focused on Sita. And hers sought Rama. Once again their eyes met, and emotions rose in tidal waves, and entire universes were submerged in them. The pain of separation was even more unbearable as she stood in his presence. What the world had to say, what events would unfold were all insignificant as time itself ceased to exist in that moment of eternity.

The children instinctively moved closer to their mother as the entire hall looked on. Tears burst from Urmila's eyes. She wanted to run and embrace her sister, but she had to keep a hold on herself. This was a public durbar and the king was presiding over it. Lakshmana's heart overflowed at seeing Sita. He was looking at his brother with a deep ache in his heart. All the sages present rose to bless her. Their hearts melted and rejoiced upon seeing her. Rishi Valmiki stepped forward and said, 'Rama! It is my greatest fortune to bring back your ever-pure, blemish-free queen along with your two sons, who are unparalleled gems. She has faced innumerable challenges by herself in these past years, but never once lost her smile nor her faith. She is your most ardent devotee. Her calm acceptance of the circumstances life has thrown at her is remarkable. A small cup can only hold a limited amount of water while the ocean has space for much more. Sometimes even impure water mixes into it but still it rejects nothing, nor does it change in its nature. Sita, like the ocean, has unflinchingly accepted the ignorance of the people of Ayodhya. She is the epitome of compassion, patience and unconditional love—just like yourself. The way the rain pours equally on the grass and the stone, you have showered your love and care on every one of your subjects. It is time the world recognizes your divinity, and that you have come to uplift humanity.' Rama bowed to the rishi and again glanced at Sita. There was deep pain in that glance. Sita at once realized Rama's heart and knew what he was going to say.

'I agree with you, O great rishi! Sita is the essence of purity and the people of Ayodhya need to realize this. She is their queen. While the sages gathered here and I know the truth, for the sake of the simple people, I must ask Sita to undergo the test of fire once again,' said Rama, steeling himself.

Rama and Sita were like two sides of the same coin. The sacrifice he put himself through for the sake of the people was the same in essence as what he commanded Sita to undergo. They never saw each other as separate. There was nothing to establish, nothing to prove. Whatever he did, she was part of it and whatever she did, he was there. If a coin were placed in fire, both sides would burn equally. The children froze. They could not believe what they were hearing. Tears were brimming in Sita's eyes. She knew that Rama was capable of changing the direction of the river of time, but he had come to play the role of a king, and thus, had to uphold the dharma of his kingdom. She had come to play her role as well. Her role was that of a daughter of a king, a devoted wife, an ideal queen, a protective mother and, of course, an extraordinary woman. Rama, throughout his life, set an example for how women should be honoured. He took an oath to marry no other at a time when it was common among royalty to take many wives to strengthen and expand the boundaries of the kingdom and build friendly ties. He uplifted the position that a wife held in society. She intended to uphold his vision. Society was such at the time that a woman's word was not sufficient proof. The words of the sages were not enough either. People wanted to 'see' with their eyes. They could not see with their hearts. It was time to lift their vision beyond the gross. Rama would never tell anyone who he really was. He was bound by the role he had chosen. Sita would have to do it instead. The ignorance of the people was the veil of separation that was unbearable for both Sita and Rama.

This clear intention rose within Sita like a delicate yet intense prayer, and the earth responded to her calling. She heard that familiar voice telling her, 'It is time, my child, come to me!' and this time Sita gave in and let go. That same instant a light rose around her, and her feet began to glow; the earth began to tremble. Sita looked straight into Rama's eyes and drank in their beauty to quench her thirst. Her eyes were overflowing with love, pain and prayer. She dissolved into the intensity of her prayer. There was only Rama, and her heart that was filled with bliss. The earth opened up and the fire in its heart rose to the surface at Sita's command. There stood the one who ruled over nature herself. The elements danced to the rhythm of her breath, flowers blossomed at her sight, life sprung up with her touch. Having given a glimpse of herself, she became one with the elements, and there was only light. There was light within and light all around. The eyes of the people were opened as the earth closed. They turned to look at Rama with a new understanding. Who was he? And what had they done? Every person in the gathering fell to their knees and bowed with their heads on the ground and tears in their eyes. It was difficult to tell if they bowed to Sita or to Rama, whose divinity she had shown to them all. Indeed, they bowed to both, for both were one and the same. Having witnessed Sita's divinity, their eyes opened to Rama.

Luv and Kush stood staring at the light, unable to fathom what the moment had revealed. Their eyes were fixed, their minds were blank and when it seemed that their hearts would burst with grief, they saw the magnificent form of their mother in the light, fully adorned and radiant, as she stood beside the infinite form of the Lord of the Universe. They saw themselves within them, they saw her loving smile, they felt her touch under their skin, they heard her voice in their heart, they felt her presence in every cell of their being and the highest knowledge of divinity illumined their intellect. They bowed to the great light in reverence and felt enveloped by its love.

Rama embraced the boys and they wept together. The sages gathered around them and allowed their emotions to flow. Father and sons were united, and Sita lived eternally in their hearts. After some moments, the sages praised Sita as the form of Devi Lakshmi herself and reminded Rama of his true nature. It was not unknown to him, but as always, he played his role perfectly. He allowed his humanness to also express itself. However, Sita had taught everyone a precious lesson through her sacrifice. When you see the world through the eyes of wisdom, there is only love, only One.

Epilogue

Take me to the place with no sights to see
For whatever my eyes fall upon reminds me of you
And I am still there
To see you.

Take me to the place where sounds cannot reach
For every whisper, every song reminds me of you
And I am still listening
To everything you say.

Take me to the place where I will feel nothing
Not your softness, not your gentle touch
For I still exist
To feel you.

Take me to the place where there is no right or wrong
For I seek only those who revere you

And I still stand
With my head bowed down to you.

Take me to the place where one remembers nothing
For I seek to forget everything but you
And I still am here
Remembering you.

Take me to the place where time stands still
For I seek to live forever in your company
And I still exist
Waiting and longing.

Take me to the place my lord where I cease to be
For this separation is unbearable
And I am torn apart
In waiting and longing

To merge is not possible
For there are no two
Remove this veil of the mundane
That you have cast over yourself
So that I may cease to exist

Let me rejoice without conflict
Let me repose in your self
Let me abide in your being
Let me dissolve in your love

Let there be
Only you,
Only you,
Only you.

Back Stories

The following are some of the 'back stories', glimpses of which have been given to the reader in the course of the book. I have shared them in greater detail here for your better understanding. They help us become aware of the cycle of cause and effect. And when we start seeing events from a larger perspective, the mind is freed from judgements, cravings and aversions. The role play becomes clear and the *leela* unfolds.

The Gatekeepers of Lord Vishnu

Jaya and Vijaya were the gatekeepers at the abode of Lord Vishnu in Vaikunta. One day, the Sanat Kumaras, the four sons of Brahma, arrived at the gate when the lord was resting. Jaya and Vijaya refused entry to the young rishis. The rishis were willing to wait. But Jaya and Vijaya had become arrogant because of the position they held. They spoke inappropriately to the rishis and were not willing to inform the lord of their arrival. They simply told them that he wouldn't want to meet them. The rishis saw that they needed to learn a lesson. 'The lord will never refuse to meet his devotees! Your arrogance has blinded you and left you bereft of humility. May the two of you return to the earth and be born as mortals. You do not deserve to be the gatekeepers of the lord!'

Jaya and Vijaya were taken aback at the turn of events. By this time, Lord Vishnu himself came outside to receive the rishis. Jaya and Vijaya fell at his feet, asking for forgiveness. The lord asked them to seek forgiveness from the rishis. 'When you take your good fortune for granted, arrogance comes up and gratefulness recedes. And it is only through gratitude that grace can flow. You must return to the earth to fulfil the words of the rishis,' said the lord.

However, at his request, the rishis softened the curse and gave them a choice. 'You may choose seven lives on earth as devotees of the lord or three as enemies before you can return to your place here.' The thought of being away from their beloved lord for seven lifetimes was too much, so they chose to be born as his enemies thrice.

The lord, in his compassion, also told them that he would himself incarnate to liberate them. They rejoiced upon hearing this, and it brought them some solace that they would be with their lord after all. At that moment, they could not envision any hatred, but soon the veil of *maya* took over and they were born first as Hiranyaksha and Hiranyakashipu. Vishnu appeared in the form of a boar and then in the fierce form of Narasimha and vanquished Hiranyaksha and Hiranyakashipu respectively. Jaya and Vijaya were then born as the brothers Ravana and Kumbhakarna to Rishi Vishrava and his wife Kaikesi. Going forward, in the Krishnavatara, they came back as Sishupala and Dantavakra before returning to Vaikunta.

The Story of Narada

The celestial sage Narada once sat in deep meditation. The god of the devas, Indra, set several tests for his penance but the sage remained untouched. He finally sent Kamadeva to disturb him, but Narada was unaffected. Lord Shiva acknowledged Narada and praised him, 'You, like me, have won over even Kamadeva! But I would not talk about this to Lord Vishnu!' Shiva smiled mischievously before returning to his meditative state. The seed of pride had sprouted in Narada's heart. He did not heed the words of Lord Shiva and rushed to Vaikunta to boast about his achievement to Lord Vishnu, who listened to him and simply smiled. Narada, feeling a little unappreciated, took his leave and began his travels around the world, keeping a watch on the happenings everywhere.

He chanced upon a magnificent city which he had never visited before and descended to investigate further. The city was ruled by King Sheelanidhi who was preparing for his daughter's swayamvara. When the sage arrived, the king was overjoyed, and his daughter Sreemathi also came forward to take the sage's blessings. Her beauty was unparalleled, equal only to Devi Lakshmi herself, and he said so to the king. 'Your daughter resembles a goddess and is fit to be the bride of Lord Vishnu!' remarked Narada, but secretly made up his mind to participate in the swayamvara.

He was smitten by her beauty and went back to Lord Vishnu to seek his help for securing her hand in marriage. If the girl was fit for Hari himself, then all he had to do was look like the lord. He shared his wish with him and said, in Sanskrit, 'Give me the face of Hari!'

'Thataastu,' replied Lord Vishnu, meaning 'so be it'.

With great enthusiasm Narada proceeded to the swayamvara and took his place amongst the participants. Whoever he met on the way smiled much more than usual, and sometimes even broke into laughter. He did wonder why but was too excited about the swayamvara and the fact that he looked like Hari to be bothered with their reactions.

Sreemathi, fully adorned and holding a garland in her delicate hands, walked towards him. King after king was introduced to her, but she didn't garland anyone. Finally, she stood in front of Narada. She gently raised her eyes to look at his face and her lips curled into a smile, followed by a shy giggle. Narada looked into her eyes and stood rooted and stunned. Sreemathi moved on and in a matter of moments garlanded someone who was behind him. Without even turning around, Narada knew it was Lord Vishnu for that was what he had blessed her for. But what enraged him was his own reflection that he saw in Sreemathi's eyes. He had a face of a monkey. The word 'Hari' had several meanings in Sanskrit and one of them was monkey. He felt betrayed, and, in his anger, thought that the lord would understand his heart only if he too were to experience the pain of separation from his beloved. And, at such a time, only those who looked like him would be able to help him. Soon enough, he saw them together, and in an instant, the palace vanished, the city was gone, and Narada stood with the lord and Devi Lakshmi back in Vaikunta. Before his thoughts could become words, the lord said, 'Narada, your thoughts will come to pass, but there is time for that. What is more important for me is that you are not entangled in the web of pride and delusion.' Narada felt remorse for his thoughts and behaviour and was grateful to the lord for opening his eyes to the highest truth. With tears of gratitude, he began singing the glories of Lord Vishnu once again.

A Celestial Intervention

When Dasharatha planned the coronation of Rama, the devas became worried. The purpose of Lord Vishnu's incarnation as Rama was to free the earth from the terror of the asuras. They lived primarily in the forests and tormented the rishis. If Rama were to become king, and get bogged down with administrative affairs, then when would he fulfil the purpose of his taking birth on this planet? The devas approached Devi Saraswati for help. They identified Kaikeyi as the person who was strong enough for this task. Devi Saraswati veiled Kaikeyi's mind temporarily and as a result wisdom took a back seat. Kaikeyi, under the influence of Manthara, asks the two boons that changed the course of the story leading to Rama's glory. In my father's narration of this story, he would say that Saraswati requested Kaikeyi to do this. Kaikeyi sacrificed her good reputation for the sake of Rama's glory and to help him fulfil his purpose. There are always many ways to perceive or understand a situation. When you look at it positively, it saves your mind from anger, hatred or from blaming anyone.

A Special Boon

Swayambhuva Manu was the son of Brahma from whom the human race came forth. Satarupa was his wife. This couple undertook severe penance for several years and experienced the presence of Lord Vishnu in their heart. They had a deep desire to have the lord as their son. The lord granted this wish and, in time, they were born as Dasharatha and Kausalya.

Brahma's Blessing

Often, when we think of the *agnipariksha*, we only recollect Sita having to walk through fire. Sita had mastery over the elements. So, it was not a surprise that she walked through the fire unscathed. But walking through fire is metaphoric for the fire in the mind that she moved through. There was the fire of doubt in the minds of many about her purity, the fire of humiliation when her character was questioned in a public gathering of thousands, but none of it touched her. The fire in the mind burns more fiercely than any physical

fire and, of these, the fire of humiliation is the most difficult
to withstand. When the gods question Rama for his act, he
tells them, 'Sita and I are inseparable like the sunlight and
the sun. She is unblemished and ever pure. I know this. But
the world does not have my eyes. They don't understand
this. Further, I have come to play the role of a human.
I have to act accordingly.' With the gods standing witness,
after the agnipariksha in Lanka, Brahma sings the praise of
Rama and Sita in several beautiful verses (to be found in the
117 sarga of the Yuddha Kanda of Valmiki Ramayana). He
ordains that whoever sings those verses with devotion will
never be touched by the fire of humiliation.

Insights from the Author

When I was a child, my father would vividly recount the stories of Ramayana and Mahabharata along with many of the Puranas. His ability to tell the story along with the story within it, and the story behind it, just kept our attention hooked and opened our minds to several new horizons of possibilities. Still there were many unanswered questions, especially about Sita and the choices that Rama made in her regard.

As I grew up, I had the opportunity to understand the wisdom and deeper meaning behind many of these events from Gurudev and this brought a completely new dimension of understanding. I was able to appreciate the strength behind the characters and the importance of role play.

Gurudev says, 'Beyond every object is infinity, beyond every event is wisdom and beyond every person is love.' This sutra has been my guiding factor in this narration of the story of Sita as an empowered woman with remarkable strength of character, purity of mind and heart, implicit trust, an unshakeable faith, conviction and devotion. Her patience and acceptance are legendary. Just feeling close to her is enough to imbibe these qualities from her. Our life is enriched by the values that she represented.

I hope that in your reading of this book, you have begun to see Sita and Rama, and the choices that they made in a new light.

My Best Wishes to all!

References

The Ramayana is one of the most loved epics and has been written by poets and authors in different ways over the years. There are over 1000 versions that exist today. The following are the scriptures that have been a reference for my work.

Valmiki Ramayana by Maharishi Valmiki
Ram Charit Manas by Goswami Tulsidas ji
Kamba Ramayana by Mahakavi Kamban
Adhyatma Ramayana by Maharishi Veda Vyasa
Adbhuta Ramayana by Maharishi Valmiki
Brihadaranyaka Upanishad

Glossary

Aarti	A ritual of circling the lit lamp in front of the deity or a person to be honoured. It literally means removing of darkness.
Adharma	Disharmony with the nature of things—as opposed to dharma.
Adi sesha	The celestial snake, on which Lord Vishnu reclines in the cosmic ocean.
Adipathi	Master, ruler
Agamas	Post-Vedic scripture conveying ritual knowledge
Agni	The God of Fire
Ahalya	A renowned sage and wife of Rishi Gautama
Ananda tandava	The dance of bliss by Shiva

Ashoka	Saraca asoca—this tree holds great prominence in the cultural traditions of the Indian subcontinent
Ashoka vatika	The beautiful garden that housed Sita when she was in Lanka
Ashram	A hermitage
Ashwamedha yagna	A sacrifice performed by rulers to establish their sovereignty
Ayurveda	It translates to 'Science of Life'. It is one of the branches of the Vedas which is also one of the oldest surviving medical system in the world.
Besan	Gram flour/chickpea flour
Bhaav	A feeling
Bhabhi	Sister-in-law
Bhaiya	Elder brother
Bhakti	Devotion
Bhavati bhiksham dehi	May you give me some alms.
Brahmakamalas	It is commonly known as Night Blooming Cereus or Queen of the Night or Lady of the Night as its beautiful lotus-like flower blooms late at night.
Brahman	Connotes the supreme unbounded consciousness, the highest universal principle

Brahmana	A sect of people who are highly educated and have knowledge of various streams of Vedas, Upanishads and the dharma
Brahmastra	An extremely powerful weapon that is generally received as a boon after long penance
Brahmavadini	Women ascetics who strive for the highest spiritual wisdom of the supreme consciousness
Brahmavadins	Ascetics who strive for the highest spiritual wisdom of the supreme consciousness
Brahmins	A sect of people who are highly educated and have knowledge of various streams of Vedas, Upanishads and the dharma
Butas	Motifs
Chakoras	Alectoris chuka, known as the crow pheasant, symbolizes intense and often unrequited, love. It is said to be in love with the moon and to gaze at it constantly.
Chakravaka	A kind of bird called ruddy goose
Champa, champaka	A large, evergreen tree with beautifully fragrant flowers that have long and thin petals
Chana dal	Split chickpeas

Chikoo	The fruit manilkara zapota, commonly known as sapodilla
Chudamani	An Indian headdress that is usually studded with jewels
Dakshina	Skilful offering
Dal bati churma	A traditional delicacy made of lentils and whole wheat
Dalia khichdi	A traditional delicacy made of broken wheat
Danavas	The descendants of Danu
Darshan	The auspicious sight of a deity or a holy person
Deva, devas	The ones having qualities that are heavenly, divine
Devi	The Divine Mother
Didi	Elder sister
Durbar	The court of the ruler where the king holds all the discussions regarding the state
Gandharvas	Celestial beings who are the keepers of harmonious sound
Garuda	An eagle-like being that serves as the mount of Vishnu
Gayatri mantra	A twenty-four-syllabled Sanskrit verse that invokes the divine to illumine the intellect
Gunagrahi	One who has the ability to imbibe the virtues

Gunas	Three primal qualities or elements of matter
Halwa	A delicacy made of sugar, ghee and flour
Har har mahadev	A popular chant meaning, 'Please take away (destroy) my sorrow and ignorance.'
Hiranyagarbha	The golden womb that is the source of the creation of the universe
Holi	An ancient festival celebrating victory of positivity over negativity. It is also called the Festival of Colours.
Indra	The lord of the devas
Ishta	Cherished, desired form of the divine that one worships
Jalebi	An Indian sweet made of batter, fried and soaked in sugar syrup
Jambu	Rose apple
Jayamala	The garland of victory
Jijaji	Brother-in-law
Kadhi	A delicacy made of curd, chickpea flour and spices
Kailash	A mountain that is considered to be the abode of Lord Shiva. It is a place filled with happiness and celebration.
Kanakambara	The scientific name is Crossandra infundibuliformis. It is also commonly called the firecracker flower or tropical flame.

Karka lagna	Ascendant in the zodiac sign Cancer
Kartavirya	A powerful king said to have a thousand arms
Kheer	A sweet delicacy made of milk, rice, jaggery, saffron and cardamom
Kinneras	Celestials who play musical instruments and sing with the Gandharvas
Kishora chandra shekhare, rati pratikshanam mama.	Verses from the Shiva Tandava Stotram
Kshatriya	One of the four sects, where traditionally people belonged to the ruling and warrior classes
Kubera	The god of riches and wealth
Kumbhakarna	Ravana's younger brother
Kumkum	A red powder made of turmeric and other herbs used to make a distinctive mark on the forehead of women
Kurma	The avatar of Lord Vishnu as a tortoise
Kusha	Sacred 'darbha' grass, known as desmotachya bipinnata
Kutir	A cottage
Laddoo	An Indian sweet made from a mixture of flour, sugar and shortening, which is shaped into a ball

Lagna	The Most Effective Point (MEP) of the Ascendant, Lagna is that point of the zodiacal belt that coincides with the position of the horizon at the time of birth, for a given place of birth
Lakshmi	The consort of Lord Vishnu. She is the goddess of wealth, prosperity, fortune and purity
Lauki	Bottle gourd
Leela	Divine play
Ma	Mother
Mahadev	Referring to Lord Shiva
Maharani	Queen
Maharishi	A great Hindu sage or spiritual leader
Mana	Mind
Manmatha	Cupid
Maya, maya shakti	The inherent power of the supreme consciousness that casts a veil/illusion of separation between the creator and the creation
Mayastra	A weapon that casts illusions and confounds the enemy
Moola bala	Literally means the source of strength, contextually refers to the most powerful army of asuras
Motichur	Literally translates to crushed pearls. It is a delicacy where chickpea flour globules are fried in ghee or oil, and soaked in sugar syrup.

Mount Meru	A sacred mountain, also called Sumeru
Nagalingapushpa	Flower of the Nagalinga tree/ couroupita guianensis
Nagapasha	It literally means 'serpent-noose', a magical lasso in which an enemy can become entangled
Nandi	The divine vehicle, vahana, of Lord Shiva
Navaratna	Nine gems
Nidra devi	The Goddess of Sleep
Odhani	Shawl/veil
Pallu	The loose end of a sari, worn over one shoulder or the head
Pandit	A scholar
Parashurama	A revered sage who is also considered the sixth avatar of Lord Vishnu
Parijata	Night-flowering coral jasmine
Parval	Pointed gourd also known as green potato
Pattabhisheka	Coronation ceremony
Pitaji	Father
Prajapati	Lord of Creatures
Prasad	A gift from God
Puja	An act of worship generally performed out of gratitude
Punarvasu	The birth star of Lord Rama
Puranas	All the mythological stories

Purushottama	Highest among men
Pushpaka vimana	The flying vehicle that Ravana had usurped from Kubera, the lord of wealth
Rabri	Sweetened thickened milk
Raga bhairav	A morning melody
Raga malhar	A melody said to have the ability to bring rains when sung proficiently
Raja dharma	Duty of the rulers
Raja rishi	A king who turned into a royal sage. A king even while ruling the kingdom reaches a state of rishi and attained self-realization.
Rajas	Rajas is one of the three gunas; it is innate tendency or quality that drives motion, energy and activity.
Rakshasa	Sons of Khasa and Kashyapa, known for their demonic traits
Rakshasi	Daughters of Khasa and Kashyapa, known for their demonic traits
Ramabaan	The arrow of Rama that never misses its mark
Rig veda	One of the four main Vedas; a very ancient collection of Sanskrit hymns
Rishi yagnavalkya	A renowned Hindu Vedic sage
Rudra puja	Prayer with ancient mantras honouring Lord Shiva in the form of Rudra

Rudra	Lord Shiva
Sadhak	Seeker
Sadhana	Spiritual practices
Sahasrarati	Sahasra means thousand and rati means adoration
Sama veda	One of the four branches of the Vedas
Sandhyavandan	Refers to a ritual that is performed at dawn and dusk that brings brilliance in the intellect and purifies the mind
Sanjeevani	A herb that heals and bestows the elixir of life
Saptapadi	Seven steps representing seven commitments that the bride and groom make to each other for a happy married life
Sastras	Weapons
Sattva	One of the three gunas. It is the quality of balance, harmony, goodness, purity, universalizing, holistic, constructive, creative, building, positive attitude, luminous, serenity, being-ness, peaceful, virtuous.
Shastras	Scriptures that prescribe the ideal way of life
Shakti	Power, energy
Shiva dhanush	Also known as Pinaka, this is the bow of Lord Shiva
Shiva linga	A symbol that represents Lord Shiva

Shiva tandava stotra	A hymn in praise of Lord Shiva that glorifies the creation as the cosmic dance of Shiva
Shiva tattva	The Shiva Principle
Simsupa	Scientifically called Amherstia nobilis; Sita sat under this tree in the Ashoka Vatika in Lanka. It is also called the 'Tree of Heaven'.
Sita Mata ki jai	Victory to Mother Sita
Spatika linga	Crystal Shiva linga
Sugandharaja	A flower with the botanical name Polianthes tuberose, known by different names across different regions, all of the names generally meaning, 'King of fragrance' or 'fragrance of the night'
Sutra	A rule or aphorism in Sanskrit literature
Swami	Lord
Swayamvara	In this context, Swayam means 'self' and Vara means groom. This was a practice where a girl of marriageable age chose her husband from a group of suitors
Tamala	Cinnamomum tamala tree
Tamas	Tamas is one of the three gunas. It is the quality of inertia, inactivity, dullness, or lethargy.
Tapasvis	One who engages in tapas/penance
Uddalaka	Uddalaka Aruni is a revered Vedic sage of Hinduism

Upanishads	One of the components of the Vedas, the philosophically oriented and esoteric texts
Uttara phalguni	The twelfth of the twenty-seven nakshatras in Vedic astrology
Vanara	A being that possessed extra-ordinary super-human abilities
Varaha	Lord Vishnu in his incarnation as a boar
Vastu shastra	An ancient Hindu system of design and architecture that promotes harmony and prosperous living by promoting positive energy and eliminating negative energies
Vedanta	Spiritual wisdom based on the doctrine of the Upanishads, especially in its monistic form
Vedas	The oldest scriptures that are the basis of Sanatana Dharma and are a source of the highest knowledge
Vijayi bhava	A blessing for victory to dawn upon you or 'may you be victorious'
Yagna	Ceremonial rites to God. The purpose of a Yagna ritual was to bring ancient yogis into direct contact with the source of the universe by connecting them with the elements—the underlying forces of creation itself.
Yoga nidra	A state of restful awareness

Acknowledgements

I would like to acknowledge Sri Shanmuga Shivachariar and Sri Sundaramurthy Shivam for helping me with the relevant scriptural references.

I would also like to acknowledge astrologers Sri Manak Sharma and Sri Ashutosh Chawla for their inputs regarding the horoscope of Rama.

I acknowledge historians and founders of Bharat Gyan, Sri D.K Hari and Hema Hari, for supporting me with many historical facts and timelines associated with this epic.

I would like to acknowledge the efforts of Pratibha Kumari for the beautiful paintings and cover illustration that she has created for my book.

I would like to acknowledge my team of reviewers Arvind Varchaswi, Srividya Varchaswi, Madhushri Tejasvi, Ajay Bagga, Khushal Choksi, Mamta Khailkura and Raghav Chanana.

I acknowledge my editors Dr Ajay Tejasvi, Harish Ramachandran and Bharathy Harish.

My special thanks to my husband Sri N. Narasimhan for his timely insights and continuous support.